Encountering Depression In-Depth

Encountering Depression In-Depth

An existential-phenomenological approach to selfhood, depression, and psychiatric practice

Patrick Seniuk

Subject: Theory of Practical Knowledge
Research Area: Critical and Cultural Theory
School: Culture and Education

Södertörns högskola
(Södertörn University)
Biblioteket
SE-141 89 Huddinge

www.sh.se/publications

Cover illustration: "Depths", Thomas Hawk,
CC BY-NC 2.0 (a re-working of the original work)
Cover layout: Jonathan Robson
Graphic form: Per Lindblom & Jonathan Robson

Stockholm 2020

Södertörn Doctoral Dissertations 176
ISSN 1652-7399
ISBN 978-91-89109-22-3 (print)
ISBN 978-91-89109-23-0 (digital)

Abstract
This dissertation in Theory of Practical Knowledge contends that depression is a disorder of the self. Using the existential-phenomenology of Maurice Merleau-Ponty, I argue that if we want to disclose the basic structure of depressed experience, then we must likewise disclose how self-experience is inseparable from depressed experience. However, even though depression is a contemporary psychiatric category of illness, it is nevertheless a historically and heterogenous concept.

To make sense of depression in the context of contemporary psychiatric practice, I show that depression has historically been characterized by two broad models of causation; that is, a phenomenon that is causally explained by either a biological dysfunction or a psychological conflict. But this stark characterization is not limited just to history; by conducting qualitative interviews with psychiatric professionals, I illustrate how this causal dichotomy remains prevalent in contemporary psychiatric practice. On one hand, the clinicians report dissatisfaction with the depression diagnostic criteria (i.e. it is impersonal or vague), while on the other hand, the clinicians also recognize that a depression diagnosis is useful insofar as a diagnosis facilitates access to various resources associated with psychiatric care. Consequently, clinicians have developed a coping strategy that is witnessed in their empathetic desire to distance patients from their depression diagnosis, which led to statements such as, "*you* are not the problem, the problem is *depression*." One consequence of this approach is that depression is artificially cleaved from the person who experiences depression, which subsequently means that depression is viewed to be something independent of oneself.

Because I argue that depression and the self are mutually implicated, it is crucial to disseminate some of the most influential contemporary models of selfhood. I show that the brainbound, situated, psychological, and narrative model of self, all have respective strengths and weaknesses. But I also go beyond these models and characterize selfhood as a developmental phenomenon that is expressed as an embodied-style. This style reflects the way in which we establish perceptual contact with the otherness, without which there could be no self-experience.

By adopting the notion of self-as-a-style, my phenomenological analysis of depression discloses the way in which an experiential structure of depression is inextricable from lived-space. More specifically, I show that depressed experience is an affective modification to the way spatial depth is experienced; things in the world are experienced as being distant, out of touch, or simply that one feels incapable of effortlessly engaging the surrounding world. Accordingly, I argue that the relationship between depression and selfhood may be characterized in two broad ways, as either a depressive-style, or as an interruption of self-style.

The distinction between depressive-style and interrupted self-style has implications for depression diagnosis and treatment. I show that persistent-depressive disorder is phenomenologically indicative of a depressive-style, whereas major-depressive disorder corresponds with interrupted self-style. In the context of depression treatment, I draw on the work of philosopher John Russon to offer an account of psychotherapy that is rooted in phenomenological sensibilities. Most notably, I show how "talk" therapy is also an existential project, one that attempts to raise our unreflective and embodied habits to the level of explicit awareness in an attempt to re-style the way in which the self is able to cope with the vicissitudes that arise from our everyday situations.

Keywords: Phenomenology, existential philosophy, psychiatric practice, Merleau-Ponty, selfhood, depression.

Abstract
Denna avhandling i ämnet den praktiska kunskapens teori undersöker hur depressionen griper in i och förändrar vår erfarenhet av oss själva. Genom att använda mig av Maurice Merleau-Ponty's existentiella fenomenologi, argumenterar jag för att vi måste beskriva och analysera erfarenheten av självet och hur den är relaterad till den depressiva erfarenheten om vi vill blottlägga depressionens grundläggande struktur.

Depression har historiskt sett förklarats med hjälp av två olika orsaksmodeller: antingen har den betraktats som en biologisk dysfunktion eller som ett resultat av en psykologisk konflikt. Gränsdragningen återfinns emellertid inte bara i historien; genom att genomföra djupintervjuer visar jag hur denna kausala dikotomi fortfarande är verksam i den samtida psykiatriska praktiken. Å ena sidan redogjorde mina informanter för sitt missnöje med kriterierna för diagnosen depression (exempelvis att de är opersonliga eller otydliga), medan de, å andra sidan, vidkände att diagnosen är användbar såtillvida som den gör det möjligt att få tillgång till den psykiatriska vårdens olika resurser. Personer som är verksamma inom den psykiatriska professionen har därför utvecklat olika strategier för att hantera detta dilemma, något som exempelvis visar sig i deras vilja att distansera patienter från deras depressionsdiagnoser, vilket ledde till uttalanden som ”*du* är inte problemet, det är *depressionen* som är problemet”. En av följderna med denna strategi är att depressionen separeras på ett artificiellt sätt från personen som lider av den, vilket också innebär att depressionen betraktas som något som är oberoende av det egna självet.

Eftersom jag argumenterar för att depression och själv påverkar varandra ömsesidigt är det viktigt att analysera några av de mest inflytelserika modellerna för att förstå självets struktur inom samtida forskning. Jag visar att den hjärnbaserade modellen, den situerade modellen, den psykologiska modellen och den narrativa modellen av självet har sina respektive styrkor och svagheter. Men jag går också bortom dessa modeller och karakteriserar självet som ett utvecklingsfenomen som ger sig till känna som en *förkroppsligad stil*. Denna stil reflekterar det sätt på vilket vi etablerar en perceptuell kontakt med annanheten, förutan vilken det inte skulle finnas någon erfarenhet av det egna självet.

Genom att använda mig av begreppet självet-som-stil, visar min fenomenologiska analys hur depressionens erfarenhetsstruktur är oskiljaktig från den levda rumsligheten. Jag visar hur den deprimerade erfarenheten är en affektiv förändring av det sätt på vilket rumsligt djup upplevs; ting i världen upplevs som frånvarande, utom räckvidd, eller så upplever den deprimerade personen helt enkelt sig vara oförmögen att utan stor ansträngning etablera kontakt med omvärlden. Därför argumenterar jag också för att förhållandet mellan depression och självet kan karakteriseras på två huvudsakliga sätt, antingen som en depressiv stil eller som ett avbrott av självets stil.

Denna distinktion mellan depressiv stil och en avbruten självstil får konsekvenser för diagnosticeringen och behandlingen av depression. Jag visar att en långvarig depressiv sjukdom - dystymi - fenomenologiskt sett vittnar om en depressiv självstil medan en kortare depressiv sjukdom motsvarar en avbruten självstil. När det kommer till frågan om behandling av depression utgår jag från filosofen John Russons verk för att visa hur samtalsterapi också kan förstås som ett existentiellt projekt som syftar till att medvetandegöra våra oreflekterade och förkroppsligade vanor i ett försök att omstilisera det sätt på vilket självet förmår handskas med de förändringar som uppstår i vardagliga situationer.

Nyckelord: Fenomenologi, existentiell filosofi, psykiatrisk praktik, Merleau-Ponty, självet, depression.

Table of Contents

Acknowledgments

A dissertation is seldom the work of a single person. Unsurprisingly, this project entails the fruit of many labourers, whose effort – in whatever way – has made this project possible. First, because this dissertation is a subproject within the larger research project: "The Phenomenology of Suffering in Medicine: Explorations in the Baltic Sea Region," it would not have been possible without generous funding from the Baltic Sea Foundation, to whom I wish to express gratitude. I also want to recognize the efforts of Ewa Rogström and Lena Casado, who graciously dealt with all the administrative challenges that inevitably emerge when living in Sweden as a non-resident. Also, I am grateful to the clinicians who agreed to participate in this research project, and I only hope that I have done justice to the insights they so generously shared me with.

I am indebted to Somogy Varga who agreed to serve as my opponent for the final seminar. His generous feedback and encouragement were indispensable to this manuscript. I also want to acknowledge the fastidious proofreading services of my friend and colleague David Payne. Likewise, I want to thank my dear friend Gustav Strandberg who agreed to translate the dissertation abstract. To my colleagues at the Centre for Studies in Practical Knowledge, your philosophical insights have been invaluable, but it is your companionship over the past five years that I cherish the most.

Over the past decade, it has been my great fortune to collaborate and work with philosophers whose shoes I could never presume to fill. In this category I include my supervisor and friend Fredrik Svenaeus, without whom this project would have never come to fruition. I have never once doubted Fredrik's commitment to me or to my work. It is not possible to adequately express here how grateful I am to have been able to work alongside Fredrik during my time in Stockholm, and I can say with certainty that I would not hesitate to do it all again. To my co-supervisor and friend Jonna Lappalainen, who so patiently read Kierkegaard with me during her free time, thank you for everything. I also want to say thank you to my co-supervisor Rolf Ahlzén for generously sharing his clinical expertise in psychiatric practice.

Finally, even though this work is thoroughly collaborative, some contributions demand special mention: first, to my parents, Wilfred and Diane Seniuk; it goes without saying that your support has made this entire process possible and I am forever grateful. Second, it is not an exaggeration to say that this dissertation would have been impossible without the incomparable friendship of Duff Waring and Jayne Davis.

Even those who know you best don't understand the glare bouncing off your eyes, the glare that prevents you from seeing up the road

Daphne Merkin, *This Close to Happy*

Introduction

x. Research aim

This study investigates two nebulous phenomena: depression and selfhood. I eschew the standard view of depression, namely as an affective disorder (or mood disorder), and argue instead that depression is more appositely characterized as disorder of the self. In contemporary psychiatric practice, "disorders of the self" have traditionally been reserved for persons diagnosed with schizophrenia, psychosis, or personality disorder, according to which altered self-experience is characterized by disintegration or fragmentation. However, this investigation contends that the diffuse nature of selfhood does not necessarily conform to a logic of selfhood that is predicated on a sense of an "intact whole." Instead, I contend that selfhood is a perceptual phenomenon that is expressed as a self-style, by which I mean a generalized manner of comportment that expresses our basic and fundamental relationship with the world. I further contend that an existential-phenomenological investigation of depressed experience corroborates the claim that selfhood is an elusive, but nonetheless ubiquitous feature of lived-experience.

To develop a novel account of depression as an affliction of the self, it is imperative that we adopt an investigative framework equal to this task. I will show that securing novel insight about depression cannot be limited to a scientific inquiry alone. Our approach must illuminate why theoretical and practical assumptions of psychiatric medicine will continue to overlook the central role of selfhood in depression if it does not address lived-experience prior to scientific thought. Not that our study of depression and selfhood is to be confined to lived-experience alone; for, psychiatric professionals are tasked with diagnosing and treating persons with depression, and if depression is indeed a disorder of the self, then it is incumbent upon us to attend to the way in which psychiatric professionals conceptualize depression and selfhood.

The relationship between selfhood and depression I am proposing will be disclosed ontologically. This means that selfhood must be investigated at the irreducible level of lived-experience, which, as we will see, is typically inaccessible to research methods employed in the natural sciences. Why? Because the world is the silent partner that backgrounds all conscious experience, and thus we cannot properly understand selfhood without specifying how selfhood is perceptually connected to the world prior to mediating concepts; selfhood is a phenomenon tied to embodied action rather than cognitive faculties. For instance, when I sit down at the computer to write, I must already possess an implicit understanding of what it means to sit. Consequently, as we will see over the course of this study, to properly describe the phenomena of depression and selfhood we must attend to our pre-conceptual experience (i.e. tacit knowledge) of the world prior to scientific objectification (or abstraction).

x.i Investigative approach

My investigation will be of interest to persons who currently experience depression (or have experienced depression previously). It will likewise be of interest to psychiatric professionals who recognize that the intersection of psychiatric theory and clinical practice is anything but straightforward. Principally though, my study of depression and selfhood aims to be salient for those working within the philosophy of psychiatry, that is, those whose work deals with conceptual and practical issues in the context of depression.

From the outset I want to establish in what way this study of depression and selfhood is to be understood as philosophical. First of all, the study is motivated by the need to make sense of depressed experience without resorting to causal explanations of that experience. Because depression is classified as a psychiatric disorder, philosophically-oriented studies of depression have typically been comparatively of less interest owing to the prevailing assumption that when we want to explain the nature of depression, we must identify its cause.[1] It is thus unsurprising that contemporary depression research across most Western countries is predominantly oriented around the positive sciences, meaning that scientific investigations amass "positive" evidence in an attempt to explain the material cause of natural phenomena. For instance, the proliferation of psychopharmacological therapies over the last quarter-century has engendered a commonsense assumption – for lay and professional alike – that the nature of de-

—

[1] A cursory search on the PubMed database returns 425,772 scientific publications on depression between 1950 and 2019.

pression is best characterized by neuro-chemical pathology, reinforcing the view that depression is a brain-based *disease.*

It is worth noting from the outset that I believe it is dubious to presuppose that depression is a brain-based disease.[2] After decades of research and development, this hypothesis has ultimately proven less fruitful than researchers had once imagined it might be (Hindmarch 2001). Since this is a critical study of psychiatric practices in the context of depression and selfhood, the existential-phenomenological perspective pursued here will incite us to disclose metaphysical assumptions that guide scientific study of natural phenomenon.

Having said this, a significant obstacle for scientists and phenomenologists alike is that depression is a remarkably heterogeneous phenomenon, giving us all the more reason to treat causal explanations of depression with caution.[3] At present, though we remain uncertain about the nature of depression itself, there is a general consensus that the phenomenon of depression is manifold (Ratcliffe 2015, Fernandez 2019). Yet, even though depression is likely a heterogenous phenomenon, this investigation argues that it is nevertheless possible to articulate what I consider to be essential structures or features of depressed experience, irrespective of possible depression types.

To shed light on the essential features of depression, we need an approach appropriate for the task. I have elected to adopt an *existential-phenomenological* philosophical framework to investigate depression for the simple reason that this approach forces us to analyze lived-experiences divested of scientific or conceptual assumptions; that is, existential-phenomenology allows us to investigate human behavior *as it is lived,* which is to say, a pre-conceptual experience of the world. As we work through this study of depression it will become clear that phenomenology "is not a particular body of knowledge; it is the vigilance which does not let us forget the source of all knowledge" (Merleau-Ponty 1964b, 110). In other words, phenomenology does not begin with pre-established assumptions about depression and selfhood, but rather aims to raise scientific prejudices about these phenomena to the level of philosophical thought.

—

[2] Generally speaking, in medicine the term disease denotes *discernable* bio-physiological dysfunctions that deviate from otherwise "normal" functioning. This essentially means that without empirical evidence of the dysfunction, the processes in question cannot be defined as a disease.

[3] Here I simply mean to say that a variety of depression types may exist, meaning that it is highly improbable that depression can be properly explained by a single cause.

The task of disclosing psychiatric presumptions regarding depression and selfhood cannot be achieved by drawing on descriptions of lived-experience alone. Psychiatric professionals routinely meet with persons who suffer from depression in ways that prevent them from living a flourishing life. As a result, since I posit that depression is disorder of the self, I believe that we also have good reason to investigate the way psychiatric professionals understand the notion of selfhood in the context of depression. Because the notion of selfhood is generally a philosophical question, the way clinicians understand selfhood in the context of clinical practice will presumably be implicit, at least for the most part.

This does not mean that clinicians are without some sense of what it means to be a self; on the contrary, I argue that clinicians (indeed, as we all do) hold implicit notions of selfhood, which can be identified in and through clinical practices. Accordingly, in addition to the phenomenological analysis of depression and selfhood, I conduct a qualitative study comprised of interviews with psychiatric clinicians across three different clinics in Sweden: two in Stockholm, and one located three hours west of Stockholm in Karlstad. By interviewing psychiatric professionals with varying professional competences, our philosophical study of depression and selfhood will take as its point of departure these clinical insights. The qualitative material gathered for this study not only offers insights into the specific challenges arising from the intersection of psychiatric theory and psychiatric practice, it also serves as a springboard for deeper philosophical analysis during subsequent chapters of this investigation. The qualitative part of this study is intended to illuminate aspects of psychiatric practice that theory alone cannot elicit. But the qualitative material alone will be insufficient in raising both depression and selfhood to philosophical awareness.

Since the overarching purpose of this study is to describe the interdependent relationship between depression and selfhood, the existential-phenomenological approach enables us to access structures of the lived-experience of depression without having to resort to scientific explanation; that is, existential-phenomenology permits us to address *how* depression is experienced irrespective of *why* it is experienced. For instance, a diagnostic tool (sphygmomanometer) can provide information that suggests I may have hypertension, yet it is not necessary that I subjectively *experience* physical symptoms of hypertension. In this instance, asymptomatic experience is at odds with the objective data derived from a diagnostic aid. This disparity suggests that we can be subjectively mistaken about our bio-physiological state of affairs. Then again, the inverse also holds true, insofar as *objective* data can fail to corroborate *subjective* experience, meaning that lived-experience also tests the veracity of objective data.

This study takes seriously the phenomenological premise that lived-experience *is* itself objective by virtue of the fact that all human experience is parasitic on a shared world, a premise that challenges the common-sense view that subjective experience distorts objective explanations of human behavior. Because depression (as well as scientific activity) is embedded more broadly in history and culture (Radden 2002), it would be remiss to presume that natural science will have the final say on the nature of depression. And while the metaphysical status of depression remains opaque, that is, with respect to *what* it is, we do not require empirical explanation to posit an incontestable fact about depression: the ability to live a flourishing life is painfully inhibited.

x.ii Philosophical framework: The field of depression studies

In light of the claim that we no longer find ourselves in the "age of anxiety" but rather are submerged in the "age of depression" (Horwitz and Wakefield 2005), it seems curious that so few philosophical monographs dedicated to depression exist. To be sure, contemporary literature reflects a significant rise in philosophically oriented inquiries into this phenomenon. However, these studies are limited in scope, and leave us wanting more comprehensive accounts. Presently, there are only three monograph length studies on depression (Ratcliffe 2015, Gilbert 2014, Tellenbach 1980).[4] The content of these studies, like mine, draw inspiration from phenomenological philosophy. What sets my investigation apart, however, is the theme of selfhood in the context of depression. My aim is to show the reader why a comprehensive phenomenological approach to depression must, if it is to uncover the essential structures of depression, attend to the phenomenon of selfhood.

My existential-phenomenological approach to depression works through lived-experience in an attempt to articulate the essential structures associated with depression. These structures, however, are not to be mistaken for physical or anatomical structures; instead, I show that these essential structures are established via perceptual experience of the world, without

[4] Of these three monographs, I will limit my analysis to the work of Ratcliffe in subsequent chapters. Herbertus Tellenbach's text is comprised of an admixture of psychoanalytic and phenomenological insights, which renders it far too broad to treat in any great detail. Likewise, Jill Gilbert's dissertation, which also employs an existential-phenomenological method, is less concerned with clinical practice and deals extensively with Freudian melancholy, a theme that lies beyond the scope of this dissertation.

which, the experience of consciousness would be limited to an isolated ego existing independent of the world. For this reason, the notion "lived-experience" means that we cannot understand human behavior without considering the relationship between oneself and the world.

The notion of "lived-experience" has increasingly gained currency among qualitative researchers across a variety of academic disciplines. But we must not lose sight of the *philosophical* implications that make lived-experience central to phenomenological studies. Lived-experience was raised, most notably, to the level of philosophy by the work of Edmund Husserl. Broadly speaking, phenomenology emerged as a philosophical movement motivated by the desire to overcome thorny philosophical issues traditionally associated with the way in which we understand and describe conscious experience. Unlike scientific investigations, which presuppose that consciousness is an object to be studied, Husserl posited that consciousness is not an object *in* the world but rather a type of experience.[5] Thus, to be conscious is to have a certain type of experience of the world, namely, intentional experience. While I will address intentionality in more detail in subsequent chapters (Chapter 4 and Chapter 5), intentional conscious reflects the fundamental way that experience is always directed toward some *thing* in the world. And while I cannot presume to do justice to Husserl's philosophy here, the continued relevance of phenomenology is perhaps attributable to Husserl's assertion that the world is the ontological *a priori* of all experience. That is, the possibility of consciousness experience presupposes the existence of the world. In mundane life, it may be easily taken for granted that all experience implicitly takes place against the background of the world.

Husserl's seminal philosophy was further developed in Martin Heidegger's ontological-hermeneutics, and later in the existential-phenomenology of Jean-Paul Sartre and Maurice Merleau-Ponty. While there is considerable variation among these phenomenological methods, they remain unified by

—

[5] The view that consciousness is a "thing" or object to be studied continues to be held by some contemporary philosophers. It is often referred to as the Hard problem of consciousness, which is basically concerned with how it is possible for brain processes (which are biological processes) to give rise to conscious life characterized by the capacity for reflection, memory, and rational thought. The crux of the problem is that there appears to be an explanatory gap between how the material brain elicits non-material life characteristic of the mind. Phenomenologists deny that there is a hard gap problem, since they reject the claim that consciousness is a thing. As we will see later in the investigation, phenomenology characterizes consciousness as a type of experience rather than something *inside* human beings.

the overarching view that human beings cannot be understood independent of their relationship to the world. In opposition to Newtonian atomism, which posited that objective knowledge of entities requires us to reduce a given entity to senseless, brute matter, indifferent to its surroundings, phenomenology contends that knowledge of things in the world is predicated on the way in which an entity stands in relation to the world.

Merleau-Ponty in particular was a vocal critic of the scientific tendency to treat objective knowledge "as a sum of things [in the world] or processes tied together through causal relations" (Merleau-Ponty 2012, xxvii). According to scientific thought, which Merleau-Ponty – following Kierkegaard – called "objective thought," to fully "know" an object in-itself, the object in question must be (artificially) suspended from its relationship to the surrounding environment. Arguably, Merleau-Ponty's entire philosophical *oeuvre* is dedicated to refuting the dogmatic certainty that scientific thought is capable of exhausting our knowledge of, not only nature, but *human behavior*. The phenomenological psychiatrist Erwin Straus, who will be important for this study, particularly in Chapter 4, shared Merleau-Ponty's sentiment concerning the limits of naturalist explanation. Straus says: "It is never debated that experience alone makes possible interpersonal relations and communication, [therefore] *science itself owes its existence to experience*" (1966c, 249, emphasis added).

Importantly, then, the phenomenological critique of scientific thought is not leveled against the pursuit of objective knowledge. Scientific thought, as Merleau-Ponty sees it, is remiss for failing to recognize that lived-experience of the world is necessarily prior to any and all possibility of objective knowledge. As Husserl recognized, causal explanations of phenomena take for granted the background existence of the world. The only way to right this error is, according to Merleau-Ponty, to "make explicit our primordial knowledge of the 'real' and to describe the perception of the world as what establishes, once and for all, our idea of the truth. Thus, we must not truly wonder if we perceive a world; rather we must say: the world is what we perceive" (ibid., xxx). Here, Merleau-Ponty has in mind Descartes' philosophical method of hyperbolic doubt, the latter of which sought an indubitable epistemological foundation to withstand systematic metaphysical doubt. As a result of Descartes' philosophical legacy, it is often believed that perceptual experience is far too erroneous to offer epistemic certainty about the world. In the end, Descartes concludes that we can indeed possess objective knowledge about the world once we recognize that the only thing that cannot be doubted is that we are thinking beings – if we think, then we must exist.

Like many philosophers, Merleau-Ponty takes issue with Descartes' failure to recognize his theoretical presuppositions about the existence of world. Descartes is certain that he exists because he thinks, but he concludes that he cannot be certain about the existence of the world. Descartes certainty that he thinks must mean, by necessity, that the very possibility of existing as a thinking being implies (and presupposes) the existence of the world. And it is for this reason that Merleau-Ponty contends that there can be no doubt that "the world is what we perceive." Moreover, Merleau-Ponty and his contemporaries insisted that because the existence of the world precedes thinking beings such as Descartes, then the way in which we know the world is not primarily conceptual or cognitive. On the contrary, concepts and cognition are secondary expressions that are derived from our primary or pre-reflective experience of the world.

What makes Merleau-Ponty's phenomenological project especially salient for this investigation is his insistence that a detailed study of human life must address the way in which we experience the world prior to our capacity for conceptual thought. His phenomenological point of entry is embodied perceptual life, a method of investigation that eschews causal or rational explanation. In order to understand perception, Merleau-Ponty contends that we must understand perception as an embodied phenomenon. It is not only Merleau-Ponty's extended meditation on perception and embodiment that sets him apart from other phenomenologists. It is equally his vehement insistence that scientific thought is remiss in assuming that human behavior is a determinate phenomenon. Accordingly, he writes:

> I cannot think of myself as a part of the world, like the simple object of biology, psychology, and sociology…everything that I know about the world, even though science, I know from a perspective that is my own, or from an experience of the world without which scientific symbols would be meaningless…my existence does not come from my antecedents, nor from my physical and social surroundings; *it moves out towards them and sustains them* (2012, lxxii, emphasis added).

Here we are offered a hint as to why Merleau-Ponty's phenomenology is an existential-phenomenology. The world of science and causal explanation is established upon the world that we take up and live as a personal project. Our lives are self-defined within a world that, prior to our birth, we had no part in determining. Yet, we carry ourselves toward the world with bodies whose contact with the world is experientially prior to anything science can tells us about it. Ultimately, then, Merleau-Ponty incites us to meditate on the world with which we are already well acquainted by virtue of our privileged perceptual access.

One of the many implications of existential-phenomenology is that lived-experience is characterized by a practical orientation toward the world. For phenomenology in general, the primacy of lived-experience is likewise the primacy of subjectivity. We will see that intentional consciousness is structured in such a way that the world is disclosed to us not by what we think, but rather through what we do. Furthermore, that practical action is a fundamental feature of a human being implies that *someone* is the source of action. In this investigation into depression, this *someone* is characterized as the self (or selfhood). The concept of selfhood is, on the one hand, a ubiquitous and familiar term that we invoke in everyday language. On the other hand, it is an especially nebulous concept that cuts across philosophy, history, and culture. For Merleau-Ponty, embodied perceptual life is ultimately subtended by the self, albeit, a specific conception of self that does not resemble what we typically have in mind with respect to the nature of *selfhood*.

In the clinical context of psychiatry, I suggest that when a patient with depression reports that she does "not feel like myself," clinicians are presented with their first significant insight into the phenomenon of depression. Hence, the phenomenological task in this investigation is to specify the way in which selfhood is necessarily interwoven with depressed experience. This is all the more crucial given that depression is *not* typically considered to be a disorder of the self, a category reserved for afflictions such as schizophrenia and personality disorders. By the end of this investigation, however, it will be clear that depression is intelligible as a phenomenon that affects selfhood. Of course, this does not mean that depression is similar in nature to schizophrenia or personality disorders. What this investigation attempts to illustrate (indirectly) is that the manifestation of depression is only possible in the context of being a self.

x.iii Investigation structure

Now that the motivating philosophical framework for this project has been outlined, it is incumbent upon us to clarify why this investigation is necessary, as well as how the study will be structured. As I already noted, the state of philosophical literature on depression is relatively limited, dwarfed by over half a century of scientific publications, medical studies, and clinical trials, related to depression. Yet, even though the philosophical literature on depression is not prolific, contemporary phenomenological studies of depression have nevertheless elicited novel insights concerning depression, which have increasingly come to exert influence on psychiatric practice.[6] By exploring dimensions such as temporality, intersubjectivity, embodiment, and affectivity, phenomenologists have persuasively described the way in which intentional consciousness is altered in depression. Surprisingly, despite increased philosophical interest in the lived-experience of depression, the relationship between depression and selfhood remains underexplored in phenomenological studies.[7] Having said this, since depression and selfhood are theoretically capacious concepts, it is understandable that scholars may have reservations about undertaking a joint study of these themes.

The inherent constraints associated with this type of project (resources, time, etc.) make this study of depression and selfhood an ambitious one. A central tenet of this investigation is that depression and selfhood are interdependent. This therefore means that insight into one phenomenon will presumably illuminate aspects of the other. The upshot of a complex study such as this is the promise of being able to provide a novel contribution to the research area. This dissertation has been organized in such a way that the argumentation of each chapter successively builds on the main claim that self-experience in depression is marked by altered spatial experience.

With this in mind, the general thesis of this investigation is that if we want to grasp how depression alters the structure of selfhood, and if selfhood is rooted in embodied perceptual experience, then we must not only investigate lived-experience, we must likewise address the way in which perception structures our spatial experience of the world. Readers

—

[6] One example is the development of the Examination of Anomalous Self Experience (EASE) questionnaire (2005), a collaborative project between psychiatrists Josef Parnas, Louis Sass, and philosopher Dan Zahavi. The questionnaire is intended to help clinicians access features of schizophrenia that are commonly experienced by patients yet fall outside the scope of standard psychiatric questionnaires.

[7] To my knowledge, there are no monograph length phenomenological studies that focus exclusively on the relationship between depression and selfhood. Ratcliffe and Stephan (2014) have enhanced the literature with their anthology exploring depression, self, and emotion. Many excellent phenomenological articles addressing depression allude to the significance of selfhood, yet such accounts are ultimately cursory or only treat selfhood indirectly.

uninitiated to phenomenology may very well ask, what can *space* tell us about *depression* and *selfhood*? When we eventually arrive at Chapter 4, I address this point in considerable detail; however, for the moment it must suffice to say that the relationship between depression, self, and space, is an existential relationship. Moreover, because space, depression, and selfhood, are related existentially, it is imperative that we pay proper attention to the way in which the self establishes contact with its surrounding world. An analysis of lived-space will demonstrate that an essential feature of depression is the way in which the experience of space is altered; things, people, and practical activity, are experienced as distant, or out of touch, or impossible, and these experiences of the world exemplify the way in which lived-experience is existentially structured by spatial *depth*.

Phenomenologically speaking, lived-space – unlike geometrical space – is imbued with practical significance, meaning that the relationship between self and world is established through the way in which we cope with our surrounding world. "My eye," writes Merleau-Ponty, "is moving or at rest in relation to a thing that it is approaching or that flees from it. If the body provides the ground or the background to the perception of movement…it does so as a perceiving power, as it is established in a certain domain and geared into a world" (2012, 292). In other words, the distance between the self and world – in lived-experience – is not characterized by an objective physical measurement; to navigate the space of my kitchen does not require that I calculate the distance between the table and myself; the distance between the table and I is an expression of the way in which I must move myself according to the "demands" of the table; it is a practical or lived situation, the significance of which calls forth a particular style of action to resolve a specific task. Once we are adequately prepared to analyze in detail lived-space during Chapter 4, I will show how self-experience in depression is characterized by an altered experience of spatial *depth*. By subjecting our otherwise normal, practical engagement with the world we will then be in a position to argue that depressed experience of depth expresses a modified "hold on" things in the world.

Even though my overarching goal is to obtain a robust phenomenological account of depression, it is imperative that we first consider how depression has become one of psychiatry's most notable (but enigmatic) objects of inquiry. To prepare for the eventual phenomenological analysis of depression and selfhood, we must first reflect upon how these phenomena are conceptualized in both the history of psychiatry and psychiatric clinical practice. Once we understand how psychiatric science has shaped the conceptual contours of depression and selfhood, I will turn my attention to psychiatric clinical practice to investigate the influence of psychiatric theory within psychiatric *praxis*. All in all, this investigation spans six chapters, subjecting depression and selfhood to historical, clinical, and phenomenological analyses. Upon conclusion, the reader will be able to appreciate why depression and selfhood are interdependent phenomena rather than mutually exclusive.

x.iv Outline of research contribution

In order to contextualize contemporary clinical practices, the initial task in this dissertation is to formulate a historical account of depression and psychiatry. In the first chapter I argue that depression has been historically characterized by the profession of psychiatry in two disparate ways: depression is caused by either biological dysfunction or psychological pathology. A secondary aim of this chapter is to show that the historical conceptualization of depression likewise led to implicit commitments about the nature of selfhood, specifically as something attributable to a biological function, or conversely, to psychological processes of the mind.

In this chapter I also address the historical development of psychiatric diagnosis, as well as some of the ongoing conflicts that remain unresolved in contemporary psychiatric nosology. The central task in this chapter is to articulate how depression has become classified as a psychiatric disorder. The history of depression and psychiatry that I offer is neither revisionist nor apologetic in nature. Instead, I outline but one way to understand the complex story of depression, up to, and including, a commentary on various ways in which depression is interwoven with contemporary Western culture.

The second chapter shifts focus from the history of psychiatry to psychiatric clinical practice. For this purpose, I conducted qualitative interviews with psychiatric professionals, including (but not limited to) psychiatrists, physicians, psychologists, and psychotherapists. In doing so, the findings from the qualitative study reveal considerable insight into some of the vexing problems that psychiatric clinicians routinely encounter in clinical *praxis*. An overarching tension that continually appeared in the interview material is the clinicians' ambivalent relationship with psychiatric diagnosis. On the one hand, clinicians overwhelmingly reported dissatisfaction with the operationalized approach to psychiatric diagnosis on account of the "impersonal" and vague symptoms used to diagnose depression. On the other hand, the clinicians also recognize that, despite the imperfect diagnostic criteria, a clinical diagnosis of depression opens the gateway for patients to receive appropriate care. But the especially salient finding from the qualitative study is that the way in which clinicians understand depression entails implicit assumptions about the nature of selfhood.

Although the qualitative findings related to psychiatric practice are interesting in and of themselves, the attitudes expressed by the interviewees need to be considered within the broader historical landscape of psychiatric medicine itself. That is, the informant's views regarding depression and selfhood are not *sui causa*; when we examine the historical contingencies of depression in Chapter 1, particularly the seminal influence of figures such as Emil Kraepelin and Sigmund Freud, it becomes clear that contemporary clinical attitudes regarding depression are informed by the way in which depression and selfhood have been conceptualized historically in psychiatric medicine. At the same time, when clinicians express dissatisfaction with the nature of psychiatric diagnosis, it is evident that their frustration is partly attributable to the fact that they lack a language that permits them to describe depression in a way that transcends the "scientific" discourse of psychiatric medicine.

The qualitative study undertaken here offers us insight into not only how clinicians currently understand depression, but provides us with a point of departure for our phenomenological investigation of depression and selfhood, developed in chapters four and five. The qualitative study is moreover crucial to the overall arc of this dissertation, inasmuch that one of the aims in the concluding chapter will be to offer clinicians a phenomenological language and a set of phenomenological insights which will enable them to better express aspects of depression and selfhood that psychiatric theory and psychiatric manuals typically take for granted. But more importantly, since this dissertation contends that selfhood is implicated in the experience of depressed patients, and that depression is a disorder of the self, then I believe we are warranted in gathering together clinical attitudes concerning depression on the basis that these attitudes will inform – however implicitly – the clinical practice of diagnosis and therapeutic treatments.

The third chapter in this dissertation marks a thematic shift. This chapter attempts to familiarize the reader with philosophical issues associated with the nebulous topic of the self. I will present what I believe are the four most salient and influential models of selfhood in the context of contemporary psychiatric practice. Putting aside the historical and practical analysis from Chapters 1 and 2, Chapter 3 is tasked with establishing the philosophical landscape with respect to contemporary views of selfhood. Until this point in the investigation, the discussion of selfhood has been limited to historical and clinical perspectives. To provide a more robust picture of the imprecise notion of selfhood, the third chapter assesses four models of selfhood (Brain-based, Experiential, Situated, Narrative), all of which have influenced contemporary philosophical discussions regarding selfhood. I also assess the respective relevance of each model in the context of psychiatry and depression.

Though each particular model of the self has merits, I argue that no one of these contemporary models of selfhood is capacious enough to encompass the ambiguous nature of lived-experience. Put another way, because consciousness experience permits us to shift between explicit self-awareness (thetic) and implicit self-awareness (operative), a robust account of selfhood must not only make sense of our ability to shift and slide seamlessly between *world*-oriented awareness and *self*-awareness, but it must also offer insight into the way in which our experiential awareness is modified in depression.

Chapter 4 is an extension of the previous chapter dedicated to philosophical analysis of selfhood. However, the central task of the fourth chapter is to develop a phenomenological – and ontological – account of selfhood by drawing extensively from the philosophy of Maurice Merleau-Ponty and Erwin Straus. The contribution of this chapter is two-fold: first, I will argue that the self is characterized by a style of action that manifests through embodied-perception. Second, in order to understand selfhood in the context of phenomenology, this chapter functions as an essential point of philosophical reference to appreciate why phenomenology is relevant for depression and selfhood, all of which must be understood through the ontology of situation. Second, in addition to the philosophy of Merleau-Ponty, I reinforce his insights by drawing on the work of phenomenological psychiatrist Erwin Straus. I argue that Merleau-Ponty's phenomenological understanding of perception is heavily indebted to the work of Straus, a significant yet underappreciated aspect in the history of philosophy. As the chapter comes to a close, we will be well placed to conduct a phenomenological analysis of the relationship between selfhood and depression.

The investigation steadily prepares the way for a phenomenological analysis of depression and selfhood, the central focus of Chapter 5. In this chapter, depression is considered from the perspective of lived-space, with particular emphasis given to the existential dimension of depth. While I acknowledge that my analysis is, in many ways, indebted to previous phenomenological investigations of depression, I also argue that embodied approaches to depression fail to properly specify the perceptual implications of embodied subjectivity (or selfhood). As the outcome of Chapter 5, the reader is offered a phenomenological account of depression, as well as two possible ways that selfhood is altered in depression: either as *depressive-style* or as an *interruption* of self-style.

In the final chapter of the study, I attend to the way in which our phenomenological findings are salient to the practice of psychiatry. First, in the context of depression diagnostics – discussed at length in both Chapter 1 and Chapter 2 – I employ the phenomenological distinction between depressive style and interrupted style to illustrate the unique way in which selfhood is altered in persistent depressive disorder (PPD) and major depressive disorder (MDD) respectively. In the case of the former, because PPD diagnoses are reserved for persons who experience depression for two or more years, I specify how PPD is diagnostically compatible with altered self-experience as disclosed through depressive-self-style. By contrast, MDD, which is acute in nature, diagnostically corresponds with altered self-experience, and is phenomenologically characterized by an interruption of self-style. Depressive-style and interrupted self-style not only bear fidelity to the lived-experiences described by many depressed patients, these two ways of characterizing depressed experience "remind" clinicians that depression cannot be fully grasped without explicit reference to selfhood.

Going beyond the issue of depression diagnosis, the phenomenological findings with respect to self-style and lived-space are also significant in the context of depression treatment. Specifically, in the context of "talk therapy" or psychotherapy, I contend that our phenomenological understanding of selfhood and depression are salient points of reference in establishing (fundamental) "meta goals" that I believe to be fundamental to *any* psychotherapeutic approach irrespective of specific professional norms and competencies guiding a particular model of therapy (e.g. cognitive behavioral therapy, psychodynamic therapy, dialectic behavioral therapy, art therapy, and so on). Hence, even though a clinician's psychotherapeutic competence will to a large extent depend on his or her professional training, we can nevertheless develop essential therapeutic goals that will subtend any particular therapeutic modality, regardless of a clinician's theoretical or practical training.

The therapeutic encounter entails certain obligations or responsibilities to be fulfilled by both clinician and patient to support therapeutic success, and these responsibilities are delineated by the overall goals of therapy. Drawing on the work of Canadian philosopher John Russon, I argue that therapy is, first and foremost, a therapeutic *project*, the overarching goal of which aims at self-transcendence or re-stylization of self-style. That is, the guiding aim of therapy is to interrogate and overcome deeply rooted embodied habits that inhibit one's ability to lead a flourishing life. For persons seeking therapeutic treatment for depression, the goal of re-stylization is contingent upon the extent to which sedimented bodily behaviors may be re-habituated, such that "success" is broadly defined by a person's ability to cope with practical situations that had previously proven to be stultifying.

Having said this, the possibility of self re-stylization is far from guaranteed in advance. Why? Self-style is developmental and unreflective, which means that it is expressed practically and pre-conceptually as we learn to navigate the world; since our self-style emerges at the earliest stages of life, our embodied way of contacting the world becomes established *tacitly* as preferred ways of contacting the world. As a result, even if we prove capable of raising embodied habits or behaviors to the level of explicit awareness, simply being aware of behaviors is insufficient to impel behavioral change.

Then again, even if habitual and embodied habits prove resistant to change, it is nevertheless the case that self re-stylization remains an open possibility for us. Clinicians are essential figures for facilitating the possibility of self-change. And even if patients and clinicians fulfill their respective *individual* therapeutic responsibilities, it must be kept in mind that a therapeutic project is also rooted in the inviolable intersubjective demand to be recognized and confirmed by an 'other self' (therapist). Put plainly, therapy is an ongoing (existential) project, the success of which depends upon intersubjective engagement. This means that a satisfactory vision of therapy should not be one that prioritizes self-directed introspection. Instead, therapeutic goals that subtend the therapeutic process itself must be navigated together by both parties. But crucially, the psychiatric professional is not simply someone who serves as a therapeutic guide; psychiatric clinicians are responsible for acting as a surrogate on behalf of reality and of others in general, the success of which is reflected in a renewed and sustained ability to be oneself.

CHAPTER 1

Looking behind and ahead: A historical discussion of depression and psychiatry

1. Introduction

Even if it was plausible to provide the reader with *the* history of depression, the ambition of this chapter is considerably more modest. For, if historians and scholars of psychiatry agree on one thing, it is undoubtedly that the field is characterized by disagreement. To illustrate, psychiatrist and historian David Healy has noted that "against a background of difficulties getting into print articles on the adverse effects of drugs, it is something to be able to say that I have never had reviews as openly vituperative as the reviews of some of the historical articles" (Healy 2014, 451). Likewise, "the history of psychiatry," says historian Edward Shorter, "is a minefield" (Shorter 1997, ix). The genesis of depression as we know it in contemporary life is, of course, an amalgamation of disparate historical facts and events. Yet, facts and events alone do not constitute a chronicle of depression. As Walter Benjamin puts it, the chronicle is the telling of history (Benjamin 1968, Sato 2015) and so the history of depression is equally the way in which it is told. Moreover, Micale and Porter contend that "psychiatry boasts no stable and consensual theoretical vantage point from which to construct itself historically" (Micale and Porter 1994a, 5). Thus, in addition to ideological and methodological disagreement about how disparate facts and events should be interpreted, there is equal disagreement concerning the way in which the story of depression ought to be told.

This chapter provides a historical picture of depression. The historical relevance of depression and selfhood is twofold: first, it is crucial that we delineate contemporary depression from the phenomenon of melancholy, so as to establish basic boundaries regarding the object of our inquiry. Second, because depression research has been overwhelmingly conducted from the perspective of natural science, in anticipation of the phenomenological analysis in chapters four and five, it is incumbent upon us to highlight how scientific prejudices of objective thought have obscured rather than clarified the phenomenon of depression. The account I offer accentuates a relatively simple, yet polarized history of depression as a psychiatric category. The twentieth century marks a particularly auspicious period of scientific discovery, and at the outset of this century, the profession of psychiatry as we now know it was merely *en route*. By the end of the century, however, psychiatry had become (and continues to be) a fully-fledged science. This emergent scientific *zeitgeist* was considered especially promising for scientists interested in "cracking" the complex code of human behavior. An enduring legacy of this historical moment is a dubious assumption that the source of "pathological" human behavior (i.e. depression) is causally attributable to mechanistic or physical malfunctioning.

But the "causal" paradigm that guided early psychiatric medicine was not the only explanatory model on offer. The organic causation model of depression was challenged by an alternative model that attributed depression's cause to psychogenetic factors (i.e. the psychological account) rather than organic ones. And even though this bifurcated picture of causation emerged early in the twentieth century, I use this chapter to illustrate that contemporary clinical attitudes regarding depression reflect considerable fidelity to this two-tiered explanation of depression.

I argue that our contemporary notion of depression is historically indebted to the work of two seminal figures: Emil Kraepelin (the biological account) and Sigmund Freud (the psychogenic account). Second, I demonstrate how the influence of Kraepelin, and Freud permeates the development of psychiatric nosology, which ultimately made possible the psychiatric category of depression. Last, I consider whether the category of depression is responsible for the "age of depression" (Horwitz and Wakefield 2005) that has come to characterize late modern life. Like many others (Hess and Majerus 2011, Micale and Porter 1994b, Scull 1999, Henckes 2011, Mora 1994), I share the view that the proliferation of depression is necessarily connected to the category of depression established in DSM-III. It seems doubtful, however, that the connection between depression and DSM alone is a sufficient condition to understand the prevalence of depression. Looking beyond psychiatry itself, I consider how pharmacology, professional integrity, and the human condition have evinced the "age of depression."

1.1 The present before the past

The most recent iteration of the depression criteria is found in the 2013 publication of DSM-5. Depression is a category of disorder that is subsumed under the broader category of affective disorders. Depression is clinically identified by employing an operationalized set of criteria – comprised of observable signs and symptoms – that guide the clinical task of diagnosing depression. Depression is in turn defined by the criteria found in *Fig. 1* below, which provides us with a considerably restricted sense of *what* depression *is*. Keeping in mind, however, that the task of this investigation is to disclose the essential features of depression, these criteria unfortunately offer little concrete insights about the phenomenon of depression itself.

This makes it all the more imperative that we specify why the symptoms associated with depression, and which constitute the content of depression's diagnostic criteria, have become the standard diagnostic tool in identifying major depression and persistent depressive disorder (formerly dysthymia). At present, a depression diagnosis is obtained by recording patient symptom reports, which are then corroborated or complimented by relevant clinical observations made by trained psychiatric professionals (APA 2013, 168):

Major Depressive Disorder	**Persistent Depressive Disorder**
A. Five (or more) of the following symptoms have been present during the same 2-week period and represent a change from previous functioning; at least one of the symptoms is either (1) depressed mood or (2) loss of interest or pleasure.	**A.** Depressed mood for most of the day, for more days than not, as indicated by either subjective account or observation by others, for at least 2 years. Note: In children and adolescents, mood can be irritable, and duration must be at least 1 year.
1. Depressed mood most of the day, nearly every day, as indicated by either subjective report (e.g., feels sad, empty, hopeless) or observation made by others (e.g., appears tearful). 2. Markedly diminished interest or pleasure in all, or almost all, activities most of the day, nearly every day (as indicated by either subjective account	**B.** Presence, while depressed, of two (or more) of the following: 1. Poor appetite or overeating. 2. Insomnia or hypersomnia. Low energy or fatigue. 3. Low self-esteem. 4.Poor concentration or difficulty making decisions. 5. Feelings of hopelessness.

or observation).
3. Significant weight loss when not dieting or weight gain (e.g., a change of more than 5% of body weight in a month), or decrease or increase in appetite nearly every day.
4. Insomnia or hypersomnia nearly every day.
5. Psychomotor agitation or retardation nearly every day (observable by others, not merely subjective feelings of restlessness or being slowed down).
6. Fatigue or loss of energy nearly every day.
7. Feelings of worthlessness or excessive or inappropriate guilt (which may be delusional) nearly every day (not merely self-reproach or guilt about being sick).
8.Diminished ability to think or concentrate, or indecisiveness, nearly every day (either by subjective account or as observed by others).
9. Recurrent thoughts of death (not just fear of dying), recurrent suicidal ideation without a specific plan, or a suicide attempt or a specific plan for committing suicide.

B. The symptoms cause clinically significant distress or impairment in social, occupational, or other important areas of functioning.

C. The episode is not attributable to the physiological effects of a substance or to another medical condition.
Note: Responses to a significant loss (e.g.,

C. During the 2-year period (1 year for children or adolescents) of the disturbance, the individual has never been without the symptoms in Criteria A and B for more than 2 months at a time.

D. Criteria for a major depressive disorder may be continuously present for 2 years.

E. There has never been a manic episode or a hypomanic episode, and criteria have never been met for cyclothymic disorder.

F. The disturbance is not better explained by a persistent schizoaffective disorder, schizophrenia, delusional disorder, or other specified or unspecified schizophrenia spectrum and other psychotic disorder.

G. The symptoms are not attributable to the physiological effects of a substance (e.g., a drug of abuse, a medication) or another medical condition (e.g. hypothyroidism).

H. The symptoms cause clinically significant distress or impairment in social, occupational, or other important areas of functioning.

Note: Because the criteria for a major depressive episode include four symptoms that are absent from the symptom list for persistent depressive bereavement, financial ruin, losses from a natural disaster, a serious medical illness or disability) may include the feelings of intense sadness, rumination about the loss, insomnia, poor appetite, and weight loss noted in Criterion A, which may resemble a depressive episode. Although such symptoms may be understandable or considered appropriate to the loss, the presence of a major depressive episode in addition to the normal response to a significant loss should also be carefully considered. This decision inevitably requires the exercise of clinical judgment based on the individual's history and the cultural norms for the expression of distress in the context of loss.

D. The occurrence of the major depressive episode is not better explained by schizoaffective disorder, schizophrenia, schizophreniform disorder, delusional disorder, or other specified and unspecified schizophrenia spectrum and other psychotic disorders.

E. There has never been a manic episode or a hypomanic episode. Note: This exclusion does not apply if all manic-like or hypomanic-like episodes are substance-induced or are attributable to the physiological effects of another medical condition.

disorder (dysthymia), a very limited

Note: The essential feature of persistent depressive disorder (dysthymia) is a depressed mood that occurs for most of the day, for more days than not, for at least 2 years, or at least 1 year for children and adolescents (Criterion A). This disorder represents a consolidation of DSM-IV-defined chronic major depressive disorder and dysthymic disorder. Major depression may precede persistent depressive disorder, and major depressive episodes may occur during persistent depressive disorder. Individuals whose symptoms meet major depressive disorder criteria for 2 years should be given a diagnosis of persistent depressive disorder (APA 168).

Fig. 1 Criteria for Major depression and persistent depressive disorder (APA, 2013).

The criteria for PDD overlap with those of MDD. What distinguishes the two categories is duration and the severity of symptoms. PDD is a low-level depression that persists over time (chronic), whereas MDD is episodic and severe (acute). A cursory glance at this matrix might lead one to wonder why it might be considered an inadequate description of depression. Does the DSM description not reflect or map onto reality? The short answer is that it does not. The complicated answer, however, is that we cannot know in advance whether future empirical research will (eventually) confirm that the DSM-5 description of depression is ultimately accurate. Having said this, clearly some maps are better than others. A map with directions drawn by a friend is likely to have less detail and scope than that of a GPS in one's automobile. Both are approximations with considerably varied degrees of accuracy.

The criteria for diagnosing depression have remained relatively stable since publication of DSM-III nearly 40 years ago. And though the DSM depression criteria have since undergone minor revisions, these revisions have largely left what we call "depression" conceptually unchanged. Having said this, there is one significant, yet subtle, change that, with the recent iteration of the depression criteria in DSM-5, has raised eyebrows. Hitherto, psychiatry's ability to discern between depression and "normal" sadness has hinged on the DSM's long-standing bereavement (or exclusion) clause, a diagnostic exception that permits clinicians to make clinical distinctions between depressive disorder and depression symptoms associated with bereavement. The exclusion clause is intended to recognize that depression symptoms elicited by grief and loss are in fact culturally sanctioned or expected affective responses to personal loss rather than depression.

Because clinical depression is a medical diagnosis, the bereavement clause acknowledged that depression symptoms are context dependent. In other words, a depression diagnosis should be contextualized so as to permit a clinical distinction between *actual* depression and ostensible depression. The DSM exclusion clause allows clinicians to diagnose depression if, and only if, the person's symptoms are not elicited by extraneous life circumstances, such as job loss or end of a relationship.

It is all the more perplexing, then, that when DSM-5 was published in 2013, the APA elected to excise the long-standing exception clause due to bereavement from the depression category. Why? Until 2013, the ability to clinically contextualize symptoms enabled clinicians to discern between depression and "normal" sadness. However, in light of this recent and unexpected conceptual shift, "the current definition [of depression] that [now] emphasizes the specific presence of symptoms departs from the contextual tradition" (Horwitz, Wakefield, and Lorenzo-Luaces 2016, 16). According to Horwtiz et al., without this diagnostic safeguard, there no longer exists the possibility of distinguishing depression from normal sadness:

> the removal of [the bereavement] criterion from the diagnostic criteria in DSM-5 indicates that far from making diagnostic progress, the recent his-

tory of the mood disorders shows significant regression in understanding the most basic of all distinctions – the difference between normal sadness and depressive disorder" (2006, 20).

Horwitz and Wakefield have a vested interest in this controversy, since they argue for a very particular conception of exception, one that turns on the distinction between dysfunction and normal sadness. From their perspective, the bereavement clause was the last diagnostic exception that could allow for this distinction: "the failure to allow exclusions other than bereavement enhanced the reliability of the MDD diagnosis because clinicians and researchers might disagree on whether depressive symptoms represent appropriate contextual responses" (ibid.). Hence, for Horwitz et al., depression manifests itself without identifiable reasons or causes.

Why should we get hung up on what is an otherwise relatively minor diagnostic change? First, it bears on the long-standing debate about the causal nature of depression: depression is either causally explained by a (biological) dysfunction, or conversely, depression is explained by way of (psychological) reasons that are related to life context. Staying with the example of grief, in the case of biological dysfunction, depression is qualitatively distinguished from grief because depression should not be explained by reference to an external circumstance; it should have no "reason." With respect to psychological reasons, depression is (potentially) indistinguishable from grief since the symptoms are symptoms of depression, regardless of reasons that endanger these symptoms. Hence, without the bereavement exclusion clause, we are confronted with a causal dilemma: depression is explained by either a naturalistic model (causal) or a psychosocial (reasons-based) model.

The second reason for addressing the removal of the bereavement exclusion in detail here follows from the first, namely that DSM-5 diagnostic criteria ignore the phenomenology of depression. It is to ask: is the phenomenology of grief identical with the phenomenology of depression? Does the experience of grief map onto the experience of depression? Even if the symptoms are similar, should we presume that the lived-experience of depression and the lived-experience of grief correspond? These questions suggest that the APA's decision to rescind the bereavement exclusion clause in DSM-5 has subsequently opened up the space to re-visit conceptual problems concerning depression.

Now that we have outlined what depression looks like as a contemporary diagnostic category of psychiatric disorder, it is incumbent upon us to make sense of exactly how this has come to pass.

1.2 Delimiting the origin of depression

It is important to reiterate that this investigation attends to the contemporary category of depression. Despite the common-sense view that depression and melancholia are interchangeable terms, the notion of melancholia is so nebulous that it would be remiss to presume that these phenomena can be reduced to a single, continuous phenomenon. One chapter alone could hardly do justice to a cultural phenomenon such as melancholia, the history of which spans over two millennia.[8] Nevertheless, the story of depression cannot be told without some consideration of the connection with melancholia, and it would be naïve to believe that a study of depression could dispense with melancholia *in toto*. In order to understand the essential structures of depression it is crucial that we sketch out the historical contours of psychiatric medicine, which as an emergent branch of medical science is responsible for the eventual conceptual shift that saw melancholia replaced with depression.

The indexical use of the term depression is best understood as a process rather than taking place at a determinate point in history. It is a slippery concept; while appearing rarely in the lexicon prior to the 19th century, it can hardly be considered a modern word. At best, we can roughly delineate a period during which depression began to denote a concrete referent. Prior to this, the nebulous concept of melancholia served psychiatry as a catch-all term for almost any form of mental disturbance.

The term depression does not emerge as the consequence of any one historical moment. According to Stanley Jackson,

---

[8] Using one of many possible examples, Karen Ross' review (Ross) of Clark Lawlor's *From Melancholia to Prozac: A history of depression,* wonders how the scope of this topic - spanning over two thousand years - can be adequately dealt with in two-hundred pages. It is crucial to be explicit about the relationship between melancholia and depression. The issue continues to divide scholars, and is one unlikely to be resolved, at least definitively. There are two general characterizations of this issue: depression and melancholia are viewed as either continuous phenomena or discontinuous phenomena. Plainly put, melancholia, with a history spanning two millennia, is roughly the same thing as our contemporary notion of depression, or the two, despite some shared features, are ontologically distinct. There are countless discussions of melancholia and the relationship to depression, some of which include: Radden (2003); Berrios and Porter (1995); Varga (2013); Lawlor (2012), and Horwitz and Wakefield (2007).

> *depression* is a relative latecomer to the terminology for dejected states [...] the term and its cognates came into use in English during the seventeenth century [...] but it was during the eighteenth century that depression really began to find a place in discussions of melancholia (Jackson 1990, 5, emphasis original).

The appearance of depression in the lexicon, while historically interesting, is of less interest philosophically. Regardless of when the word first appears in the literature, what concerns us here is *what* the term denoted: depression as a symptom, or depression as a category. Since the term melancholia was too inclusive, it referred to a range of conditions that included manic states, depressive states, psychosis, and varieties of insanity. Like most of the early psychiatric categories, melancholia was strikingly capacious, meaning that our familiar categories of schizophrenia and depression would have at one time been synonymous with melancholia.

The conceptual disintegration of melancholia in the early twentieth century coincides with changes in the physical location of clinical practice. Patients with psychiatric symptoms were funneled away from the physician's clinic and into hospital-based care. With unfettered access to patients and the ability to conduct longitudinal observations, the new clinical setting allowed clinicians to record increasingly detailed descriptions of a patient's symptoms and behavior. Increasingly refined observations led to a realization that manic features were not proper to cases of melancholia. Concurrently, melancholia became understood as an affliction aligned with intellectual faculties rather than emotional faculties. More importantly, patient observations overturned the dominant view that melancholic illness was irreversible, i.e. permanent (Berrios 1988, 44). These modifications, which arose in the mid-to-late nineteenth century, are attributed to the seminal clinical work of Emil Kraepelin.

1.3 Kraepelin: Psychiatric idol

If the history of modern psychiatry is said to begin with French alienist Phillipe Pinel (Shorter, 1997, 12), then the modern category of depression likely begins with Emil Kraepelin.[9] Prior to Kraepelin, views on the putative etiology of mental illness vacillated between mental pathology (e.g. Pinel, Esquirol) and disease of the brain (e.g. Griesinger, Maudsley). Long before

—

[9] Alienists were essentially proto-psychiatrists, clinicians tending to patients in asylum care suffering mental-alienation (Shorter 1997, 17).

depression became a formally designated category of disorder, explanatory (or causal) frameworks for mental disorder were already polarized. But what makes Kraepelin iconoclastic is that his research *was not about* etiology *per* se. On the contrary, Kraepelin "put biological psychiatry behind him, deciding to concentrate instead on a psychiatry based on bedside observation of patients over time… declaring himself agnostic [concerning causation] (Shorter, 1997, 106). Kraepelin did not altogether eschew organic causation, he merely recognized that the etiology remained elusive. In this way, Kraepelin was "not primarily a clinician or a theorist but a researcher and classifier" (Radden 2009, 259). Nevertheless, he remained associated with the "biological model," which is one of the two poles that characterizes the way we have come to understand depression. It is important to keep in mind that Kraepelin believed that the in-patient setting of the hospital, which was conducive to longitudinal observation of illness course and prognosis, would elicit better results than working with slides in the laboratory. Then again, the patients with whom Kraepelin had contact did not exhaust the (potential) spectrum of depressive illness. Patients treated at the hospital did not suffer from "the blues"; Kraepelin's patients were unambiguously "mentally ill."

Kraepelin's observation-based methodology became the inspiration for contemporary psychiatric nosology, inasmuch that his talent for meticulous and detailed descriptions is a particular trait the DSM has striven to emulate: "DSM-5 is designed to better fill the need of clinicians, patients, families, and researchers *for a clear and concise description*" (APA 2013, 5, emphasis added). Not only did Kraepelin initiate descriptive practices in psychiatry, he also altered the course of nosology by borrowing from the medical model of disease. His clinical work led him to conclude "that there were a number of discrete psychiatric illnesses, or diseases, each separate from the next. Depression, schizophrenia, and so forth were different just as mumps and pneumonia were different" (Shorter 1997, 108). Psychiatry, though, proved less receptive to the Kraepelin perspective (Decker 2013, 341).

Kraepelin's longitudinal studies would lead him to divide psychiatric illness into thirteen groups, two of which are generally held to be the most influential for contemporary psychiatry: *Dementia praecox* (i.e. schizophrenia today) and *manic depressive insanity* (i.e. bi-polar mood disorder) (Radden 2002). Interestingly, of the thirteen groups, these two were the only *non-organic* psychiatric illnesses, meaning that they were without brain lesions or obvious brain abnormalities, traits that were identifiable in syphilitic illnesses. Kraepelin also cast doubt on the contemporaneous view that the prognosis for mental illness was deteriorative. Hitherto, consensus had been that most patients were chronically ill, and therefore incurable. Kraepelin's detailed studies contradicted this view, demonstrating that the illness often remitted or that it was episodic rather than chronic. His conclusion, then, was that not all forms of insanity were irreversible, and they could be subdivided into distinct groups according to prognosis, which in essence was to say that mental illnesses could be delineated into homogenous groups or kinds. Kraepelin's use of prognosis to organize mental illness was rooted in a very basic matrix: illnesses that remitted were affective in nature, while the nature of conditions that failed to resolve were cognitive (Lawlor 2012, 137). And even though Kraepelin's fastidious observations were not the ultimate foundation for the category of depression, his approach is widely acknowledged as the precursor to contemporary psychiatric nosology, out of which depression was made into a homogenous category.[10]

The notable, albeit subtle, contribution Kraepelin made to depression was to transform its sense. Previously, depression denoted a symptom, whereas Kraepelin applied it as a "general category" (Decker 2013, 301). The category, in turn, stipulated a variety of melancholic states. For instance, his famous textbook of psychiatry posited two main categories (or nosological groups):

> bringing together in one category psychoses that he considered to be deteriorating in nature and in another category psychoses that he considered to be non-deteriorating. In the first group (*die Verblödungsprocess*) were those conditions that were to constitute his notion of dementia praecox [...] in the second group (*das periodische Irresein*) he brought together mania, melancholia, and circular insanity, thus discontinuing the presentation of mania and melancholia as separate disorders (Jackson 1990, 189).

Kraepelin's description of depression – which bore little to no resemblance with depression as it is described in DSM-5 – remained clinically active as late as the turn of the twentieth century. Hence, although depression is not directly the result of Kraepelin's work, "his version of depressive symptoms has *constituted the basis for diagnosis and classification* for depressive disorders up to the present" (Lawlor 2012, 140, emphasis added). Moreover,

---

[10] This should not be interpreted to mean that the phenomenon of depression is homogenous. The point is that depression would eventually become a distinct categorical entity, which was not continuous with other mental illnesses.

with respect to biological psychiatry and the putative neurological basis of depression, Kraepelin was either prescient, or at least inspirational, insofar as he "placed a heavy influence on internal factors rather than the external events like the death of a loved one, romantic issues, or money problems. Even these events, which might seem on the surface to have caused depression, would in fact be due to innate internal factors" (ibid., 140-141).[11] The removal of insane features, and emphasis on emotional disturbance rather than intellect, precipitates a substantive shift toward the affective disorder of depression.

What makes this a point of relevant interest? It is taken for granted that the term depression was initially used to denote a symptom rather than a syndrome or disorder. In 1867, German physician Wilhelm Griesinger, who was a significant influence on Kraepelin, said of melancholia

> *the general result* of these (mental and cerebral) processes is depression or a painful state of mind [...] Observation shows that the immense majority of mental diseases commence with a state of profound emotional perversion, of a depressing and sorrowful character (Griesinger 2000, 225-226, emphasis original).

On the one hand, the "medical" view of melancholia (or soon to be depression) passes from Griesinger on through to Kraepelin. On the other hand, Kraepelin's method of observation led him to subsume melancholia and mania under the grouping term "depressive states," which then further subdivided into four categories according to severity: melancholia simplex, melancholia gravis, stupor, and involutional melancholia (Lawlor 2012). The inchoate historical emergence of depression arguably begins to take shape as it passes from descriptor (symptom) to indexical (thing). Despite appearances, this transition is far from innocuous. It provokes an ontological question, not only regarding disease and disorder, but reciprocally, concerning the way we conceptualize subjectivity (or the basis for all experience). As we will see in Chapter 3, as depression slowly transfigures into a discrete category, the movement from depression "as symptom" to depression as "entity" represents a (surreptitious) transfiguration of what means to be a self, a distinction between having an illness or being ill. As we move further into the chapter, we will see how the conception of depression is connected to the concept of self.

—

[11] This is the general premise of Horwitz and Wakefield in their influential book (2007) published a century after Kraepelin's seminal work on classification.

1.3.1 Freud: Psychiatric zenith and nadir

The theoretical development of Freudian psychoanalysis is one of – if not *the* – most influential, and for many, most problematic moments in the history of psychiatry. We witness a profession whose initial flirtation with Freud's iconoclastic ideas developed into an infatuation, and eventually came to monopolize both psychiatric theory and practice for nearly half a century.

Freud's psychiatric legacy provokes disagreement among historians. Notably, Shorter insists it is Kraepelin, "not Freud, who is the central figure in the history of psychiatry" (1997, 100). Shorter is unreserved in his critical view of Freud:

> Freud was a neurologist who did not see patients with psychotic illness. His doctrine of psychoanalysis, based on intuitive leaps of fantasy, *did not stand the test of time.* By contrast, Kraepelin and his data cards provided the single most significant insight that the late nineteenth and twentieth centuries had to offer into major psychiatric illness (ibid., emphasis added).

Shorter's evaluation that Kraepelin eclipsed Freud is not unmotivated. His portrayal of psychoanalysis is generally unflattering, particularly since he believes that the progress of modern psychiatry is internally validated through the duration of its concepts. Since psychoanalytic theory resisted falsification (Popper 1963), the practice had no claims to status as a science.

It is a fitting coincidence that Kraepelin and Freud were born only three months apart in 1856. Their divergent methods reflect the historical polarization of psychiatric theory: biological psychiatry of Kraepelin at the one end, and psychopathological psychiatry of Freud at the other. To be clear, Freud did not deny that biological life underpinned mental life. But he insisted that most mental illnesses were not explained by biological processes. Mental illness (or neurotic behavior) was a consequence of stultified psychic processes that were the result of psychic traumas experienced during personal development, giving rise to the clinically significant result that the internal psychic conflicts manifested in deleterious personal behaviors.

Though the approaches of Freud and Kraepelin are theoretically and methodologically divergent, they may both be credited with literally reconfiguring the physical space of psychiatric *praxis*. Just as Kraepelin opted for the in-patient setting of the hospital over the lab, Freud's psychoanalytic method moved psychiatry out of institutions (including the lab) and into the private clinic. And though the migration to private practice had begun prior to Freud's influence, the positive uptake of psychoanalytic theory, which placed emphasis on an empathic analyst-patient relationship, expedited the move toward private practice, transforming a trickle into a stream.

With respect to the conceptual development of depression, we need not engage in an extended exegesis of Freud's psychoanalytic theory.[12] What concerns us here is the relationship between psychoanalytic theory and psychiatric epistemology. While Kraepelin was (unknowingly) preparing scaffolding for the development of psychiatric classification, Freud was undermining the clinical relevance of classification itself. In the hospital, Kraepelin tended to patients with severe illnesses (psychotic), whereas Freud's own patients had illnesses that were "neurotic," or less severe, in nature (Shorter 1997, Horwitz 2007). Once again, for Freud, the illness in question was not causally attributed to an organic dysfunction. Instead, the illness was a manifestation of psychic conflicts played out within the patient's conscious and unconscious inner world:

> As we have learned, the symptoms of the neuroses are basically substitute gratifications for unfulfilled sexual wishes [...] It now seems reasonable to formulate this statement when a drive impulse undergoes repression, its libidinal portions are turned into symptoms (Freud 2004, 97).

To put it concisely, "neurotic" illnesses arise when irrational desires from the unconscious dimension of psychic life impinge upon our rational decision making capacities. For Freud, the repression of one's natural desires necessitated that these desires be displaced onto other dimensions of one's life. Repeatedly frustrated desires, in turn, manifest unconsciously as behaviors (neurotic) that are at odds with the demands of everyday life, and consequently engender varying degrees of suffering due to this psychic conflict.

From the Freudian perspective, even though mental illness may result in suffering that is equal to that experienced in somatic diseases, unlike Kraepelin's model, the illness was not ascribed the status of being an entity. In other words, "Freud rejected the 2,500-year old tradition that postulated physiological causes of pathological depression and adopted a psychogenic theory of causation" (Horwitz 2007). Therapeutic impetus behind psycho-

—

[12] Since the category of depression pre-dates Freud, his work only touched on melancholia. His most famous text on the topic is "Mourning and Melancholia" (see Radden 2000). However, with respect to the historical development of depression as a concept, his essay is dedicated to the internal psychic dynamics of melancholia, which is beyond the scope of this chapter.

analysis obliged patients to make conscious the unconscious dynamics of which they had hitherto been ignorant. By establishing an ongoing therapeutic with an analyst, the patient could hope to eventually bring to light developmental traumas that plagued her unconscious life. Even though neuroses could be of a certain type (e.g. compulsion neurosis), no two patients would suffer from the same causal event. Each case was developmentally unique, which ultimately rendered any impetus to observe the course or outcome of an illness moot. Cognizance of the psychical conflict engendering neurotic behavior could only become apparent to both patient and analyst through a protracted process of analysis. Accordingly, there was little impetus for psychoanalysis to abide by any formal classification system, for each patient would – in principle – resolve the psychical conflict, regardless how it might be classified.

We can begin to see how psychogenesis came to stand in opposition to the biological model of causation (pathophysiology). And though these two perspectives are polarized, both entail implicit ontological commitments regarding the nature of the self. The "psychological" (i.e. psychogenic) account of depression leads to the conclusion that the illness is not an entity, but a behavioral expression of stultified personal development. The patient, or subject, who experiences depression, *is* ill or disordered: "symptoms of depression resulted from the depressed person's unconsciousness turning inward of hostility toward another person" (Horwitz 2007). In contrast, the depressed patient on the biological account *has* an illness or disorder. The underlying causal mechanism is independent of the patient's subjectivity: "Even many cases that seemed to arise normally from external influences such as deaths, quarrels, unrequited love, infidelity, or financial difficulties actually were manifestations of disorders that stemmed from innate dispositions" (ibid., 77). Here, the sense of innateness does not correspond to character or personality, but instead denotes genetic or biological pre-disposition. This means that, if the pathophysiology behind depression was to be empirically validated, we would have circumscribed an organic process or state that is exclusive of who the patient is.

When the philosopher of science Carl Hempel addressed the APA in 1959 regarding psychiatric taxonomy, he amplified the need for psychiatric classification to discern between a "case" and the individual:

> An individual case of the kind here referred to is best understood to be a particular human being at a given time, or during a given time span, in his life history: this construal allows the possibility that a person may belong to

> a class representing a certain illness at some time, but not at all times, during his life (Hempel 1965, 138).

Coincidentally, though Hempel is referring to mental illness in general, the case Hempel employs as an example is psychotic depressive reaction. He argues that the category of depression (or any mental disorder) is not a kind of thing, but that individual cases exemplify the classificatory concept of depression. And though Hempel does not equate categories with entities, he nonetheless reinforces the biomedical model of disease by appealing to a basic dichotomy of presence and absence – i.e. to have or not to have – with the caveat that borderline cases will undoubtedly arise. With luck, the concept or category under which individual cases are grouped will (eventually) be corroborated by empirical evidence drawn from psychiatric research.

1.4 The story of becoming a thing

For various reasons, the reputation of psychiatry is marked by ambivalence. The issue of etiology has been an especially salient preoccupation of many critics. At present, the etiological basis of depression continues to prove elusive, and, moreover, despite the considerable achievements in medical science, the causal mechanisms of depression remain enigmatic. Psychiatric etiology remained highly eclectic well into the twentieth century, and indeed this was a compelling reason for Kraepelin to organize his patient observations in accordance with symptom descriptions rather than the underlying cause. Without causal evidence, psychiatry required an approach to nosology (or classification) relying on descriptions rather than explanations.

Psychiatric classification is broadly concerned with ordering or arranging individual disorders based on typically presented signs and symptoms. The number of signs or symptoms that must be present to warrant a diagnosis is what constitutes the diagnostic criteria of a disorder. Recall that a major depressive disorder is one of several disorders under the umbrella category of affective disorder. In section 1.1, it was said that there are nine possible signs or symptoms associated with MDD. If four (or more) symptoms of the nine are reported by a patient or observed by a clinician, then the diagnostic *criteria* are satisfied and thus the diagnosis is confirmed.

What makes this historically significant? First, psychiatric categories have proven to be dynamic with respect to quantity and quality. Second, prior to the inaugural version of DSM (and up until DSM-III), psychiatric categories were loosely applied and descriptively inconsistent across the profession. Even though physicians such as Kraepelin had established rough category schemas derived from illness outcomes, there was no definitive agreement across the profession about how to classify, a problem exacerbated by geographical variations.

Until the DSM and ICD were published, formal diagnostic categories for mental disorder were scant. Taxonomic discourse – pertaining to how to classify and arrange nature – was far from unanimous. The very possibility of establishing veridical classifications hinged on a more primary problem, namely whether there was any logical basis for identifying "essential" properties of an entity. For instance:

> The deep problem with such essentialistic approaches is that they are not easily open to empirical verification. If expert taxonomist A claims that plants should be initially divided on the basis of their fruiting bodies and expert taxonomist B on the nature and shape of their leaves, they will develop internally consistent but distinct taxonomies. On what basis can we compare one with the other – as each achieves its own internal goals? (Kendler 2009, 1937).

The problems faced by the botanist were (and remain) no different from those of the psychiatrist: What concepts are best suited to validate mental illness? Just prior to Kraepelin and Freud, nineteenth century French alienists classified according to the "cause of the disorder ... the substratum ... the clinical ... outcome ... actuarial... phenomenological ... 'natural' ... psychological... and disease course" (Berrios, 107). Alternatively, we can say that this list employed by alienists, when taken as a whole, constitutes "the nosological entity" (Jablensky 2012, 79), which indicates a 'disease' or syndrome.[13] The nosological entities in early psychiatry bear little resemblance to what we find in modern classification (DSM). At the time, disorders included: "mania, lypemania, monomania, dementia, paralytic insanity, and idiocy; to which some added stupidity" (Berrios, 106). In contrast, the relatively recent publication of DSM-5 contains 297 disorders, which are subdivided into 22 categories (APA 2013). The confused state of classification in pre-DSM psychiatry attributable to clinical pluralism and the absence of theoretical uniformity:

---

[13] The distinction I employ between disease and syndrome is not theoretically robust, but the point is to point out that the nosological entity in psychiatry may be a disease (with evidence of underlying pathophysiology, among other requirements) or a syndrome (where a cluster of signs and symptoms hang together in some way, but it remains unclear how or why).

> The proposing authors (including luminaries such as Pinel, Griesinger, Kahlbaum, Kraft-Ebing, Wernicke, Kraepelin and Breuler) each brought to their classifications both wide clinical experience and a range of assumptions about what constitutes the essential features of psychiatric illness ... Just as diverse botanists, using distinct essential criteria, developed incompatible taxonomies, so various expert psychiatrists, using different validators to implement their concept of the essential nature of psychiatric disorders, proposed a bewildering array of different possible nosological schemes (Kendler, 1937).

Prior to the era of DSM-III and ICD-8 in the 1980s, the object of psychiatric inquiry was vague and uncertain, with classification disarray continuing well into the twentieth century, remaining diffuse and porous (Lawlor 2012). At the same time, it was becoming increasingly clear that if psychiatry was to solidify its status as a scientific branch of medicine, its theoretical and methodological eclecticism would be an obstacle. Foundations for a robust profession required a shift from inchoate and vague outlines, to concrete, distinct, and reliable ways to identify disorders such as depression.

So, despite psychiatric developments at the turn of the twentieth century, a cohesive psychiatry practice remained elusive. Certainly, despite the varied geographical pace of development and orientation, psychiatry was not totally devoid of basic consensus internationally (Pichot 1997, 48). Unfortunately, scientific research cannot establish a solid foundation according to basic agreement. How could psychiatry in the West, then, eventually coalesce into a uniform branch of scientific medicine that would end up introducing the category of depression?

1.5 The loss of melancholia

Up until the late nineteenth century, melancholia was an extremely promiscuous and wide-ranging notion designating mental illnesses, and it is upon this historically capacious spectrum that many want to carve out a tiny slice we now call depression. Regardless of the metaphysical status of depression (whether it has always existed as a kind of thing, or if it is simply a modern category), it is dubious that the symptoms observed in the asylum or early psychiatric wards, which have ultimately motivated our current descriptive categories (i.e. Kraepelin), are aligned with depression as a specific phenomenon.

Before the DSM definition of depression, it is reasonable to assume that there existed persons who suffered from "depression," however, this group of people remained unaccounted for since the severity of their illness – compared to psychotic patients – was not pronounced enough to warrant institutionalization. Since the signs and symptoms associated with melancholia were so indiscriminate, the modern depression category did not come into being by virtue of supplementing the existing category of melancholia. Instead, depression was established by *stripping away* irrelevant signs and symptoms, much like peeling an onion. Even still, it would be overly simplistic to assume that the core symptoms of the DSM-5 category of depression are simply a pared back version of melancholia once purged of its excesses.

Until roughly 1970, attitudes toward depression remained inspired by Freud – and later Rudolph Meyer (Lawlor 2012). Though I have emphasized the influence of Freud in early psychiatry, the rise to prominence of psychoanalysis cannot simply be reduced to the influence of Freud alone. The development of analysis is complicated by a variety of circumstances, many of which go beyond issues internal to psychiatry itself.[14] For instance:

> Writing the history of psychoanalysis is rather like writing the history of twentieth-century cultural weather: Its presence is so constant and pervasive that escaping its influence is out of the question. And precisely because of its inescapable character, it cannot be isolated from the myriad striking events (sic) that can more straightforwardly be singled out as part of the histories of science, of medicalization, of great ideas [...] of all the other movements to which it might apparently belong (Forrester 1994, 174).

But historical facts and figures will not adequately illustrate how psychoanalysis came to suffuse psychiatric theory. This is a multi-faceted transition, which if outlined in its entirety, would take us well beyond the scope of this investigation. But minimally, we need to illustrate how psychoanalysis established a foothold in North America – and ultimately western Europe – by considering the conditions under which psychoanalysis was positively received in psychiatry. At the same time, this cursory sketch will pre-figure why the success of psychoanalysis could not be sustained after publication of DSM-III in 1980.

The seed of psychoanalytic theory emerged on European soil, but its roots

became firmly planted in the United States. Up until the first decades of the twentieth century, the United States was without any tradition of psych-

[14] For an account of how psychoanalysis came into prominence see (Shorter 1997), (Lawlor 2012), (Micale and Porter 1994)

iatry in comparison to Europe. Here there are minimally two aspects for us to consider. First, the space of psychiatric treatment was transforming. With a move toward community-based care, and under the influence of the nascent field of neurology, "psychoanalysis was important in anchoring American psychiatrists in the office" (Shorter 1997, 160). It puts one in mind of "Goldilocks," meaning that the situation in America was "just right" for analyst-psychiatrists to ply their trade. This led to

> rapid and considerable growth in terms of the number of specialists, support from public opinion, and financial contributions from government agencies. This growth and the large sums allocated to psychiatry for teaching and research purposes were considered with awe in the European countries impoverished by war (Pichot 1997, 49).

American psychiatry is notable for the swiftness of its proliferation. There is little doubt that financial and state support expedited the positive reception of psychoanalytically informed psychiatry. Crucially, however, "what was specific to the United States was the intensity of the movement (ibid). The "new" psychiatric medicine was on fertile ground.

The second – and more significant – point to note is the geo-political situation of the United States during the 1930s. The political climate in Germany during this period was both an existential and professional threat for many intellectuals in psychiatry. It became clear that European soil was becoming inhospitable for their endeavors:

> World War I made a big difference in public acceptance of psychoanalysis, perhaps because Freud's views of death instinct and aggression seemed to illuminate the war's awesome irrationality. In 1920 Freud argued that two fundamental instincts existed – the and death instincts, or Eros and Thanatos, rather than just the sexual instinct as he had previously believed. After the war, it became the rage to include psychoanalysis in one's therapeutic palette. Many clinics that previously would have nothing to do with psychotherapy were now proclaiming their attachment to psychoanalysis (Shorter 1997, 158).

Despite Shorter's disdain for Freud and psychoanalysis, he presents a sympathetic portrait of the challenges faced by European psychiatrists during the War (and inter-war) years. The flourishing of European psychiatry (and psychoanalysis) "underwent a momentous change. The rise of Nazism in Germany and Austria snuffed out literally from one moment to the next the rich scientific discipline of psychiatry" (ibid., 160). The result was that "fascism drove many analysts who were Jewish from Central Europe to the United States, where they lent the stripling little American movement the glamour and heft of the wide world" (ibid., 166).

A younger generation of American psychiatrists were put in contact with the refugee psychiatrists who were widely extolled, and as devotees of these analysts, the new émigrés, "in alliance with the younger generation of Americans," were successful in influencing "the training institutes that had budded in the 1930s to ensure the orthodox teaching of a given body of doctrine, in opposition to [...] eccentric training that had previously prevailed" (ibid., 169). Adolph Meyer is one of those psychiatrists who relocated and was to be transformative for the profession. Meyer initially extended the ideas of Kraepelin, but in a reversal, would ultimately distance himself from Kraepelin's biologically oriented psychiatry in favor of a psychobiology (Gelder and Freeman 1999, 103), something of a precursor to the psychodynamic approach defining contemporary therapy.

This period of upheaval with respect to depression is particularly noteworthy. Though the first world war was by no means any less of an existential threat than the second world war, there is little doubt that the holocaust, labour camps in different theatres of war, as well as the sheer number of casualties, fundamentally unsettled human attitudes about life. Cultural responses to World War I and II, such as art (e.g. Cubism), literature, and philosophy (e.g. existentialism), reflect a shift in fundamental beliefs about what it means to be human in a world that is indifferent to human suffering. Of course, the effect of war was transformative well beyond the private sphere of life. Many soldiers returning home from the front manifested symptoms of trauma, most of which had not previously been clinically observed. To aver that psychiatry was *radically* revolutionized by the war period would be something of an overstatement, and yet it is simultaneously the case that psychiatry would be forever changed.

The traumatic period of World War II held positive implications for this "new" psychiatry. Psychiatrists returning from theatres of war testified to the efficacy of psychoanalytic-oriented methods. The treatment of soldiers along the front required entirely new and unorthodox methods that deviated from standard practices applied in in-patient hospital care. This led many psychiatrists to conclude that pre-existing standards of psychiatric care were insufficient for treating patients at home, as well as at the front lines of battle. Soldiers stationed in war zones could not be institutionalized in hospitals as inpatients – something that remained common practice at home, particularly since the prevailing belief was that the "insane" needed to be removed from their "noxious environments" (Decker 2013, 7). It was thus becoming clear that psychiatry was near both its theoretical and clinical limit.

1.6 Psychiatric image: Reliable classification, or reliable integrity?

The success of psychoanalysis could not outstrip its own shortcomings. Indeed, the war had forced clinicians to re-orient therapeutic attitudes. But the experience of war simultaneously proved to undermine the psychoanalytic conceptual framework. Soldiers returning home from war began presenting human behavior for which the psychoanalytic doctrine (and concepts) could not account. The vicissitudes of war had evinced signs and symptoms that did not fit into the standard psychiatric categories and the nomenclature available to military psychiatrists, most of whom could not adequately account for the psychological issues that were presented by the soldier-patients (Grob 1991, 428.). Psychodynamic labels like 'neurosis' did not square with the psychosomatic disorders that psychiatrists were now confronting.

In light of the novel symptoms that were being observed, the United States Army and Navy were compelled to create their own classification system, one that would eventually give rise to the inaugural American Psychiatric Association publication of DSM-I in 1952. A second version (DSM-II) was published after the World Health Organization issued the International Classification of Diseases (ICD) in 1968 (Cooper and Sartorius 2013, 17). Yet, even with this initial attempt to formalize and concretely establish a classificatory scheme – one indebted to Kraepelin's early work – American psychiatry remained largely unchanged and toothless. A principal reason for this was the fact that the DSM was intended "to reflect, not to change, the current practice of psychiatry" (Kirk and Kutchins 1992, 28). Thus, the arrival of the DSM was not a watershed moment, for it did not depart from the theoretical influence of psychoanalysis. Nonetheless, once DSM-III was published in 1980, the course of psychiatric practice would be irrevocably altered.

In the last quarter of the twentieth century, the development of psychiatry in the United States underwent substantial change. The DSM became the definitive point of reference for psychiatric epistemology, nosology, as well as epidemiology. Because the DSM is typically touted as the "official" diagnostic manual for (American) psychiatry, it is easily taken for granted that the *International Classification of Disease* (ICD) has always been the international benchmark for diagnostic coding in medicine. That the DSM-5 – and not ICD-10 – has become synonymous with psychiatric diagnosis can be attributed to the fact that psychiatric training programs in the United States inculcated clinicians with diagnostic precepts associated with the DSM (Reed 2010). Likewise, insofar as ICD is a compendium that classifies all forms of disease, with only one chapter devoted to mental disorders, the content of the ICD is considerably broader in scope than the DSM. Hence, the publication of DSM (and its subsequent iterations) gradually permitted the American Psychiatric Association to carve out a professional niche that was expansive in scope but limited in kind. It became a dedicated classification "book" of mental disorders, the putative authority of which has led many to euphemistically characterize the DSM as the psychiatric "bible."

At the same time, from an epistemic perspective, the DSM is considerably different from the ICD insofar as it is "closer to a nomenclature of diseases than to a classification. A nomenclature of diseases lists all diseases and provides a description of their chief characteristics" (Sartorius 2015, 205). When one considers the ICD as a classification of diseases, "[it] is no more than a tool to group the diagnoses of diseases or disorders into a smaller number of groups. Makers of a classification do not decide whether a particular condition should be called a disease or not" (ibid.). In other words, the ICD represents what the DSM ideally sought to achieve: a *descriptive* catalogue of disorder or disease. But the DSM extends beyond a simple description of disease; the considerable influence American psychiatry exerted on contemporary psychiatry, *vis-à-vis* the DSM, gained traction in 1980 with the release of DSM-III by "taking the bold step of *providing each of the diagnostic terms with an operational definition*. This was an important step for psychiatry which at the time did not have an accepted professional language" (Sartorius 2015, 205). In other words, the release of DSM-III provided clinicians with a formally structured point of reference to determine if, and under what circumstances, a series of signs and symptoms qualified as a mental disorder.

Even though I have focused considerably on the relationship between psychiatry and the DSM, I want to caution against over-inflating the authority of the DSM, since psychiatry is, after all, a professional *practice*. Even the precepts of the manual must be applied and interpreted according to the individual symptoms presented by each patient. Diagnosis is a practical endeavor that must incorporate a conceptual schema with clinical reality, a prospect that always poses intractable problems. Here we see how the story of depression is invariably situated within the larger genesis narrative of the DSM.

Early iterations of the DSM (DSM-I and DSM-II) were simply extensions of the American census bureau collection of statistics. Both versions reflected the psychoanalytic sensibility that saturated psychiatry between 1952 and 1968, respectively. The attempt to establish a cohesive theoretical psychiatric "medicine" (i.e. grounded in psychoanalysis), as opposed to one grounded in empirical evidence, made psychiatry highly vulnerable to criticism. As Karl Popper famously pointed out in 1945, psychoanalysis could not be considered scientific knowledge in the absence of rigorously applied scientific method, according to which a specific theory could be subject to falsification. Psychoanalytic explanations of behavior, according to Popper, could not be scientific given that particular forms of behavior or neuroses could not be falsified; that is, they could not be disproven. Consequently, a formidable obstacle to psychiatry's incumbent theoretical principles was the absence of an empirically vetted classification schema which would permit clinicians and researchers to reliably identify and diagnose depression.

For all the successes of psychoanalysis, post-war psychiatry increasingly became mired in an atmosphere of uncertainty. The scientific legitimacy of psychiatry was seriously threatened by unresolved issues regarding reliability and validity. In medicine, reliability denotes a level of confidence that individual clinicians, if presented with the same case, can reach the same diagnosis. Validity, however, has been less important for psychiatry, since validity effectively addresses whether or not the diagnosis of depression is empirically true.

Problems with poor diagnostic reliability undermined psychiatry's status as a medical science. Even if psychiatrists *could* reliably diagnose depression, there was scant evidence to confirm whether or not diagnostic labels corresponded to valid or "real" disorders. During the 1960s and 1970s, a burgeoning anti-psychiatry movement exploited psychiatry's inability to empirically validate disorders such as depression. Amongst other things, they argued that the nature of psychiatry was not medical, but a form of social (and therefore political) control that policed the boundaries between normal behavior and social deviance. Prominent figures of this movement, such as Thomas Szasz, Theodore Sarbin, R.D Laing and Thomas J. Scheff (Wakefield and First 2003) leveled serious criticisms against psychiatry, which motivated (or forced) the APA to publish a third version of the DSM

(DSM-III) in an attempt to refute mounting criticism against the profession: "Nothing is more basic to a profession or a science than the validity of its core concepts [...] As criticisms mounted, the definition and classification of mental disorders emerged as an enormously important problem for psychiatry" (Kirk and Kutchins 1992, 23). Evidence of the profession's indiscriminate clinical use of concepts, definitions and diagnostic terms, lent credence to the anti-psychiatry sentiment that psychiatry was scientifically bankrupt. Outside the profession, psychiatry was portrayed unfavorably, as arbitrary and unscientific.

Low inter-rater reliability, coupled with the theory-laden approach of psychoanalysis, cast doubt on psychiatry's scientific rigor. A considerable limitation to psychiatry's claim to science was the eclectic use of psychiatric nomenclature, which consequently inhibited reliable, predictable, and successful communication among psychiatric professionals. The obvious remedy was to consolidate psychiatric communication that would not only inspire professional integrity (e.g. different psychiatrists making the same diagnosis), but likewise offer psychiatric researchers with well-defined categories to guide the search for underlying etiological mechanisms that would explain disorders such as depression. And if psychiatric researchers *could* identify the cause(s) of depression (and mental disorder in general), psychiatry's status as a branch of science would be vindicated.

1.7 DSM-III and the new landscape: Depression, and description

When the APA published DSM-III in 1980, the trajectory of psychiatry changed in a myriad of ways. This was especially notable with respect to depression. The DSM-III represents a shift in the psychiatric ideology. In the attempt to distance itself from psychoanalytic theory, the DSM-III reflected (neo) Kraepelin sensibilities. Drawing from Kraepelin's work on classification and description, the DSM-III attempted to erase doubt concerning its status as a medical profession. Without "hard" evidence, a necessary requirement to validate a disease or disorder, it was imperative that the new classification scheme of DSM-III demonstrated psychiatry's bio-medical foundation. Hence, the historically broad spectrum of symptoms, which had been taken as indicative of melancholia, were being pared back to a set of core, empirically vetted, symptoms, that could be clinically identified with consistency.

An undeniably positive consequence of psychiatry's bio-medical status is that psychiatric syndromes such as depression had reason to be taken seriously, and it likewise meant that the sufferer was ultimately not responsible for his or her suffering. Medical illnesses are broadly characterized as a pathological state or process that interferes with one's life without it having been voluntarily brought upon oneself. Illness is thus beyond one's control and something for which we are not held responsible. Intuitively, it would be absurd to claim a person is blameworthy for having cancer.[15] We can say that illness, which has now come to include mental illness, impedes personal autonomy. As psychiatry reinforced its image as a specialized medical practice, depression becomes characterized – not something worthy of blame but – as an uninvited threat to one's autonomous way of life.

A less positive outcome of psychiatry's status as medicine is that, much like biomedicine, psychiatric classification and taxonomy is deeply inspired by naturalist taxonomy. The premise, then, is that there exist psychiatric (brain or mind) disease entities that may be classified or grouped based on essential properties or traits defining that group, the prevailing practice in disciplines such as botany and zoology. But since scientific knowledge about the causes of depression remains elusive, the only recourse for psychiatry is to categorize disorders according to form, as opposed to content; that is, psychiatry relies on descriptive data to outline depression in the form of typically observed symptom clusters or features. And while one of the foremost goals in depression research is to specify mechanisms or pathologies underpinning depressive disorders (thus broaching the "content"), the continued inability to identify the relevant empirical evidence required to validate the category of depression means that some philosophers of psychiatry have strong reservations that mental disorders like depression will ever prove to be natural kinds.[16]

In the absence of causal explanations validating the presence of depression, psychiatric classification is predicated on a rather large assumption (or prescience?) that despite the *current* lack of explanatory evidence concer-

—

[15] As the nature of health becomes a moral imperative, there exist increasingly fewer clear-cut cases. For instance, a smoker's chances of lung-cancer are significantly increased compared to a noon-smoker. Yet, it is not logically sound to claim that the smoker caused her cancer. There are certainly exceptions where smokers are not diagnosed with cancer. In this respect, it would be difficult to comprehend why the smoker with cancer is blameworthy while the smoker who is cancer-free is above moral evaluation. Moreover, this is further problematized by the fact that, even if the smoker had *never* smoked, it is possible that she could, despite this, ultimately develop lung-cancer.

[16] Philosopher Dominic Murphy is a notable exception (Murphy 2006), and has been a target for many philosophers of science who argue that the "natural kinds" or realist position is untenable, c.f. Cooper (Cooper 2007) (Cooper 2006), Bolton and Hill (Bolton and Hill 2004).

ning depression, this lack is merely indicative of the current state of scientific research. Hence, until depression researchers demonstrate depression's physiological pathways, the DSM category of depression functions as a placeholder until psychiatric research finds more auspicious avenues of investigation. As I stated earlier in section 1.3.1, the descriptive categories in the DSM are intended to be *provisional* categories subject to revision in light of novel psychiatric findings.

In 1980, the publication DSM-III made considerable inroads in enhancing inter-rater reliability by introducing an operationalized approach to diagnosing depression. This achievement was underpinned by philosophical concepts taken from analytic philosophy, as well as neo-Kraepelin inspired perspectives. Taking inspiration from Hempel's lecture to American psychiatrists in 1965 (see sec 1.3.1), the APA approach to psychiatric diagnosis in DSM-III was operationalized (Parnas and Bovet 2015, 273). Hempel opined that "an operational definition of a concept will have to be understood as ascribing the concept to all those cases that would exhibit the characteristic response if the test conditions should be realized" (Hempel 1965). For Hempel, observation itself may fulfill "test conditions," which is to say that depression may be diagnosed if clinical observation confirms "characteristic responses" that are indicative of the concept depression. In addition to the insights of Hempel, the category of depression in DSM-III was overwhelmingly the result of research data developed by a group of researchers in St. Louis that came to be designated as the Feighner criteria.

Much like Hempel, the Feighner criteria adopted a neo-Kraepelian stance toward psychiatry. With DSM-III, psychiatric epistemology and classification was imbued with scientific sensibilities that were not visible in previous DSM publications

> although researchers concurred that a separable, psychotic form of depression existed, they could not reach a consensus about the nature of non-psychotic types of depression [...] They disputed how many forms neurotic conditions took and even whether they had any distinct forms at all (Horwitz, Wakefield, and Lorenzo-Luaces 2016, 9).

All that could be agreed upon concerned the underlying structure of depression, namely that one form was bio-physiological, the other psychogenic. Otherwise, at the time there existed upwards of twelve different systems to classify depression, none of which were of the same "opinion about how depressions should be classified," nor was there "any body of agreed findings capable of providing the framework of a consensus" (Kendell 1976, 25). Unsurprisingly, publication of the influential paper by Feigner et. al., which proposed a validated category for mental illness, was positively received by the psychiatric community in 1971.

The group of researchers in St. Louis asserted that their "new" diagnostic criteria for depression were validated by five steps: clinical description; laboratory study; delimitation from other disorders; a follow-up study, and a family study (Feighner et al. 1972, 57). The authors contended that these steps validated the criteria for depression (along with thirteen other psychiatric illnesses), which would in turn elicit high clinical inter-rater reliability. Under the category of "Primary Affective Disorder," the Feighner article proposed eight criteria for depression: dysphoric mood; duration of at least one month, and five of the following additional symptoms must be present (1) poor appetite, (2) sleep difficulties, (3) loss of energy, (4) agitation or retardation, (5) loss of interest in usual activities or decreased sex drive, (6) feelings of guilt/self-reproach, (7) decreased ability to concentrate, (8) suicidal thoughts (Feighner et. al., 1972, 58).

Though the Feighner criteria episode may appear to be nothing other than a relatively minor moment in psychiatric history, it was truly seminal for psychiatry. The work of Feighner et al. aligned depression and the DSM-III with the progressive image of psychiatric medicine. Whether, however, psychiatric medicine lives up to this standard remains an open question. In one sense, the publication of DSM-III was nothing short of a transformation for psychiatry and depression: "DSM-III formulated depression in a radically new way relative to the previous 2500 years of medical diagnosis" (Horwitz, Wakefield, and Lorenzo-Luaces 2016, 15). In another sense, the transformation of depression criteria in DSM-III did not truly offer any meaningfully novel criteria. Rather, the novelty in DSM-III lay in the new *standardized* process to diagnose depression.

It is worth noting here that the depression criteria famously associated with Feighner et al. was not foreign to psychiatry at the time, owing to the fact that their detailed criteria drew extensively from a model that had already been put forward by Cassidy et al in 1957. Closer examination shows that the group of St. Louis researchers made only minor amendments to the criteria developed by Cassidy et al. (Horwitz, Wakefield, and Lorenzo-Luaces 2016, Kendler, Muñoz, and Murphy 2010). Moreover, the supporting evidence used to justify the depression criteria "was very limited. Only one of the five publications cited in the footnotes to the [Feighner et. al] article provided empirical substantiation [...] This was a study by Walter

Cassidy and several colleagues" (Horwitz, Wakefield, and Lorenzo-Luaces 2016, 13). Why is this significant? Because the Feighner criteria for depression "*became almost the sole basis for the DSM-III diagnosis*" (ibid., 14, emphasis original) and yet the criteria for depression in DSM-III were neither radically new, nor were they empirically grounded.

With DSM-III, the APA believed that it had resolved the problem of poor professional communication, the result of which was enhanced inter-rater reliability. The operational language resulted in a manual that standardized:

> (a) *diagnostic criteria,* and (b) *algorithms,* or decision rules, for each diagnosis. Rather than merely describing each diagnosis as DSM-I and DSM-II had done, *DSM-III* explicitly delineated the signs and symptoms comprising each diagnosis and the method by which these signs and symptoms needed to be combined to establish each diagnosis (Lilienfeld and Landfield 2008, 16 emphasis original).

Once again, depression was not radically transformed by the criteria *per se*, but instead what we find is a change in taxonomic terminology. Major depressive disorders were distinguished from bipolar disorders, and in an attempt to purge psychoanalytic theory from its ranks, "DSM-III eliminated the diagnoses of depressive reaction and neurotic depression" (Gruenberg, Goldstein, and Pincus 2005, 4). In DSM-I and DSM-II, psychotic depression (which included mania) was distinguished from neurotic forms of depression. Neurotic depression, on the other hand, was understood as a psychological defense mechanism that belied a primary problem connected to anxiety.

1.8 The politics of depression

The DSM-III sought to redress the psychoanalytic influence amid pressure to establish professional integrity. The previous approach, devoid of formal categories and strung together by eclectic theoretical content, was jettisoned in favor of operational criteria that would elicit more precise diagnostic outcomes at the clinical level. Still, the DSM was not intended to replace clinical judgement. The APA concedes that the DSM is not a precise tool and is not intended to function in the same way as say a thermometer does in taking a temperature: "we recognize that mental disorders do not always fit completely within the boundaries of a single disorder" (APA, xli). Although psychiatry fought hard to establish specific criteria to create disorder categories, the DSM is intended to be subordinate to the authority of clinical judgment when establishing a diagnosis. Thus, it would be incorrect to view psychiatric practice solely as an expression of the DSM. What clinical judgment cannot determine is the range of diagnostic *possibilities* that remains within the borders of the disorder categories. So, while a good clinician may decide to overrule DSM guidelines, the possibilities of *what* a clinician may decide upon is delimited by the DSM.

As to defining precisely *what* depression *is*, it was far from a neutral affair. The production of DSM-III involved numerous committees, taskforces, and consultants. With respect to depression, competing professional interests about how to classify depression made it impossible to assuage one and all. Whether changes to a category were accepted or rejected had little to do with science. Most decisions were influenced by psychiatric politics. And still, despite political motivations, much of the debate implicitly continued to remain tethered to causation.

The prevailing problem was whether depression should be represented as one or two disorders. A two-disorder model allows room for an internal-external distinction among depressions. Prior to the third revision of the DSM in 1980, depression was divided in this manner: endogenous and reactive (also neurotic depression).[17] The desire to expunge psychoanalytic terminology from the psychiatric nomenclature meant neurotic depression was unsatisfactory. Initial drafts that dropped the label were unsurprisingly not well received by influential analyst-psychiatrists. Robert Spitzer, who at the time was chairman of the APA, was pulled in many directions by competing interests. The first draft proposed a distinction between major and minor mood disorders (Shorter 2013). Insurance companies were quick to oppose the distinction, since minor conditions would not solicit reimbursements. In response, the revision taskforce adopted episodic (acute) and intermittent (chronic) mood disorders. Again, analysts opposed this new iteration because it failed to map onto their categories. To complicate matters further, biologically oriented psychiatrists had serious doubts about whether endogenous and reactive depression was truly distinct. Hence, disagreement arose as to whether there were one or two depressions.

—

[17] Shorter has pointed out that the endogenous-reactive distinction has, with time, been misappropriated by psychiatry. In 1920 Kurt Schneider had applied this distinction to denote a difference between body feeling and life feeling. Both types could be precipitated by forces outside the person. By contrast, endogenous and reactive came to represent causal distinctions: depression with internal cause and with external cause.

Jumping ahead to the final iteration of the draft that would constitute DSM-III, major mood disorders (i.e. major depression) – against the wishes of insurers – supplanted the previously proposed "recurrent depression" while minor depressive disorder (dysthymia) replaced chronic affective disorder. At a late stage in the drafting process, Spitzer – without consent from the taskforce – conceded ground to the analyst faction by conflating dysthymia with neurotic depression:

> This was actually quite a stunning achievement. Spitzer had collapsed the two depressions of melancholia and nonmelancholia, in use in psychiatry for over two centuries, into a single depression, called major depression, and ensured that it was the only diagnosis you could get into unless you were seeing a psychoanalyst and could qualify for neurotic depression (Shorter 2013, 138).

Despite this change, two forms of depression continued to exist. But as Shorter notes, almost all depressions would qualify as "major" depressions. The new problem with this characterization was that the scope of depression was overly inclusive. Depression diagnosis became expansive. The DSM had re-organized depression in such a way that the criteria made it very difficult to discriminate between "depression" and "normal" sadness.

1.8.1 DSM: Good, but good enough?

The publication of DSM-I and its seven subsequent revisions has been a perennial source of controversy. The anti-psychiatry movement, to which I drew attention earlier in the chapter, is but one extreme example. The attempt to classify (abnormal) human behavior *vis-à-vis* the medical model poses thorny philosophical problems. Indeed, many of the objections leveled against the DSM have been warranted, several of which were forceful enough to induce the APA to reassess categories of disorder that critics deemed problematic.[18]

The DSM undoubtedly has limitations. It is often (rather unfairly) portrayed as the psychiatric "bible," a characterization that overlooks the manual's flexibility. The tendency to ascribe monolithic status to the DSM has become commonplace, even though it is – in principle – merely intended to be implemented as a guide to the diagnostic process. But the putative

—

[18] Here I have in mind the controversial designation of homosexuality as a disorder category in DSM-II, which was subsequently removed in DSM-III. For further discussion on this issue see (Kirk and Kutchins , Cooper).

biblical status of the DSM is not simply due to its content. It is easily overlooked that the DSM is a definitive resource for the economic relationship between clinicians and insurance companies. Not only is the DSM (and ICD) a tool for psychiatrists, it is essential for patient insurance claims, the approval of which requires appropriately notated diagnostic coding listed by the DSM or ICD.[19] Clinically speaking, the DSM provides clinicians with a *reliable* point of reference to identify clusters of behaviors (i.e. signs and symptoms) in order to distinguish depressed people from non-depressed people. Note, however, that the DSM does not make claims concerning *what* is reliably being identified other than a cluster of symptoms that represent "depression."

Because the DSM is a practical resource for clinicians, the question whether or not the category of depression is valid is a matter to be determined by psychiatric researchers in the future. In the clinical context, concern with diagnostic validity is subordinated to diagnostic reliability, since the clinical mandate is to ensure that patients who suffer from depression receive appropriate treatment, irrespective of how suffering is caused. There is no doubt that the DSM and ICD have enabled clinicians to diagnose and treat many persons who suffer from depression. These guides enable clinicians to put a name to the cluster of symptoms that interfere with one's life, which effectively legitimatize and substantiate the illness experience associated with depression. As a result, since depression is accorded medical status by DSM and ICD, these diagnostic guides have helped mitigate social stigma that has been an all too common problem for persons suffering from mental illness.

Hence, whether or not depression is a valid category is a question best answered by psychiatric researchers. As I have intimated, in the clinical context, whether or not the category of depression is sound is less important than the ability to repeatedly organize and identify individual illnesses. In the second chapter, I use qualitative interviews with psychiatric clinicians to illustrate the extent to which psychiatric theory does not seamlessly dovetail with clinical practice. But before we address clinical attitudes concerning depression, I want to further specify why the relationship between diagnostic reliability and diagnostic validity is acrimonious rather than harmonious. For instance, even if we accept that diagnostic validity is not

---

[19] The relationship between psychiatry and insurance companies in the United States certainly exacerbated the need for diagnostic coding to ensure patient claims are approved, However, the ICD coding system long predates that of the DSM. Irrespective of insurance claims, diagnostic codes are in fact regularly employed in all areas of medicine.

essential to clinical *praxis*, why should we presume that the DSM diagnostic criteria or algorithms used to identify depression are *themselves* sound? That is, do the signs and symptoms of depression reliably represent the phenomenon of depression?

Indeed, when the criteriological approach was first introduced in 1980, contributors to the DSM revision acknowledged that "their criteria [was] a tentative first step that awaited future validation" (Horwitz, Wakefield, and Lorenzo-Luaces 2016, 14). Even Robert Kendell, who would eventually be appointed head of the Royal college of Psychiatry in the United Kingdom, himself wrote that "no evidence has been offered to suggest that it is anything more than a convenient strategy" (Kendell 1976). As a result, even at face-value, the *practical* nature of the DSM is inherently fraught with theoretical limitations. Emphasis on the putative pragmatic value of the DSM has subsequently meant that "the wholesale, and largely arbitrary, adoption of one among a number of competing ways of defining depression perhaps accounts for why – more than 30 years after its promulgation – research on depression has yet to yield any major breakthroughs" (Horwitz, Wakefield, and Lorenzo-Luaces 2016, 17). Likewise, "the discipline of psychiatry has failed to identify a single biological marker or gene useful in making a depression diagnosis" (Gruenberg, Goldstein, and Pincus 2005, 10). The clinical reliance on reliable (but unvalidated) depression criteria has led to the subsequent criticism that psychiatric research cannot validate depression as a category of disorder because the diagnostic criteria are what guide psychiatric research. If empirical research in depression is reliant on the DSM category of depression to determine the nature of depression, then it is not unreasonable to ask whether or not the lack of scientific breakthroughs in depression research is a consequence of hitherto having relied on an impoverished category (signs and symptoms) that guides scientific research?

As such, an impediment to depression research is that if the diagnostic criteria do not adequately describe depression, then it is foreseeable that empirical research will likewise be unable to adequately delimit the phenomenon of depression. The point is not that we should reject the future possibility of identifying biomarkers, since it is reasonable to adopt a "wait and see" attitude about future scientific discoveries regarding depression. But because depression researchers take their cue from the DSM categories, if the operationalized criteria fail to adequately articulate the phenomenon of depression then we have good reason to believe that extant research paradigms (e.g. serotonin, norepinephrine, imbalance theories) may continue to "miss their mark," as it were. A balance must be struck between optimism and cynicism, for it is unwise to blindly subscribe to the operationalized approach to diagnosis assuming that scientific promissory notes will ultimately be fulfilled.

Until now, I have traced the way in which depression has become a psychiatric category, electing to portray the emergence of depression as a consequence of the development of psychiatry itself. As I have described above, with the advent of DSM-III (and its subsequent revisions) the number of depression diagnoses skyrocketed. At the same time, one must consider whether the advent of depressive disorder is the sole reason for the proliferation of depression diagnoses? How are we to make sense of *World Health Organization* statistics that suggest, "globally, depressive disorders are ranked as the single largest contributor to non-fatal health loss" (WHO 2017, 13)? A consistently overlooked feature of depression is the way in which signs and symptoms hang together. The operationalized approach to depression diagnosis is adept at picking out individual symptoms, yet in doing so the operationalized approach fails to recognize the way in which the individual symptoms hang together as a whole. Which is to say, depression symptoms affect an individual, a *self* through whom depression is manifested. And this is what makes depression unlike other illness experiences, insofar as the symptoms of depression not only indicate that something is wrong but that *something is wrong with me*. A consequence of the operationalized approach to diagnosis, the aim of which is to describe and identify individual symptoms of depression, is *that who I am* bears no relation to the symptoms I experience. And yet, as I will argue in the following chapters, distress engendered by depression is not isolated to a particular bodily location; depression is experienced as being everywhere, which is but one way to say that depression is an all-encompassing type of *experience* that transcends individual symptoms. Hence, to characterize depression by appealing to specific symptoms is not only to misunderstand the phenomenon, it is also a misunderstanding of experience itself, which may be provisionally characterized in the following – albeit ambiguous – way: experience expresses depression and depression expresses experience.

1.9 Epic or "epidemic?"

Until now, this chapter has addressed almost exclusively the conceptual and historical development of depression. This is but one side of the story of depression. Given that psychiatry remains committed to the strictures of medical science, it is of course entirely reasonable to say that psychiatry treats depression. And while this basic characterization is correct in a broad sense, the "medical" nature of psychiatry often obscures the relationship between psychiatry and its service users. Psychiatry does indeed treat depression, but it does so only by virtue of the fact that first and foremost psychiatry treats *people* who suffer from depression.

If the WHO's stark statistics regarding rates of depression are accurate, then we are reasonably warranted to ask *why so many people continue to seek psychiatric help for depression*? I want now to set aside issues concerning professionalization in psychiatry, which have been the central focus of the chapter so far, by shifting our attention to three non-psychiatric developments that have fanned the flames of our so-called depression "epidemic."

A recognized development catapulting depression into the psychiatric limelight is the intimate relation between the psychopharmaceutical industry and psychiatric practice. Second, irrespective of psychiatric categories, it behooves us to enquire about the extent the vicissitudes of modern life have prompted higher rates of depression.

The relationship between psychiatry and the pharmaceutical industry is one of mutual dependence. Arguably, scientific credibility of psychiatry is (and continues to be) complimented by developments in pharmacological science. The advent of life-saving pharmacological therapies during the twentieth century (e.g. penicillin, vaccines) effectively led to a complacency about specific drugs targeting and correcting particular pathologies. After the discovery of penicillin, bacterial infections that had previously proven fatal were no longer the automatic death sentence they had once been; vaccinations for polio and measles curtailed the threat of community spread, but they also assuaged existential anxieties that tacitly accompany significant threats to human existence as such.

Prior to the development of anti-depressants in the second half of the twentieth century, psychiatric drugs did not target or correct specific pathologies. The early class of psychiatric drugs available to patients effected the body in non-specific way (e.g. sedatives, tranquilizers), and for a long time there were no auspicious alternatives. Contrast this state of affairs in psychiatry with that of somatic medicine, where researchers had fortuitously stumbled upon novel *disease specific* treatments (e.g. penicillin) that would forever re-define medical practice and enhance the quality of human life. Bearing in mind that at that point in time psychiatry remained under the theoretical influence of psychoanalysis, the advent of anti-depressants effectively initiated a gradual theoretical transition, from analytic oriented psychiatry toward the more scientifically promising and biologically oriented psychiatry. Now that psychiatry possessed well-delineated categories of mental disorder, the logical presumption was that every mental disorder warranted a corresponding drug that acted on a specific pathology. The psychiatric shift toward disorder specific drugs reflected the profession's internalization of "the 'magic bullet' model" of somatic medicine "that had led to the discovery of the sulfa drugs and antibiotics [and] was simple in kind. First, identify the cause or the nature of the disorder. Second, develop a treatment to counteract it" (2011, 47). In technical terms, this approach constituted a disease centered theory of drug action (Moncrieff and Cohen), one that would quickly become the *status quo* of psychiatric treatment.

Psychiatric drugs became part of the clinical repertoire between the 1940s and 1950s. One of the first widely used drugs was a tranquilizer marketed in North America under the name Chlorpromazine. Psychiatry benefited from unintended discoveries that had emerged indirectly from unrelated research. For instance, an obvious drawback with psychiatry's reliance on analgesics or anesthetics was that these interventions effectively made patients unconscious. But thanks to the new drug-oriented research paradigm, researchers unintentionally stumbled upon drugs that induced similar effects as Chlorpromazine without the unwanted side-effect of rendering their patients unconscious.

1.9.1 Anti-depressants: Failed cure

The class of drugs developed specifically to treat depression emerged in the 1960s. Here, the specific details of the "anti-depressant" story are rather complex. Nevertheless, the basic trajectory of the development of anti-depressant drugs begins with of "tricyclic" and "monoamine oxidase inhibitors" (MAOI). Due to the significant side-effect profile of MAOIs, this class of drug fell out of favor with clinicians upon the "discovery" of what we now colloquially refer to as "anti-depressants." Upon arrival of this class of drugs, some members of the psychiatric community were convinced that anti-depressants would effectively put an end to the blight of depression.[20] These drugs, which have become the standard intervention to treat depression, have become a ubiquitous feature of Western culture. Generally speaking, "anti-depressant" is a colloquial term that refers to a broad class of drugs that are effectively variations of a theme: "Selective Serotonin

—

[20] For instance, see Peter Kramer (2016, 1994)

Reuptake Inhibitor" (SSRI), "Norepinephrine Selective Reuptake Inhibitors" (NSRI), and "Norepinephrine reuptake inhibitors" (NRI).

Anti-depressant awareness was augmented considerably by the successful marketing of Prozac (SSRI) in 1985 by Eli Lilly. The discovery of serotonin and norepinephrine led to the subsequent hypothesis that depression was causally attributable to depleted levels of the neurotransmitter, thus leading to widespread acceptance that depression is caused by chemical imbalances. Although the imbalance theory of depression emerged as early as 1961 (Healy 2004b), its notoriety skyrockets after the publication of DSM-III in 1980, at which point psychiatry established a specific category to describe depression *and* a drug that targeted specific neuro-chemical pathologies.

It goes without saying that the influence of anti-depressant drugs is in no small part explained by a dramatic rise in rates of prescription. Of course, this alone cannot account for the increased consumption of anti-depressants. For instance, depression awareness campaigns in the United States and United Kingdom coincided with the release of DSM-III. Both campaigns were funded by Eli Lilly, which generated "eight million brochures titled *Depression: What you need to know* and two hundred thousand posters" (Healy 2004b). The aim of these campaigns was to "alert physicians and third-party payers in health care to the huge economic burdens of untreated depression" and to "show physicians how many cases of depression they were missing – to shame them into detecting and treating depression" (ibid., 10). In addition to educational campaigns aimed at clinicians, the elevated position that anti-depressant drugs now enjoyed was reinforced by the (mis)perception that they were "silver-bullet" cures for depression.

Depression diagnoses during the twentieth and twenty-first centuries cannot be understood independently from the way in which depression is conceptualized. The psychiatric historian Edward Shorter believes that we have little reason to doubt that depression has always existed: "it is unlikely that the frequency of serious depression, which has deep genetic roots in brain biology, ever changes over time" (Shorter 2013). Shorter, like Horwitz and Wakefield (2007), argues that the rise in depression is a consequence of false-positive diagnoses. But the rise in false-positive diagnoses is not a consequence of indiscriminate diagnosis; the problem is rather that the depression criteria insufficiently distinguishes depression from normal sadness, thereby blurring the distinction between illness and normalcy.

Shorter also puts forth a thesis that anti-depressants have shown themselves to be unsatisfactory in treating depression. He argues that prior to the arrival of anti-depressants, early psychiatric medications (e.g. Barbiturates) were considerably more effective in neutralizing depression than SSRIs. Similarly, Robert Whitaker has adamantly argued that the "new" anti-depressants have themselves caused or exacerbated depression (Whitaker 2011). Broadly speaking, Whitaker contends that the SSRI/NSRI imbalance theory is unfounded

> psychiatry then reconceived the drugs to be 'magic bullets' for mental disorders, the drugs hypothesized to be antidotes to chemical imbalances in the brain. But that theory, which arose as much from wishful thinking as from science was investigated and it did not pan out (ibid., 85).

According to Whitaker, serotonin reuptake inhibitors made depression *worse*. How? For one, he notes that the studies touting rates of anti-depressant efficacy only assessed the short-term use of the drugs. Without longitudinal studies investigating long term responsiveness, there was little or no data on rates of depression relapse. Because the imbalance model assumes that depression is explained by neurotransmitter abnormalities, SSRIs were created with the intention of correcting physio-pathologies. Whitaker is not alone in arguing that our confidence in anti-depressants is overinflated. Jacob Stegena's recent work on "medical Nihilism" reinforces Whitaker's reservations regarding the effectiveness of anti-depressant treatments: "If a cause is neither necessary nor sufficient for the disease in question, then intervening on that cause will not be sufficient to eliminate disease" (2018, 65). Given the high likelihood that depression is causally multifactorial rather than monocausal, it is unclear why anti-depressants are presumed to be effective for most people with depression even though there is no comprehensive way to determine the specific cause of depression upon which this class of drug is intended to act.

While Stegena's worry about anti-depressants concerns the how empirical evidence is used to support claims of their efficacy, Whitaker, however, goes a step further to argue that anti-depressants, in fact, elicit the opposite intended effect. In other words, rather than correct neurochemical imbalances, anti-depressants cause neurochemical imbalances

> serotonin reuptake channels are blocked by the drug [Fluoxetine (Prozac)]. The system's feedback loop is partially disabled. The postsynaptic neurons are 'desensitized' to serotonin. Mechanically speaking, the serotonergic system is now rather mucked up (Whitaker 2011, 81).

When patients cease using medication, so the argument goes, the rate of depression relapse is of greater statistical significance than in patients who received no pharmacological treatment. The discontinuation of an anti-depressant treatment elicits a rebound effect, the result of which is a significant rise in long-term rates of depression. The ironic conclusion, then, is that instead of diminishing depression, increased use of anti-depressants may exacerbate the incidence of depressive illness.

Here we have two unique but interrelated arguments that attempt to make sense of the increased prevalence of depression. Compelling as they are, these arguments on their own cannot account for the increase in depression. Even if the arguments obtained, they only make sense of depression post-diagnosis. They do not address why so many people seek psychiatric help in the first place. One way to answer this question – if there even is a final answer – is to look at the *practice* of psychiatry.

The intersection of factors, which includes the publication of DSM-III, the marketing of SSRIs, and educational campaigns aimed at decreasing stigma, go a long way in explaining why people began to seek medical attention. But according to Horwitz and Wakefield, the problem was not that more people "realized" they were depressed. As I have already noted, they argue that the depression criteria from DSM-III to DSM-5 are insufficient for distinguishing between depression and normal sadness. The title of their well-received book captures the problem succinctly: *The Loss of Sadness*. According to the authors, the increase of depression diagnoses is not best explained by the fact that there are simply more people with depression. On the contrary, the rise in depression diagnoses corresponds to the medicalization of everyday emotions in psychiatry.

1.9.2 Normal depression: Too much or too little?

Like the story of depression, understanding the putative pathologizing of sadness is complicated. Why do people feel so unwell that they seek out the clinic? On the one hand, with the publication of DSM-III and its subsequent versions, criteria-based diagnosis and the advent of anti-depressants has meant that most cases of depression are diagnosed in primary care (Goldberg and Goodyer 2005, Regier, Goldberg, and Taube 1978, Callahan and Berrios 2004). In the early nineties Leon Eisenberg asked:

> What can be done to improve the care of medical patients with psychosocial distress? [...] The answer does not lie in referral to mental health specialists; there are simply too few, and most them are in clustered cities. Any realistic

> hope of change must rest on improving the quality of care in the general medicine sector (Eisenberg 1992, 1083).

One way to view the relation between depression and primary care is that depression has become "normalized" and thus flattened out. That is, most cases of depression are perceived – contradictorily – to be normal depression. Hence, general physicians are educated on how to "spot" the signs of depression that often closely resemble the "blues."

There remains an intractable problem between depression and primary care. Clinicians such as Eisenberg believe depression remains *under diagnosed*, while Horwitz and Wakefield argue that depression is *over diagnosed.* To complicate matters, both positions can be justified by appealing to the depression criteria; poor specificity and sensitivity will affect increased prevalence of both false-positive (too many) or false-negative (too few) diagnoses. Despite efforts to increase diagnostic reliability, any given diagnosis is invariably tied to clinically dependent factors. One factor is a particular clinician's conception of depression etiology. A hardline "bio-psychiatrist" will likely accord little weight to a patient's life-context, whereas a psycho-social oriented clinician will be more fastidious when discerning depression from life situations that elicit expected and culturally sanctioned emotional responses; emotional distress due to the end of a relationship would, for example, be an expected and appropriate response. The DSM cannot determine what causes depression, it only describes what it looks like. In principle, it is entirely plausible that two different clinicians will not arrive at the same diagnostic conclusion – not on account of unreliability, but due to divergent conceptions of depression among individual clinicians.

1.9.3 Show me the money

It is difficult to investigate the rise of depression diagnoses without attending to economic motives. The discourse of publications issued by organizations such as the WHO often monetize the consequences of individual illnesses, or diseases. The economic quantification of depression, which draws upon disability statistics related to decreased production or high costs associated with sick leave, serve as evidence that improved treatments, and diligent depression diagnoses, are warranted. Quantifying depression economically is ostensibly intended to minimize the way in which illness interferes with one's quality of life. Good intentions aside, what should not be overlooked is how negative economic effects caused by high rates of depression serve as a catalyst for developing new ways to deal with depression. Arguably, then, improving depression treatment and care is not an entirely benevolent endeavor.

We should not underestimate the extent to which depression awareness campaigns, public health projects, and clinical training, are motivated by a desire to mitigate economic losses, employee absenteeism, and decreased productivity at work, all which are consequences associated with depression: "this shows how powerful market trends have become in influencing medicine, so that the nonmedical component tends to outweigh the medical component in conceptualizing depression today" (Sato 2015, 307). Contrary to the logical – or operational – concept of depression derived from the DSM, psychiatric epistemology is not a self-enclosed domain:

> The dynamics governing the relationship between the medical/nosological component, a nonmarket norm, and the nonmedical component, in which economic/financial factors including market trends play an increasingly powerful role, seem to be critically important in understanding the depression concept today (ibid.).

Psychiatric science intersects with external stakeholders, who establish alliances with commercial interests (e.g. psychopharmacology). The notion of nonmarket norms suggests that goods, services, or practices – the moral status of which is viewed to be beyond commodification – are vulnerable to the influence of psychiatry. The most salient example is our repeated reference to the medicalization of normal sadness, a type of experience many believe should not be commodified.

We cannot mention economic interests and depression without drawing attention to the contentious relationship between psychiatry and depression.[21] With respect to awareness campaigns, Moynihan et al. lament that:

> Within many disease categories informal alliances have emerged, comprising drug company staff, doctors, and consumer groups. Ostensibly engaged in raising public awareness about underdiagnosed and undertreated problems, these alliances tend to promote a view of their particular condition as widespread, serious, and treatable. Because these "disease awareness" campaigns are commonly linked to companies' marketing strategies, they operate to expand markets for new pharmaceutical products (Moynihan, Heath, and Henry 2002, 886).

—

[21] This topic has received extensive attention. See (Healy 1997), (Healy 2004a), (Elliott 2011), (Cosgrove and Krimsky 2012) and (Maj 2010).

The development of innovative depression medications is, of course, not devoid of good intentions. After all, psychopharmaceuticals are specifically indicated for persons who *suffer* – often severely – from depression. Nevertheless, the process of channeling drugs from early pipeline research all the way to the clinician's prescription pad, puts the best interest of patients in conflict with the interests of various stakeholders who produce drugs for market consumption.

The general claim is that, too often, novel drugs are introduced with the intention of maximizing profit, which in stark terms means dominating market share. Hence, the overarching goal of pharmaceutical company A is to encourage clinicians to prescribe their product more than company B, C, D, and so on. Whether it is immoral to profit from drug sales and development is a valid question, but one that we cannot answer here. For our purposes, the question is whether it is immoral for *clinicians* to profit from drug sales and development? This question, I think, is directly relevant to the increase in depression diagnoses. Aside from financial incentives to compose positive drug reviews, or to attend (all expenses paid) pharmaceutical symposia in desirable locations, the critical problem is the insidious relationship between DSM review committee members and their respective financial ties to pharmaceutical companies. When the DSM undergoes revisions, each disorder category is reviewed by a dedicated committee. Why is this a problem? According to Lisa Cosgrove and Sheldon Krimsky, when the APA was preparing revisions for DSM-IV:

> Of the 170 DSM panel members 95 (56%) had one or more financial associations with companies in the pharmaceutical industry. One hundred percent of the members of the panels on 'Mood Disorders' and 'Schizophrenia and Other Psychotic Disorders' had financial ties to drug companies. The leading categories of financial interest held by panel members were research funding (42%), consultancies (22%) and speakers bureau (16%) (Cosgrove and Krimsky 2012, no page).

The experts responsible for deciding which disorders exist also determine the criteria for a specific disorder; all too often such experts financially benefit from companies who have an interest in seeing new disorder categories created. This is particularly true if a pipeline drug appears promising at modifying certain behaviors, for which as yet no category exists.

1.9.4 The Existential predicament: I, you, me, we

We have posited several reasons that could account for the rise of depression, but we still have not answered the question: Why have an increasing number of people felt the need to seek out psychiatric care? Why are people sad? Unfortunately, I think that this is a question without a definitive answer. Moreover, the answer will likely be a normative one; definitions of well-being must be considered in the context of cultural meanings of a given epoch. Steven Pinker has recently argued that life in the twentieth century is empirically less violent, more equal, and overall a "better" period of human history in which to be alive (Pinker 2011). Even if this argument is accurate (which is open to debate), it cannot account for the existential predicament of being human. With respect to depression, the biological explanatory model is indifferent to existential considerations. Sadness is sadness, depression is depression. The psycho-social model of depression, on the other hand, takes life conditions to be a pertinent component in making sense of depression. Yet, the question as to why people seek help in the first place still remains.

Relative to preceding generations, our current historical predicament has become increasingly secular. The changing relationship between human cultural practices and religion has led to significant changes in self-understanding. The relationship between God and oneself has arguably been supplanted by the relationship of the self to oneself. Put another way, if our finite existence lacks transcendent meaning with which we might *explain* the meaning of human activity, we cannot help but pose questions concerning who we are, and how to make sense of life as an individual within a community of others. Freud remarked that

> unhappiness is much less difficult to experience [than happiness]. Suffering threatens us from three sides: from our own body, which being doomed to decay and dissolution, cannot dispense with pain and anxiety as warning signals; from the external world, which can unleash overwhelming, implacable, destructive forces against us; and finally, from our relations with others. The suffering that arises from this last source causes us more pain than any other (Freud 2004, 15).

Unlike Pinker and those who share his view, Freud paints a less positive picture of human life. To be sure, Freud's original publication of this text was in 1931, which coincided with the wave of fascist ideology in western Europe. Even still, were Freud alive in the twenty-first century, I submit that he would have likely maintained his lugubrious view of human life. It is true that Freud's meta-psychology forces him to commit to a negative view of human existence.[22] But in doing so, he captures something fundamental about the nature of being a person.

Philosophical traditions such as phenomenology and hermeneutics have long held that life and culture cannot be separated from history. Each one of us is born into the world that is not of our making, and we cannot help but take up this history that precedes us. What is perhaps troubling about being a self is that it is an unending task. It is never complete, we know it to be a task that cannot be finished, and yet we have no choice but to take it up despite awareness of the impossibility of fulfilling this task. In a radio lecture series in 1948, Merleau-Ponty opined that:

> Everyone is alone and yet nobody can do without other people, not just because they are useful (which is not in dispute here) but also when it comes to happiness. There is no way of living with others which takes away the burden of being myself, which allows me not to have an opinion; there is no 'inner' life that is not a first attempt to relate to another person (Merleau-Ponty 2004, 67).

The insight shared by both Freud and Merleau-Ponty is that existence is not inherently characterized by sadness or depression, but that existence is inherently developmental. Because we are bound to the world and to other people, we invariably undergo "traumas" that affect how we comport ourselves in relationships, and life in general. Certainly, then, sadness or its emotional derivatives are unavoidable consequences of personal life. The struggle to balance the needs of the "I" with the demands from the "we" is perhaps one of the most significant sources of emotional turmoil. Sadness manifests in degrees of severity, and likewise interferes with one's life to a greater or less extent. The equation that determines the magnitude of suffering experienced through sadness cannot be solved:

> Our emotional life in general could thus be construed as the defenses we have constructed in order to cope with the challenges we have faced in our efforts to assert the centrality of the claim that "I matter." The world con-

—

[22] Freud's meta-psychology is broadly defined by two opposing forces, Eros and Thanatos. These two forces are roughly indicative of an unconscious psychic framework structured by libidinal drives (Eros) and the "death drive" (Thanatos). The latter represents an unconscious imperative to repeatedly sabotage or destroy one's conscious existence, and thereby places the Ego or subject in conflict with her rational life.

> fronts us with a variety of obstacles, challenges, and assaults, and our emotional life is our developed style for carrying on in the face of such opposition (Russon 2003, 77).

If we follow Russon, we can sidestep the potential objection that characterizing life as inherently negative or as a struggle is a normative, albeit pessimistic, claim. This pessimistic view of life, so the objection would go, is but one (narrow) way to depict life. And though this is somewhat true, we must recall that the initial question asks why people are increasingly seeking help for sadness and depression? What Russon captures is the subtle ways in which our sense of self and our dispositions unfold over time, a drawn out process that cannot be explicitly identified. There is no one way to definitively understand why the affective dimension of our lives has increasingly become a source of suffering. Any answer needs to consider the formidable intersection of culture, economics, history, technology, politics, and ethics. What we can say with certainty is that we (as individual selves) are subjected to circumstances that determine – in part – who we are.

Another possible objection may hold that the briefly outlined existential considerations do not adequately answer the question why people are depressed. It is true that interpersonal relations and selfhood will not, on their own, provide us with answers to the question of depression. However, if we situate the existential dimension alongside the growth of pharmacology, the normalization of depression, economic interests, and the medical imperative to relieve suffering, individuals experiencing emotional distress are increasingly likely to interpret their situation as being remediable. The proliferation of depression awareness and mental health hygiene has pervaded Western culture in such a way that persons who traditionally have suffered in silence are encouraged to utilize psychiatric resources that are intended to improve their lives.

Looking ahead to the coming chapters, we need to consider to what extent "sadness" and "depression" are conceptually appropriate characterizations of lived experience. If we return to the DSM-5 depression criteria outlined at the beginning of this chapter (section 1.1), it is incumbent upon us to ask whether the signs, symptoms, and experiences of depression are effects of the condition, or rather inextricable parts of depression itself? Moreover, under the auspices of utility, does the category of depression ultimately impoverish what is an otherwise complex and heterogeneous phenomenon? When the discourse regarding sadness and depression take place largely within descriptive or scientific boundaries, our ability to investigate human behavior is limited to the narrow confines of common sense or objective thought; the way we understand ourselves in relation to the world is consequently an abstraction of our lived-experience of the world. Consequently, self-understanding is presumed to necessitate the isolation of oneself from the surrounding milieu. As we will see in the next chapter, while scientific knowledge is essential to many domains of life, it cannot absolutely exhaust knowledge of human life. And when we turn to phenomenological philosophy (chapters 4 and 5), it will become evident that the possibility of objectively *explaining* our human situation is always preceded by *experiential* acquaintance with that which is to be explained. To illustrate what I mean, in order to objectively describe how the retina is implicated in visual perception, it would presuppose that I tacitly know what it *means to see*. But this presupposition is difficult to recognize given that in the act of seeing we rarely reflect upon *how* we do so. With respect to depression, we must familiarize ourselves with such presuppositions by looking beyond the DSM-5 criteria which ultimately cover over our pre-understanding of depression that is derived from our lived-experience of depression. Or again, our task is to reacquaint ourselves with depression prior to scientific understanding.

1.10 Conclusion

This chapter began on the assumption that the history of depression may be told in various ways. I have given an account of depression that focuses on the historical tension to which the Freudian and Kraepelin perspectives gave rise. Neither the biological nor psychogenic explanatory models are the sole work of Kraepelin and Freud, but their fingerprints remain permanently impressed upon depression as we now know it. Development of the DSM is underscored by a tension attributable to the Freud-Kraepelin polarity. There is no doubt that the category of depression emerged in response to a phenomenon that, in addition to causing extreme suffering, radically alters human experience. But as I argued, the category was also established based on principles of utility to ensure reliability, both of which were intended to buttress the medical-scientific foundation of psychiatric nosology. Despite having remained relatively stable since DSM-III, the diagnostic criteria for depression seem to provide little genuine insight about the nature of depression. Accordingly, the DSM category has not led to substantive insights about *what* the category of depression designates.

The task of subsequent chapters will be to inquire into why the nature of depression cannot be adequately grasped without appealing to phenomenological philosophy. Even though a historical overview of depression and psychiatry is indispensable for an investigation of this nature, we cannot rely on history alone. We will eventually need to address the lived experience of depression if we want to fully describe the relationship between selfhood and depression. But before we make sense of the relation between depression and selfhood, in the next chapter I want to assess the way in which psychiatric history is (if at all) intertwined with contemporary psychiatric practices. Hence, given that we have until now meditated extensively on the knotty *conceptual* problems related to depression and psychiatry, the next chapter will consider depression and psychiatry from a concrete, *practical* perspective. Accordingly, in Chapter 2 (and beyond) I present findings from my qualitative research which demonstrate how historical legacy of causal explanation continues to inform the way in which clinicians are conceptually orientated toward depression and selfhood.

CHAPTER 2

The psychiatric professional and practice: Interpreting clinical perspectives and doing depression and selfhood with words

2. Introduction

The previous chapter outlined a historical rift in the way psychiatry has conceptualized the cause of depression. I contended that the development of both the biological and psychogenic models of depression are fundamental to psychiatry's complex history. However, while we can now appreciate one way of understanding the history of depression, a subsequent question is whether or not history alone can satisfactorily reveal the complex nature of depression? Shifting our focus from psychiatric history to psychiatric practice, this chapter utilizes qualitative research to demonstrate how the causal paradigms of depression, as outlined in Chapter 1, are not mere relics of history. In this chapter I argue that contemporary psychiatric practice remains informed by psychiatric history.

History helps us to make sense of depression's conceptual development, but it would be remiss to assume that depression and psychiatry are simply the sum of historical facts. As Greg Eghigian puts it, "we have a great deal to yet learn about how clinicians, researchers and clients have historically understood, used and valorized the tools of the trade" (2011, 210). To move beyond an historical appraisal of depression and psychiatry, the logical point of departure is to investigate present psychiatric practices. History is grounded in concrete practices, and clinicians are bound to the history of psychiatry just as much as they constitute the way it unfolds in the present and future. My interest in the clinical perspective is relatively modest when compared with qualitative research conducted in the social and behavioral sciences, where the aim is to collect data as a means to investigate cultural, social, or economic relations that constitute a specific practice. For this investigation, what interests us how the psychiatric concept of depression intersects with clinical reality. However, the central question for this investigation also asks: how do clinicians understand the notion of self? Assuming, as I do, that depression may only be understood as something that manifests via self-experience, then we have reason to believe clinical encounters with depression are equally encounters with problems of the self.

Drawing from interviews that I conducted in Stockholm, Sweden, this chapter claims that the historical rift regarding the way in which depression is conceptualized remain operative in contemporary practice. A hermeneutic-phenomenological interpretation of the qualitative material will further illustrate that clinical attitudes regarding depression unearth tacit conceptions of selfhood. This chapter has four broad aims. The first task is to articulate exactly *who* is a psychiatric professional? Second, I outline my interview methodology and provide a selection of informant responses that I believe to be instructive for this investigation. The third task is to analyze the interview material using an interpretive framework inspired by the hermeneutical sensibility found in the work of Paul Ricoeur. The final portion of the chapter will provide a cursory reflection on the relationship between the self and depression according to clinical attitudes expressed in the interviews.

2.1 Delimiting the field: What do we mean by psychiatry?

To sketch out the trajectory of depression's historical development, we had to acquaint ourselves broadly with the professional development of psychiatry. To a certain extent, we worked from the assumption that the psychiatric profession is – in principle – defined by the group of people who possess specialized medical knowledge. As a result, psychiatry is defined by its professional authority, where authority implies certain responsibilities, powers, and knowledge that are acquired during medical training.

Professionals and scholars across various disciplines have meditated extensively on how to demarcate the boundaries of psychiatry. While it is possible to define psychiatry by referring to its *object*, it has historically proven to be a moving target:

> Note that these boundaries are not limited by decisions of the profession, by its desire for influence or power, or by the deliberations of a committee writing a diagnostic manual. If the latter does its job well, it does not decide what the boundaries should become, it describes the boundaries that exist at that time, [...] people who were not previously viewed as psychiatric pa-

> tients achieved that status because the psychiatric profession developed the ability to help them (Michels and Frances 2013, 566).

The science of psychiatry, as Michels and Frances understand it, is a bottom-up endeavor; it is descriptive and responsive to its object of study, in that it seeks to find out what exists and to respond accordingly. This implies that there exists a recursive dynamic between psychiatric knowledge and the empirical object of psychiatry. When a hitherto unknown phenomenon is observed, psychiatry is obliged to adjust accordingly. Scientific knowledge specific to psychiatry is, as with all sciences, not absolute. But as a human science, psychiatry must proceed on the assumption that knowledge of the clinical object may be – even if only in the future – objectively exhaustible. However, defining psychiatry solely on the basis of its object ignores the relation between the *practice* and its abstract object. How, then, should psychiatry be defined?

For instance, conflicting empirical evidence regarding the etiology of depression may lead to epistemic factions among individual clinicians (e.g. when a random control trial fails to corroborate the therapeutic efficacy of SSRI in depression), something that may consequently polarize clinical practices. The long-standing tension between adherents of the dominant bio-reductionist paradigm and those who adopt a pluralistic approach characterized as the bio-psychosocial approach, are but one instance of the way empirical data can be divisive. But as psychiatric science develops (or stagnates) – how plastic are psychiatric concepts in clinical practice? Might a clinician's conception of illness or suffering, for example, overdetermine her specialized professional knowledge of depression? Specifying a definition of psychiatry requires that we map out the full scope of psychiatric *praxis* that in reality transcends the extant boundaries of psychiatry erected solely with reference to medical authority

> the philosophy of psychiatry can help to clarify the descriptive and definetional power of the language of psychiatry; and the hermeneutic disciplines can show how *the interlocutor (clinician) contributes* to the construction and interpretation of the psychiatric object (Berrios and Marková 2015, 48, emphasis added).

It is crucial, then, that psychiatry not be defined solely by reference to its empirical or descriptive object. Since psychiatry is, after all, a practice, an adequate definition of psychiatry should ultimately be professionally inclusive rather than exclusive.

If medical authority is deemed to be a satisfactory measure of psychiatry's professional boundaries, our definition will only capture a narrow and idealized account of what constitutes "psychiatry." Since psychiatrists are *de facto* medical physicians, what most obviously sets them apart from auxiliary mental health clinicians is professional accreditation. A psychiatrist is medically trained in ways that auxiliary mental health professionals are not. Then again, the latter are qualified in ways that the former is not. Why, then, is competence in psychiatric medicine not an adequate representation of psychiatry as a whole?

Let us provide a provisional answer in the form of a question: "*where* is psychiatry taking place?" (Eghigian 2011, 203, emphasis added). Psychiatric practice is not limited to the psychiatric ward or the psychiatrist's private clinic. As Eghigian sees it, "the work in which contemporary psychiatry has been involved – the treatment of mental illness and the promotion of mental health, or what might be referred to as mental health care – is not a singular, autonomous enterprise" (ibid.). The reality of psychiatric practice is that the boundaries are porous, a point we will be able to investigate further now that we have become acquainted with the multifaceted functions of the DSM.

Depression is instructive as to why a strictly medical definition of psychiatry does not encompass the full scope of psychiatric practices. The DSM-5 is a widely accessible resource that is not under lock and key of psychiatric professionals. The diagnostic manual is equally essential for auxiliary mental health professionals. It is obviously particularly salient for diagnosing depression. That the majority of depression diagnoses are provided by primary care physicians is by no means an overstatement. The historical research of Callahan and Berrios leads them, for example, to claim that "primary-care doctors provide most of the care for patients with depression. Experts do not debate this fact…" (2004, ix). Save for patients who experience severe, major (or psychotic) depressive episodes, the majority of depression cases may never come into contact with psychiatric services, be they hospital in/out-patient services, or through direct consultation with a psychiatrist. Of all interventions available for depression treatment, only electroconvulsive therapy demands the oversight of a psychiatrist. When compared with schizophrenia, the frequency of contact between a psychiatrist and depression is considerably less. Yet, depression *qua* depression is nevertheless a psychiatric category of disorder defined according to *psychiatric* epistemology, research, and theory.

Some psychiatrists are trained and accredited to provide psychotherapeutic treatment, but more often than not "talking cures" generally remain the domain of psychologists, psychotherapists – or less commonly, psychoanalysts and social workers. In Sweden, for instance, as of 2011 only 12% of licenced psychotherapists were licensed physicians (Hadlaczky, Stefenson, and Wasserman 2012), a number that has remained stable since 1996. With respect to depression, the distinction between psychiatrists and other mental health clinicians, by virtue of their respective clinical competence, should be called into doubt. Returning to the case of Sweden:

> Specialist psychiatric care can be approached directly or through GP referral. Upon their arrival, patients are evaluated by either a psychiatrist (approximately 25%), a psychologist or a psychiatric nurse; patients are subsequently offered pharmacological treatment, psychotherapy, or both. Patients with less severe problems are referred to GPs in primary care (ibid., 359).

The statistics above refer to mental disorders in general and not depression alone. However, most common were problems surrounding substance abuse and depression. The Swedish case is by no means intended to be indicative of Western psychiatry as a whole, but it is by no means an exception. If only one in four patients is evaluated by a psychiatrist, 75% of patients make contact with clinicians who do not possess the "psychiatric competence" or "authority" of a psychiatrist *cum* medical physician. In the context of how clinical practice actually functions, we are justified to assume that the boundaries of professional responsibility and authority are quite porous. This said, it remains the case that psychiatry – in principle – represents the zenith of mental health professionals, for it is psychiatric discourse that determines what does and does not constitute a psychiatric disorder.

The psychiatric physician holds a distinguished place in the community not only because professional identities are highly valued, but because the major professions have an epistemically distinct place in the community. Schön approvingly cites sociologist Everett Hughes, who contends that

> the professions have struck a bargain with society. In return for access to their extraordinary knowledge on matters of great human importance, society has granted them a mandate for social control in their fields of specialization [...] and a license to determine who shall assume the mantle of professional authority (Schön 1987, 7).

A distinctive feature of professional knowledge is that it is reserved for a select portion of the population. Medical professionals are a minority community whose specialized knowledge is sought by community members, for whom such knowledge (in many cases) is essential to well-being and health. The privileged position of physicians in society reflects, in part, a social identity that is granted authority by virtue of possessing specialized knowledge. It has long been recognized that the structure of the clinician-patient relationship is underscored by a power imbalance. But what of the power and hierarchical imbalance that exists among mental health care clinicians themselves?

Our attempt to properly characterize psychiatry uses what could be termed the 'criteria of authority.' For instance, "only the professions," says Schön, "practice rigorously technical problem solving based on specialized knowledge" (1983, 21-22) and "the systematic knowledge base of a profession is thought to have four properties. It is specialized, firmly bounded, scientific, and standardized" (ibid., 23). Psychiatry is certainly specialized, putatively scientific, and standardized, but the claim I am putting forth is that the professional boundary is not reified. If this is correct, then "psychiatry" is a pluralistic field practiced by a multiplicity of professionals possessing unique professional competencies. With an expansive practical field, the medical and symbolic authority reserved for psychiatrist *qua* physician is decentralized. For this reason, the boundaries of psychiatry are not defined by, or limited to, psychiatric medicine.

Having said this, the professional boundaries of psychiatry are not determined by clinical practices alone. Recall from Chapter 1 that there exists an intimate relationship between the DSM and health insurers. In many, if not most countries, insurers will not reimburse claims for psychiatric care without a DSM or ICD diagnostic code. Regardless of professional competence, all mental health care providers are subject to the bureaucratic administrative demands imposed by insurers. Insurance companies ride on the coattails of the DSM's success, which has eventually given rise to the quasi-hegemonic mandate that all reimbursement claims be coded according to the DSM diagnostic coding system. "Since the late 1960s," argues Racheal Cooper, "it has been standard practice for medical insurance companies to request a DSM diagnosis before they will consider reimbursing for psychiatric treatment" (2004, 18). In Chapter 1 we examined the knotty intersection between psychopharmacology, diagnosis, and insurance, with respect to depression. In the context of this chapter, we are concerned more broadly with what is properly "psychiatric." Like Cooper, Halpin contends that "the *DSM as institutional tool* constructs a 'customer' via institutional processes *aligning professional practices* with insurance and pharmaceutical companies, producing receipts, reimbursement, and revenues" (Halpin 2016, emphasis added). Halpin captures something important about the internal structures of psychiatric practice, but we must treat this claim with caution. Private insurance is a serious impediment for many in need of healthcare in the United States; for many service users, it is the gateway to mental health treatment. In countries with "universal" healthcare schemes such as Sweden, United Kingdom, and Canada, the relevance of personal health insurance is markedly reduced.

Then again, reimbursement schemes are not solely aimed at service users. Governmental agencies responsible for managing financial resources in healthcare demand that clinics submit medical billing codes to ensure clinicians are remunerated. In many countries, reimbursement for services rendered by a psychiatric clinic is approved by the governmental agency on the condition that patient investigations are accompanied by the relevant DSM diagnostic code, a unique and specific number that serves to identify a specific medical diagnosis.

To close this section, I propose we adopt a liberal or wide notion of psychiatry that accentuates the professional pluralism within "psychiatry." Note that my intention is not to redefine psychiatry as such. For the purposes of this investigation, psychiatry must be employed consistently even though it is not consistently limited to traditional psychiatric settings. We need not look further than the DSM itself for corroboration:

> The information [in the DSM-5] is of value to all professionals associated with various aspects of mental health care, including psychiatrists, other physicians, psychologists, social workers, nurses, counsellors, forensic and legal specialists, occupational and rehabilitation therapists, and other health professionals. The criteria are concise and explicit and intended to facilitate an objective assessment of symptom presentations in a variety of clinical settings— inpatient, outpatient, partial hospital, consultation-liaison, clinical, private practice, and primary care— as well in general community epidemiological studies of mental disorders (APA 2013, xii).

Going forward, unless otherwise specified, the term psychiatry will be used to denote any professional whose work brings him or her into contact with persons who suffer from mental disorder, a broad umbrella term under which we still recognize diverse professional competencies.

The upshot of this characterization is that it unfetters us from the dualist ontology that permeates the common-sense phrase “mental health”. The “mental” in mental health is juxtaposed with the “biology” of *bio*medicine. The term psychiatry is by no means neutral and bears its own – often negative – set of connotations. Denoting psychiatry in this way makes it possible to escape the categorical division of *psyche* and *soma* traditionally applied in medicine. Moreover, psychiatry is a nebulous practice whose specialized clinical practices cannot be understood in isolation. The overlap of professional responsibility, in addition to the demand for inter-professional communication and cooperation, suggests that attempts to rigorously delimit what is proper to each professional group (e.g. general physicians, psychiatrists, psychologists, etc.) will prove to be artificial.

Some psychiatric professionals will object that this broad characterization devalues the specialized competence achieved through rigorous medical training. This objection, however, fails to appreciate that our new characterization of psychiatry does not equalize professional status within psychiatry. As we stated above, heterogeneous professional competencies remain distinguishable parts of the whole. This objection is unfortunately motivated by anxiety over the precariousness of professional integrity and professional identity, which in spite of DSM reforms that sought to resolve theoretical disarray in order to preserve psychiatry’s professional identity, has never quite been assuaged. Beneath an institutional façade, psychiatry quietly continues to endure an identity crisis: “It is a truism,” says Katschnig, “that psychiatry is split into many directions and subdirections of thought. Considering that a common knowledge base is a core defining criterion of any profession, this split is a considerable threat to the coherence of our profession” (Katschnig 2010, 23). This “threat” is not to psychiatry as such, rather a threat to the *unity* of the profession:

> Many would argue that our discipline has gained in status by a tremendous increase of knowledge acquired over the past decades. However, there are indications that psychiatry’s diagnostic and therapeutic knowledge base is in a credibility crisis and that the coherence of our discipline is threatened by the existence of *de facto* ideological sub- groups [...] Other professions are more and more claiming segments of our held of competence; and our image in society and in medicine is less positive than many of us might think (ibid., 26).

The inclusivity of this boundary that I have proposed has the dual merits of flexibility and utility. It also aims to depict the profession *on the ground*, as a practice that is more than the sum of professional rules and knowledge. For this reason, I have opted to meet with a variety of clinicians rather than just psychiatrists, for as we will see, the nature of psychiatric *praxis* is less than straightforward. Moreover, by shifting our focus to the clinical perspective, I will employ the qualitative material gathered from interviews with psychiatric professionals to illustrate how psychiatric discourse constrains the way clinicians understand depression and selfhood.

2.2 Interview methodology

This qualitative study is motivated by several questions: How do psychiatric professionals of understand depression? How does the DSM influence practice, if at all? And, indeed, do either of these questions provide insight into the way clinicians understand the self? In addition to any insights derived from the interviews, the opportunity to meet with clinicians was equally instructive, if for no other reason than to become familiar with the day-to-day reality of clinical practice. Within the philosophy of psychiatry, the literature is often remiss by employing generalized assumptions about clinical reality, the correctness of which are rarely called into question. Though a qualitative investigation by no means secures certainty about the correctness of such assumptions, we nevertheless minimize the potential to mischaracterize or speculate about what psychiatry looks like in the clinic.

All interviews were conducted in Stockholm, save for two, which took place at the psychiatric out-patient hospital in Värmland, Karlstad, a three-hour train journey west of Stockholm. In Stockholm, interviews were split between two clinics: Clinic A, a provider of specialized care for affective disorders and patients of all ages, and Clinic B, a provider of psychiatric care for children and adolescent patients. Informants participated voluntarily in the research and provided consent based on information sheets that were provided in advance. Informants were recruited from these clinics based on a pre-existing (but limited) relationship with the Centre for Studies in Practical Knowledge (CPK) at Södertörn University. Since the informant sample was one of convenience, those interviewed at the respective clinics were naturally sympathetic to the relationship between philosophy and psychiatry. As is often the case with most qualitative investigations, in the interest of methodological transparency, the sample group for this investigation was not assumed to be comprised of neutral informants. Similarly, the material is not purported to represent universal psychiatric attitudes. Conversely, recruiting putative neutral informants is only an ideal. Informants are unlikely to participate if the particular research theme is perceived to be of little value or interest.[23]

All interviews were conducted in English and voice recorded. The informants were explicitly instructed that they retained the right to remove themselves from the research before the interviews were transcribed.[24] Fig. 2 provides a simple breakdown of the participating informants, while Fig. 3 lists a breakdown of the informants' clinical specialties:

<table>
<tr><th>Informants</th><th>Gender</th><th>Position</th></tr>
<tr><td rowspan="2">16</td><td>4 Males</td><td>2 Psychologists (1 CBT, 1 psychodynamic)
2 Psychiatrists</td></tr>
<tr><td>12 Females</td><td>1 Psychiatrist
2 General physicians
2 Psychiatric nurses
2 Psychodynamic therapists
5 Psychologists</td></tr>
</table>

Fig. 2 Participant breakdown

[23] Some qualitative researchers go so far as to claim that 'good' informants will have critical perspectives. Davies suggests that "good informants are 'marginal' in some respects in their own society [...] who thus becom[e] more aware of the assumptions and expectations of their own society" (Davies 2008, 90). The extent to which the lack of informant neutrality is problematic will vary according to the particular research context. However, if there is any doubt about the motives of the informants with whom I met, I believe we can assuage possible reservations: first, it would be dubious to assume that all the informants held critical or philosophical perspectives. And even if it were the case, this would not necessarily irreparably taint the material, since the investigation could alternatively be framed as an investigation of critical clinical perspectives rather than so-called normal psychiatric perspectives. Second, professional institutions such as medicine are not without internal criticism from its own members. It would be difficult to imagine that a profession might develop or evolve totally devoid of dialectical processes when we consider an example like inter-generational co-mingling of professionals, where the dynamic nature of training and new knowledge can lead to professional disagreement. Last, a successful practical knowledge investigation should begin with critical distance. In the absence of the latter, there would exist no impetus to investigate the practices of a given profession.

[24] One participant requested to be removed from the study, while two interviews were not admissible due to language barriers.

Clinic A	Clinic B	Värmland hospital
1 General physician 2 Nurses 2 Psychotherapists 3 Psychologists	1 Psychiatrist 1 General physician 4 Psychologists	2 Psychiatrists

Fig. 3 Distribution of Professions

The interviews were designed according to the "active interview" model, an approach that promotes a semi-structured and "open-ended" interview process. The questions were intended to serve as points of entry, making allowance for unforeseen and unexpected directions that the interview might take. Methodologically, this approach "eschews the image of the [informant as a] vessel waiting to be tapped in favour of the notion that the subject's interpretive capabilities must be activated, stimulated, and cultivated" (Holstein and Gubrium 1995, 16). The interviews were conducted in a group format, consisting of two or three informants per interview. To encourage openness and to reduce possible unease concerning the critical judgment of one's peers, the clinic coordinator placed informants in groups based on professional or personal affinity. This format was employed to encourage discussion among the informants themselves, but also to reduce nervousness about being interviewed in English. The informants' responses often led to follow-up questions that were spontaneous and unscripted. Furthermore, unanticipated responses from the informants made for richer analysis and drew attention to aspects of clinical life that the scripted questions would otherwise have failed to address.

2.3. Approach to the qualitative material

The reader is reminded that the orientation of this investigation adopts a phenomenological-existential interpretive framework. Chapters 4 and 5 will deal extensively with phenomenological philosophy, but for the purposes of this chapter, I want to briefly specify why this investigation differs from so-called phenomenological investigations that have become an increasingly fashionable method of choice for many qualitative researchers.

Approaches that apply phenomenology to empirical investigations often adopt the following method: an introduction to phenomenological philosophy; an ambiguous description of how to do phenomenology, and a short section on findings. Ultimately, the confounding problem in phenomenological methodology is the term "method."

The crucial point for this chapter is that the term "method" in phenomenological qualitative studies is not indicative of the sensibilities associated with method in phenomenological philosophy.

This said, it would be unfair to dismiss all qualitatively inspired phenomenological research simply because some of the scholarship is less than satisfying. The problem is generally one of application. In what way should phenomenological philosophy serve an empirical investigation? To illustrate this issue, the work of Van Manen (2014), which is intended to aid qualitative researchers in designing phenomenological investigations, often employs descriptions laden with phenomenological jargon, such that when researchers begin the pivotal work of interpretive analysis, the methodological precepts are rather vacuous. Below, Van Manen contrasts phenomenological analysis with grounded theory or conceptual analysis, which have long been preferred methods in social and behavioral sciences

> 'analyzing' thematic meanings of phenomena (a lived experience) is a complex and creative process of insightful invention, discovery, and disclosure. Grasping and formulating a thematic understanding is not a rule-bound process but a free act of 'seeing' meaning that is driven by the epoch and the reduction (Van Manen 2014, 320).

On the one hand, we can appreciate Van Manen's attempt to differentiate phenomenological interpretation from traditional qualitative interpretive strategies that often disseminate data by way of codification or frequency analysis. On the other hand, Van Manen's precepts unfortunately do not provide us with a practical sense of how the phenomenological method ought to be applied to the phenomenon being investigated. Researchers often rely on Husserl's transcendental phenomenology as the central feature of their method, perhaps due to misconceptions about the practical utility of Husserl's phenomenological method. As a consequence, under the auspices of Husserl's notion of the *epoché,* researchers wrongly assume that the quintessential feature of the phenomenological method is the imperative to "bracket" out one's presuppositions or prejudices regarding the phenomenon in question. This is further complicated when researchers indiscriminately employ phenomenological concepts from different phenomenological philosophers.[25] There are various reasons why this *à la carte* approach to phenomenological research is problematic, but the overarching concern with "phenomenological" researchers borrowing widely from the phenomenological tradition is that they risk treating the phenomenological method as a homogenous notion. Why are these considerations significant for our own investigation?

It is important to recall what type of study this investigation is *not*. In this book's introduction, I made it clear that my qualitative study of psychiatric clinicians should not lead the reader to conclude that this research is sociological, psychological, or anthropological. Likewise, it is paramount that we distinguish "scientific phenomenology" from phenomenological philosophy. Stella Sandford provides an excellent characterization of this problem, which warrants quoting at length:

> Researchers in these [professional] practice disciplines [healthcare and nursing], who use phenomenological research methodologies are engaged in empirical studies involving data gathering and analysis. While their analyses might in some way be based – often several steps removed – in phenomenological philosophies, from wherever one stands within the heterogeneous discipline of philosophy it is clear that they are neither doing philosophy nor claiming to do so. Further, the non-philosophical status of these analyses have been used to defend their description as "phenomenological" against the charge that they bear little or no relation to the philosophies from which they claim to derive their methods. That is, the charge that they are not really "phenomenological" because they are remote from philosophy is countered with the argument that this is to confuse phenomenology (as developed and practiced by Husserl, for example) with scientific phenomenology (the application of insights from philosophical phenomenology in the social sciences (Sandford 2016, 53).

I concur with Sandford that scientific phenomenology is not interchangeable with philosophical phenomenology. However, it does not follow that qualitative material is anathema to phenomenological investigations. Quite the opposite, the phenomenological tradition has history of incorporating literature, art, and case studies, as rich sources for philosophical analysis.

—

[25] Recently, there has been a series of rather antagonistic exchanges between Zahavi, van Manen, and Smith, regarding how phenomenology is to be applied in qualitative research. Zahavi has explicitly referred to Van Manen to exemplify how phenomenology has been misappropriated by qualitative researchers. In response, Van Manen claims Zahavi is (wrongly) advocating a "tribal" attitude – or is policing – who can and cannot conduct phenomenological research. See Zahavi (2019), van Manen (2019), and Smith (2018).

That said, the key feature that makes phenomenological philosophy essential to this investigation is that phenomenological analysis always begins with lived-experience, whereas scientific phenomenology often begins with *abstractions* of lived-experience; the latter subjects lived-experience to objective interpretation, and thereby neglects to account for the way in which our most primary experience of the (habitual and non-conceptual) world is taken for granted. In the next section, I employ the phenomenological-hermeneutic thought of Paul Ricoeur to illustrate that without a proper phenomenological vocabulary, clinicians often struggle to characterize depression and selfhood beyond the conceptual boundaries of psychiatric epistemology.

2.3.1 To the descriptions themselves: The clinical view

Out of the collected interview material, the informants' responses consistently return to two overarching issues: 1) the way in which clinicians relate to both the DSM and diagnosis in their practice and 2) repeated emphasis on the sharp demarcation between the practical structure of adult psychiatry and of child psychiatry. I want to pick up this thread by beginning with selections from the clinicians' responses regarding both of these issues.

Until now, our reflections on the DSM have been almost exclusively historical in nature. I showed that the DSM category of depression is – in principle – a clinically ideal "portrait" of depression. But I also argued that the DSM alone does not define practice. A subsequent question of importance, then, is how do clinicians appropriate the DSM ideal in practice? To explore this question, psychiatric clinicians were asked to comment on the importance of the DSM for their own practice. I have elected to sample a significant number of excepts from the interviews so as to justify my claims about the way in which clinicians encounter depression and selfhood:

> I would say very much and not at all. In a way the DSM is like, what the patient describes quite often fits in with what's said [in the DSM], that it's like a photocopy in black and white, you know, you take a picture view and you make a bad cheap black and white picture of it.
> *Psychologist, clinic A*

> The diagnostic system with psychiatry, it's on loose grounds and shaky grounds, and I really know they are remodelling the DSM, and there has been ample, ample criticism – so it's not even controversial, in many ways – from the people who make the diagnostic system themselves, and then they can help, of course, if they can help in this way of using it as a basis for negotiation for trying to understand, for trying to talk about [depression].

And again, if you say, "Your diagnosis is depression", okay, "What does it mean for you?" It's one thing if your finger is broken or have diabetes, you know whatever. From the illness model, there's a strict cause for it. And we lack that totally in mental health. It does not exist, period. But it fits the medical model, and psychiatry is a profession within the framework of medicine. And I don't say that it doesn't help to gain some understanding, that's not what I'm saying. But you have to really treat it with great care.
Nurse, clinic A

Sometimes, but...I think I can also say it's just one way to make meaning. And now we have "this" way [makes a hand gesture like a box].
Psychotherapist, clinic B

Diagnosis is useful, I think, to be clear. But the usefulness is in, I think, sometimes for the patient to have an explanation and feeling of finding others with the same [condition]; "I'm not alone," "I am one of a community." And psychiatric diagnosis lets them find themselves [among] others with the same problems…to have an explanation; psychiatric diagnoses sometimes look like an explanation and you can get the feel of an explanation, but really it isn't an explanation, *it's a name*. So, sometimes I'm not really comfortable with patients accepting my diagnosis as an explanation: "Oh that's why I have this problem in life," because I don't give an explanation why they have a problem, *I've given them a name of their problem…*

[…continued]

I would say nearly all clinicians, I guess more in Sweden than in the United States, use the DSM and the ICD as categories but you don't follow the protocol lines, yes and no, but you use categories and place in categories. And that I think it's the only way to use it functionally.
Psychiatrist, Karlstad hospital

I have to adapt to the paradigm that we are living in right now, what they have given us. And that right now is very much this kind of sub-specialist, depression, or anxiety, or whatever, so from that view it's very, very important and I have to adapt to that, and do whatever is required of me. And that is to do this first interview, get their background, then together with the doctor, end up with a psychiatric diagnosis. But in a way, it is a problematic description.
Psychologist, clinic B

That's one reason why I became dissatisfied with child psychiatry, it's very much about diagnosis, eliciting reports of the symptoms and finding the diagnosis. And maybe, in a way, placing a label on the problem and then explaining everything with that label.
Psychiatrist, Karlstad hospital

> I think we are very pressed from Försäkringskassan [Swedish social insurance]; "read DSM," that's the bible. So, it's more a problem because they are also very [rigid], and you have to – they meet a doctor and it's like God. It's important when I do assessments. Because the diagnosis that I apply should be reasonable, of course. It should capture the difficulties that person has, and you should be able to communicate it to other people so the person can get the help they need... A diagnosis is like a label that you stick to someone. So maybe there's a reason for doing it, to communicate what sort of area the person has difficulties in.
> *Psychotherapist, clinic A*

> Well, it's important – I don't use it trying to understand my patients and trying to get them help. I don't use it as a guideline to know what kind of treatment they need. I use it because our system needs us to use it, and I use it when I do investigations, that's when you have a discussion with a doctor about what diagnosis to give [...]. Well, I could do my work without DSM in treatment, but I can't do investigations without DSM. Because a key thing to the investigation is that it provides a diagnosis.
> *Psychologist, clinic B*

> We have to diagnose when we see a patient; we have to give a diagnosis; we can't ignore it; our system just hates it [when we don't diagnose] ... and also the boss. So, we have to give a diagnosis.
> *Psychologist, clinic B*

> You have to write something in the file. I lack a little respect for the DSM
> *Psychologist, clinic A*

> DSM-IV is very limited. It is a very, it's very abstract, they line up all these criteria then say none of the above if there's another explanation, I mean, there are very few cases that you can say "this is depression and has to be treated like this". And that is a problem because that, of course, makes it different for different people.
> *Psychiatric Resident, clinic B*

The clinicians' responses above reveal deeply ambivalent attitudes concerning their relationship to the DSM. One the one hand, the informants view the DSM as an impersonal classification tool. Yet, on the other hand, a DSM diagnosis facilitates patient access to psychiatric care. By way of illustration, one psychologist above noted that: "We have to diagnose when we see a patient." Contrast this statement with that of the psychiatric resident who, in the above excerpt, stated that: "DSM-IV is very limited. It is a very, it's very abstract, they line up all these criteria then say none of the above if there's another explanation, I mean, there are very few cases that you can say 'this is depression and has to be treated like this.'" For many clinicians, then, the imperative to diagnose is often compromised by the perceived lack of concrete ways to characterize depression.

I have highlighted what I believe to be the most relevant remarks depicting the diagnostic dilemma faced by clinicians, insofar as a dilemma is defined as a choice between two equally unsatisfying options. Diagnosis is (ostensibly) intended to provide a representation of the patient, which the clinicians repeatedly point out, requiring that patient descriptions be translated into the operational diagnostic language of the DSM. Yet, despite their skepticism about diagnostic "labels", clinicians also acknowledge a positive function associated with diagnosis. The diagnostic label is useful insofar as it gathers together – under one term – a series of inchoate experiences and symptoms that impinge upon the well-being of patients. The flip side of the practicality of a diagnosis is more strictly bureaucratic, insofar that a diagnosis is the key that opens the gateway to care.

The responses also reveal that clinicians are highly sensitive to the impersonal process of diagnosis. As medical practices increasingly turn toward models of patient-centered care,[26] it is unsurprising that the informants expressed dissatisfaction with applying "objective" categories to diagnose the *person* before them:

> Sometimes it's really helpful for a patient to know "this is not really me," "I'm having a sort of disturbance, that I can adjust and will go back to my normal state." It's good for them sometimes to know that, that it is a sickness or that [it's something] people can get. It's a syndrome that exists.
> *Psychiatric nurse, clinic A*
>
> I usually take care to explain to the patient, this is something to describe the state you're in right now, *but it doesn't relate to who you are as a person.*
> *Psychologist, clinic B*
>
> I try with the same approach, "this is a construct," "diagnostic systems change, and right now it's like this but perhaps it will change in 10 years, so…
> *Psychologist, clinic A*
>
> I try to say that to many of my patients, that diagnosis is a social construct and it's a description of a certain type of problem, and when it looks like this, we call it depression. So sometimes I have that kind of conversation

[26] The term patient-centered care is here meant to be broadly defined, one reason being that there is no general consensus on a definition. Generally speaking, the term denotes a practice model that emphasizes patient participation in his or her treatment, which might include soliciting his or her preferences, desires, and so on.

> with the patient [...] I think diagnosis is some kind of acknowledgment that it's okay that I'm not feeling right or well...or sick, or something like that, maybe confirmation.
> *Psychologist, clinic B*

> They are the people they are, regardless of diagnosis.
> *Psychologist, clinic B*

> Well I can do, then, what we call psycho-education, where I can be like 'Well, anxiety works in this way', 'Some things you can do is exercise', stuff like that, speak about it in that way.
> *Psychologist, clinic A*

> For me, people have troubles and people want to understand and put a name on what troubles they have, and that changes during the course of time and the course of cultures, and contexts. But maybe the causes of the troubles are very much the same, 100 years ago from today [...] I was reading something about the Dalai Lama, and he says that your mind is your most powerful healer. That's what immediately came to my mind. So of course, the way that you think about your ailments will make a difference.
> Director, *clinic B*

> All these descriptions of human behavior are going to change. In 10 years, 20 years, we'll look for different things. There's a lot of new knowledge coming in and it will change. It's not handed down from above. But the way people function and the problems, that's a real condition, that's true; whether you call it something or not [...] but they are the people they are regardless of diagnosis.
> *Psychologist,* clinic A

The tension between impersonal diagnosis and diagnosis as a gateway to care, draws attention to practical coping strategies developed by the clinicians. This sample group of clinicians showed themselves to be sensitive to the fact that the diagnosis does something – affectively – to the patient. Clinicians themselves, however, make no reference to the specific use of any "strategies." General dissatisfaction with DSM and pressure to apply a diagnostic label suggests clinicians have developed techniques and strategies that permit them to retain some sense of agency and power as clinicians. The specific strategy of distancing patients from their diagnosis, however, points to a deeper philosophical issue, namely that the distinction between patient and diagnosis unavoidably makes use of a tacit notion of self. We will analyze this point in more detail shortly, but first we must summarize the second issue regarding child psychiatry and the informants' views on practice.

2.4 Child psychiatry: Toward an ontology of situation

An additional theme of note that may be drawn from the clinicians' interview responses is that adult psychiatry and child psychiatry are practiced in disparate ways. Specifically, the clinicians convey the extent to which child psychiatry is practically and theoretically discontinuous with adult psychiatry. This distinction is especially of interest to us since, as the informants' responses will demonstrate, the structure of the clinical encounter in child psychiatry tacitly employs phenomenological sensibilities.

In adult psychiatry, clinicians typically meet patients in a one-to-one setting. Unlike adult practice, clinicians in child psychiatry do not meet patients individually but instead meet the child with his or her family constellation (or "system"). Adult practice gathers together two horizons, that of the patient and the clinician. Clinical attempts to achieve patient understanding rely on patient self-reports, which is consistent with the assumption that adults are (rationally) self-sufficient: a consciousness *inside* a person that is intimately acquainted with all thoughts, feelings, and experiences. Adult practice begins (at least initially) on the assumption that this acquaintance is possible by one's capacity for self-reflection. Broadly speaking, the object of adult psychiatry is comparable to the self-contained monad. Treatment of depression in adults is typically two-pronged: psychopharmacological or talk-therapy (or a combination thereof). Each intervention is aimed at distinct dimensions internal to the patient: one biological, the other cognitive. In the case of the former, treatment attempts to correct a pathology or dysfunction, while the latter seeks to modify behavior by reorganizing cognitive or psychological content.

Unlike adult practice, pharmacological intervention in child psychiatry is generally reserved for extreme cases of depression. Before all else, the principle task is to make sense of the family constellation in which the child is situated:

> It's a very special situation here, because you're not dealing with a person, you're always dealing with a system or even two systems. So, I actually see a lot of what I've done over the years is protecting patients from chemicals that they didn't need.
> *Psychiatrist, clinic B*

> Well, a big difference between child and adults in psychiatry is the fact that [with children] you work much more with the system, you work with the family. And usually, not always of course, usually the child or teenager has another caring institution around her. That I think is an important dif-

> ference. Even adults can have it, but it's not the same – people don't feel responsible for an adult the way they feel responsible for a child or teenager. For example, when I have a patient with depression and on anti-depressant medicine, I can not only talk to the child, I can also ask the parents how they feel the progress has been. That helps, absolutely.
> *General physician, clinic B*

As seen above, the problem may not be *in* the patient as such. Problems emerge from entangled relations that orbit the child's constellation. What the informant implicitly expresses above is that children and teenagers are unable to fully take responsibility for choices or actions, classic hallmarks of what is considered to constitute agent autonomy. This informant suggests that child psychiatry has an added asset in the form of a quasi "truth tracking" that is not available in adult practice. Self-reports provided by a child may be tested against caretaker observations, who intuitively would seem most suitably positioned to observe a child's behavior. Likewise, broadly speaking, we are inclined to believe that caretakers concern themselves with the best interests of the child. As we will see momentarily, while caregivers do generally conduct themselves in accordance with what they consider to be the child's best interest, even the most contentious caregivers who report their observations with acuity may fail to recognize that they themselves are implicated in the situation, the child's constellation. Caretakers or other members of the constellation may not *cause* a patient's behavior, but they motivate behavior as co-constituters of the very constellation they otherwise fail to grasp. This is because they cannot step out of this constellation situation: *They are the situation.*

A formidable challenge for clinicians in child psychiatry is to discern between disorder and discord. Often, it is the case that there is nothing "wrong" with the patient *per se*:

> I had such a child today, two parents neither of them capable of handling a beautiful little 6 year-old, they don't know how to hold the child, you know internally, they don't know how to hold the child, they're not capable of it, I think they are in too deep trouble in their own lives and it's no part of our brief here to treat them, you know, in a very convoluted way you could sort of help them navigate into a situation in our organization in which it became apparent to them that they need help. But even then, we can't even refer them to somebody.
> *Psychiatrist, clinic B*

This instructive example reiterates that the primary task in child psychiatry is to make sense of the child's constellation. Moreover, constellation is not simply a series of dynamic relationships: it is the child being-in-situation, a pre-reflective world orientation that is contingently structured by what stands out as significant or meaningful, issues that concern the child and that demand resolution. Persons intimately involved in the child's life are the most proximal points of contact and thus co-constitute the meaningfulness or significance of the child's constellation. Because a child's contact with the world is equally contact with multiple interpersonal relations, all attempts to understand the child is at the same time an attempt to understand the child's intersubjective relations. This is not a clinical task that merely supplements primary diagnostic findings. It is a necessary demand placed on the clinician. Why? As this psychiatrist claims:

> Absolutely half, at the very least, half of the parents of the children who have reason to come here are incapable of parenting. How do you fix that?

Some forty years earlier, in the work of R.D Laing, a vociferous critic of psychiatry, we find a similar sentiment

> when the situation has 'broken down' to the extent that an outside agency is brought in, not only may some or all of those in the situation not themselves see what the situation is, but also *they may not see that they do not see it* [...] We have to discover what the situation is *in the course of* our intervention in the situation (Laing 1971, 34-35, emphasis original).

The clinician's views concerning child psychiatry repeatedly make it clear that the imperative in child practice is to bracket the diagnostic attitude in favor of illuminating the intersubjective relations that structure the lived world of the child. The phenomenologically relevant nature of child psychiatry is the way in which the conceptualization of a person (or self) is not restricted to the patient's inner world. For child psychiatry, children – as selves- are understood *à propos* of things and people that are drawn into their orbit.

Having said this, we must make it clear that the informants do not suggest that child psychiatry is clinically superior (epistemically or ontologically) to adult psychiatry. The constellation model we have sketched out here does not necessarily depend upon a phenomenological framework. That is, we do not need phenomenology to appreciate that the family unit exerts influence on the development of children. Likewise, it might be argued that the meeting structure in child psychiatry only differs from adult practice by virtue of the underdeveloped status of the child. What appear to be distinct practices, the argument might hold, are in reality not altogether discontinuous *if* child and adult are taken to be the same phenomenon. In other words, the object of inquiry remains particular to one person, but unlike adult practice, child psychiatry is unable to fully access the inner world of the child. On this assumption, child and adult psychiatry share the same goal of disclosing internal rational conflicts. However, what makes child psychiatry unique is that the object of inquiry is an underdeveloped or not-yet-adult. Just as an acorn entails the potential oak tree, the child is intrinsically a soon to be adult who will eventually develop into an autonomous agent. But until the developmental schedule is realized, the child's capacity for rationality remains latent, which gives credence to the necessity of third-person reports by a child's caregivers who are entrusted with providing a cohesive overview of the child's behaviors, preferences, habits, and so on

> that person [the child] is mostly constitutionally incapable of doing anything other than, at best, responding to my questions. *They can generally not generate a narrative, they do not have a "looking at myself" perspective, they don't really have self-mentalization* [...] you would never be able to run a child psychiatry without access to their caretakers, there wouldn't be any way because the kids are just not capable in most instances in giving you a really representative view of what's going on or what's going wrong.
> *Psychiatrist, clinic B*

This informant's response characterizes the child patient in terms of unrealized potential. The child's capacities are measured against those of an adult: "mentalization," "narrative," and "looking at myself perspective" are features generally ascribed to persons considered to be autonomous agents. Likewise, the capacities in question exemplify the association between inner experience and rational agency. A distinction between child and adult patients, then, would presumably rely on developmental benchmarks that aid in externalizing the patient's inner "world." The problem with this objection is that it presumes that the nature of selfhood is overwhelmingly characterized by internal life. It likewise presumes that adult caregivers – as fully realized rational adults – are able to provide a transparent overview of the child's situation, which unfortunately takes for granted that they themselves are constitutive features of the situation in question. The main distinction, then, between child and adult psychiatry is predicated on the assumption that the constellation model is necessary for child psychiatry on the basis that we cannot fully grasp the world of the child without outside observers. The implicit problem is that the child-self is *under*developed, and in turn presupposes a notion of self that couches selfhood in a matrix that emphasizes cognition, rationality, physiology, as well as experience. What does this mean for our investigation? In the forthcoming chapters, we need to further investigate the phenomenon of self in order to understand some of the inherent philosophical problems that accompany the view that self is derived from physiological and cognitive processes. For the moment, we must set this objection aside until the next chapter, where I shall assess conceptual issues related to selfhood in considerable detail, and will argue that phenomenology is well suited to redress the conceptual problems that confront any tenable account of selfhood. For the moment, however, I want to now return to the interview material for a final time to argue that clinical *praxis* is impinged upon by a dearth of phenomenological vocabulary that would permit clinicians an alternative way of *doing* depression.

2.5 Interpreting diagnosis as event: Doing depression

Why adopt a phenomenological and hermeneutic perspective to interpret the qualitative material? Patients are invariably caught up in the "world" of clinical psychiatry, meaning that experiences of depression are structured – directly or indirectly – by clinical assumptions *about* such experiences. Based on the assumption that subjectivity is modified in experiences of depression (Svenaeus 2014, Aho 2013, Fuchs 2005, Ratcliffe 2015), we have good reason to believe that the way clinicians understand their patients is equally salient when investigating the phenomenon of depression.

It may be helpful here to remind the reader that interviewed clinicians overwhelmingly reported ambivalent attitudes concerning the intersection of psychiatric epistemology and practice. Most respondents describe an unease associated with the institutional imperative to abide by those psychiatric strictures imparted by the DSM. Informants repeatedly expressed dissatisfaction with the operationalized diagnostic model, and though it does indeed offer a very generalized representation of a patient, strict adherence to DSM precepts too often effaces the complexity or totality of the person *qua* patient. Clinicians are consequently uneasy about how diagnosis affects the way patients understand themselves. Informants also described the disparity between the way in which the clinical encounter is structured in child psychiatry and adult psychiatry. We now need to consider the informants responses with a critical eye to justify why we believe clinical *praxis* discloses operative notions of the self. Using hermeneutics and phenomenology, we can reconsider how the diagnostic encounter is existentially significant with particular focus on the self.

I want to offer a simple example of why selfhood is a particularly important issue for psychiatry. For a patient who has fractured her leg, clearly *something* is wrong; by contrast, for the depressed patient, not only is something wrong, whatever that *something* is must ultimately be expressed through *me*. The manner in which a patient interprets her illness is not limited to subjective experience. Because the clinical encounter is an event predicated on dialogue, the clinician's conceptions of depression and self are not affectively neutral. As Svenaeus compelling argues, "medicine is an interpretive meeting, which takes place between two persons (the doctor or some other clinical professional and the patient) with the aim of understanding and healing the one who is ill and seeks help" (Svenaeus 2001, 39). Svenaeus also notes that research regarding the clinical encounter "has not focused on the meeting itself, but rather upon the effect that the meeting might have on outcomes such as health, compliance, patient satisfaction and patient autonomy" (ibid., 39). The claim, as I understand it, is that interest in the clinical perspective has focused largely on the way clinicians influence service user satisfaction as opposed to the way clinicians interpret or conceptualize the nature of the illness itself. The orthopaedic surgeon's conceptualization of a fractured tibia is independent of who the patient is, save for his or her recovery goals. The fractured tibia itself is not injurious to the self in quite the same as the experience of depression. Operative (pre-reflective) conceptualizations of depression are highly relevant features of the clinician's situation, particularly since an encounter with a depressed patient is not an encounter with depression itself; it is an encounter with a self through whom depression is expressed. The conduit for depression is the self. The problem cannot be located independent of the expressive behavior that define who we are.

Sense or meaning is essential to our study of depression, particularly as we delve further into the phenomenological analyses of depression and selfhood in subsequent chapters. Likewise, meaning and understanding are the hallmarks of hermeneutical investigations. Recall how the informants characterized the diagnostic encounter: 1) describe the patient's state by means of a diagnosis; 2) apply the official diagnosis (e.g. medical charts, etc.), and 3) recognize that something has happened with the diagnosis. With this in mind, we can interpret the diagnostic meeting using Ricoeur's hermeneutics of discourse. One qualification is that Ricoeur considers discourse in the context of written texts. However, we can put textuality aside and still maintain fidelity to his logic of discourse by exploiting the significance of orality and language, which according to Ricoeur, are expressed *via* speech acts as a discourse event. And as we will see, clinicians appear to be attuned to the way in which the patients restructure existential signification through the diagnostic encounter.

Discourse, according to Ricoeur, is nested within several levels. The basic structure of discourse is characterized by two aspects: the dialectic of the event, and meaning (1981, 133). In so far as discourse is an event, we mean that "something happens when someone speaks" (ibid., 133). Hence, an event *is* by virtue of a) temporality, b) the person who speaks, and c) intentionality (it is about something). With respect to intentionality, the "aboutness" character is mediated by language, a world in language. Crucially, however, Ricoeur notes that

> while language is only a prior condition of communication for which it provides the codes, it is in discourse that all messages are exchanged. So discourse not only has a world, but it has an other, another person, an interlocutor to whom it is addressed (1981, 133).

Language is the system or abstract framework that is *used*. Language itself is a-temporal, whereas dialogue and exchange endure, cease, or become interrupted. Taken together, the event character of discourse is marked by time, self, and world.

The second aspect constituting discourse is meaning. Meaning is complicit in discourse on the basis that meaning surpasses the event character of discourse. "If all discourse," says Ricoeur, "is realised as an event, all discourse is understanding. What we wish to understand is not the fleeting event, but rather the meaning which endures" (ibid., 134). Again, this formulation is justified by the function of intentionality, namely that language is meaningful insofar as we take it up in order to express something about the world. For this reason, meaning surpasses the event, not by virtue of saying, but rather *vis-à-vis* what is said.

2.5.1 Doing depression with words

We are now in a position to describe the most salient component of discourse that applies to the psychiatric encounter, specifically how meaning is related to speech acts. Relying on the work of Austin and Searle, Ricoeur exploits the affective nature of speech. More specifically, through speech, meaning surpasses the event of discourse as intentional exteriorization. Speech acts are *one* act comprised of three aspects: the locutionary, illocutionary, and perlocutionary. Locutionary acts signify the act of saying in the form of a proposition (e.g. when giving a diagnosis, clinicians tell the patient you have depression). Illocutionary acts do something with what is said (e.g. I diagnose you, I pronounce you, I hereby confer, etc.). The illocution is an officiation or authoritative declaration. The perlocutionary act is signified by what is said, "a sort of stimulus which produces certain results" (Ricoeur 1981, 135). The latter presents us with the most relevant aspect of the clinical encounter, particularly with respect to meaning and patient self-understanding:

> The perlocutionary act, being primarily a characteristic of oral discourse [...] is the least discursive aspect of discourse: it is discourse *qua* stimulus. Here discourse operates, not through the recognition of my intention by the interlocutor, but in an energetic mode, as it were, by direct influence upon the emotions and affective attitudes of the interlocutor (ibid.).

Perlocutionary acts are not necessarily empirically obvious. The act is affective if it is characterized as having a capacity to "move" or be "moved" by something. The affective nature of the perlocutionary act is an essential component in structuring meaning or sense. In other words, the force of what is said to a patient (illocutionary) is underscored by intentionality, such that the communication between clinician and patient is necessarily meaningful. Moreover, the stimulus of what is said is imbued with the capacity to reorganize both one's sense of the world or one's world orientation. For example, to be informed that a loved one is dead will (under most circumstances) affect me in such a way that the meaningful organization of the world is ruptured; the horizon of meaning becomes indelibly reconfigured.

I want to proceed by considering the diagnostic meeting in adult practice as the unfolding of an *event as discourse*. To be situated in the clinical encounter, which is more broadly an event, obscures the hermeneutic nature of the event. In other words, the relation between (psychiatric) epistemology and ontology (pre-understanding of depression) is not thematized but remains operative

> the properly *epistemological* concerns of hermeneutics – its efforts to achieve a scientific status – are subordinated to *ontological* preoccupations, whereby *understanding* ceases to appear as a simple *mode of knowing* in order to become a *way of being* and a way of relating to beings and to being (Ricoeur 1981, 44, emphasis original).

Put another way, while knowledge is reflected in action, the action is subsumed by the event. If the event is characterized, in part, by a communicative coming together of clinician and patient, then the event emerges through language. In what way is the event character of the diagnostic meeting realized in discourse? "If all discourse," as Ricoeur says, "is realised as an event [then] all discourse is understood as meaning. What we wish to understand is not the fleeting event, but rather the meaning which endures" (ibid.). Temporality limits the event; it is fleeting, and is fixed to one point. Meaning, on the other hand, transcends the event and sustains itself. We find a similar sentiment in *Truth and Method* when Gadamer says:

> Every finite present has its limitations. We define the concept of "situation" by saying that it represents a standpoint that limits the possibility of vision. Hence essential to the concept of situation is *horizon*. The horizon is the range of vision that includes everything that can be seen from a particular vantage point (1994, 302).

The ephemeral event is subtended by horizons of meaning. To be situated is to have certain concerns or lines of force that are not fixed to the temporal event. For example, a diagnosis of depression transcends the clinical meeting in numerous ways. The diagnosis in turn re-orients the patient's horizon: What does it mean to be depressed? How will this affect my life, my job, my relationships, my need for certain medications, and so on and so forth. As Gadamer puts it: "'to have a horizon' means not being limited to what is nearby but being able to see beyond it" (1994, 302). In psychiatry, "regained health may require a new self-understanding," whereas in biomedicine, at stake is "not the patient's self-understanding, but his regained health" (Svenaeus 2001, 145). Why is the nature of the psychiatric meeting discontinuous with what occurs in biomedicine? Let us consider this question according to the logic of discourse as event.

A diagnosis as speech act can be presented as follows: the locutionary act as fact, "you have depression," the declarative force of the illocutionary act,

"I hereby diagnose you," "I declare you," and so on."[27] It is important to note that the illocution or declaration must be tied to a context, which provides sense to the declaration and elicits affective force. For example, let us imagine a scenario where I meet a psychiatrist at a dinner party. After having engaged in conversation he or she tells me that I am depressed. Here, the declaration would lack the force it otherwise has in the clinical situation. For, it is in the context of the clinic that the speech act of a depression diagnosis generates its significance. This is especially true since depression diagnoses must always be properly coded (ICD or DSM) in the patient's file. In this way, psychiatric practice is preserved through the concrete context in which psychiatry takes place, that is, the literal psychiatric institution.

Clinical practice cannot be reduced to individual acts or actions that constitute the whole. Practices stand in relation to meaning and interaction. The former, according to Ricoeur, "testifies to the fact that the unit of configuration constitutive of a practice is based upon a particular relation of meaning, that is expressed by the notion of constitutive rule" (1992, 154), which functions to "rule over the meaning of particular gestures and [...] make a particular hand gesture 'count as' waving hello, voting, hailing a taxi, and so on" (ibid, 155, emphasis original). Borrowing from another of Ricoeur's examples, moving a chess piece is itself an act or a gesture, which only takes on the meaning in the practice of a chess game. With respect to the interactive nature of practices, which are more than just rules, they "are based on actions in which an agent takes into account, as a matter of principle, the actions of others" (ibid.). This leads to the claim that, "to refer to, to take account of, the conduct of other agents is the most general and most neutral expression that can cover the multitude of interactions encountered on the level of this unit of action, known as practices" (ibid.). The interpretive nature of the diagnostic situation, as we have suggested, is far from neutral. Psychiatric epistemology is hardly a domain constituted from the descriptive facts of the textbook. Clinicians inherit and preserve the history of psychiatry both through acquired knowledge and the development of *praxis*. In the last chapter, we repeatedly emphasized that depression may be historically understood by a tension between paradigms of

---

[27] The claim is not that clinicians use this phrasing. What the illocutionary acts are intended to represent is that there is a contextual requirement for the diagnosis. For example, I cannot pronounce my friend and partner to be married. It is meaningless without the force assigned to someone who has the power to confer a legal or religious union of marriage.

causation. In contemporary practice, interpretation remains enmeshed within this tension. The DSM specifies that clinicians should take account of extenuating life circumstances that might otherwise explain the patient's symptoms. Clinicians who conceive depression to be tightly connected to a biological dysfunction (c.f. Horwitz and Wakefield) follow the tradition in which external factors (e.g. relationships, work, emotions) do not hold explanatory force with respect to depression. Clinicians steeped in a psycho-dynamic tradition (including education), on the contrary, are more likely to consider exogenous circumstances as essential characteristics of a depressive disorder.

This notion of practice links up with the idea of speech acts that I have outlined above. In particular, the constitutive rule functions to ascribe meaning to the clinical encounter in its totality, meaning that it transcends the boundaries of the physical setting such that meanings continue to be affective beyond a particular clinical encounter. It is only in the context of the situation as a whole, that is, a whole predicated by pre-understanding of precisely what actions *count* in the encounter between patient and clinician. What interests us the most here is the meaning or sense that is engendered (or re-made) through the act of perlocution. Which is to say, by diagnosing the patient, his or her self-understanding is changed. The perlocutionary act may elicit a positive sense, "I feel relieved now that I know what's wrong," or conversely, a negative sense, "I feel ashamed of myself," but it is clear that patients will not remain absolutely unaffected. Diagnosis is a response to the question motivating a patient to seek help: What is wrong with me?

So, although illocutionary acts are declarations made by an individual, they are simultaneously declarations that bear the weight of the psychiatric tradition, of psychiatric practice. To investigate the force of perlocutionary acts, the intuitive approach would be to explore patient experience in the clinical encounter, given that the clinician's diagnostic declaration intends toward the patient. Of course, this perspective is essential for a phenomenology of depression, and we will address patient self-understanding in the final section of this chapter. For the moment, our interest remains with the event character of the psychiatric diagnosis. Turning our attention to the interview material, it will become evident that there exists a tight connection between acts of perlocution and problems of explanation.

Recall how the informants described the tension between diagnostic imperatives and clinical reality. Overall dissatisfaction with DSM diagnostic categories subsequently engendered a strategy that clinicians apply to minimize patients from over-identifying with their diagnoses. This coping strategy raises two further points. First, as the responses illustrate, the informants characterize the DSM using terms such as "construct," "temporary," and "unstable." In doing so, the clinicians attempt to bracket the historical tradition to which they belong. But nevertheless, the tradition remains preserved, not only by means of diagnosis, but also in the way depression etiology is conceptualized. Let us highlight some salient examples found in the responses cited above:

> "maybe the causes of the troubles are very much the same, 100 years ago from today."
>
> "the problems, that's a real condition, that's true; whether you call it something or not."
>
> "*They are the people they are*, regardless of diagnosis."
>
> "this is something to describe the state you're in right now *but it doesn't relate to who you are as a person.*"
>
> "it's really helpful for a patient to know "this is not really me," "I'm having a sort of disturbance, that I can adjust and will go back to my normal state." It's good for them sometimes to know that, that it is a sickness or that [it's something] people can get."

To supplement the above examples, let us introduce several responses that we have yet to consider:

> [Someone] says 'I have anxiety', they are often diagnosed with anxiety. And that of course is not correct, it's just a copy-paste of the word they used, and that, I think too – I don't know if it's really, but maybe in some sense – connected to this lesser stigma in society. Anyway, it's a problem and it's making the diagnosis of these psychiatric disorders harder. And in those cases, I think psychiatry has very little role in helping people suffering; our treatments don't work, medicines don't work, psychotherapy maybe not –if it works, it's overkill; what works is find another job, quit alcohol, work on your relationship...
> *Psychiatrist, Karlstad*
>
> Absolutely, we know that the mind, from meditation and exercise, can really alter the way you experience pain; it can make you calmer, lower your blood pressure and pulse, and that is only your mind doing that. There's some help from breathing and things…
> *Director, clinic B*
>
> You can work with thoughts, emotions, physical responses, sensitivity to your body and all that, and to me it's like body and mind, body and soul,

> they express each other, it also affects each other. And it's all at the same time; it's a unit and two separate things. For me it's not a big deal. I think it's very natural that because we have a mind, and we can plan things, we can see how things might go tomorrow, but at the same time we can use our mind to worry a lot, to see catastrophes, to the worst possible scenarios, and the mind – the brain – can't tell the difference from what is actually a threat here in the room or what is just a fantasised threat [...] So the brain responds to your thoughts, especially if you are worried and then you start to catastrophize, then the brain registers that.
> *Psychologist, clinic B*

> So, then you have to kind make them [the patient] be more detached ... anyway, speak more detached from it.
> *Therapist, clinic A*

> I would say the internal factors are different, more than the external. Because I think the external factors can be the same for two patients, but one you see is depressed and the other one is just sad, maybe. And that's also what it goes back to if we talk about biologically, chemically, some people are more prone to depression.
> *General physician, clinic A*

These responses reflect how the historical tensions concerning depression etiology remain present in contemporary practice. The technique of distancing patients from the diagnosis is intended to protect, or even empower patients with a renewed sense of agency. But even so, the desired intention does not always elicit the desired effect:

> We can say that the diagnostic language in some cases will position the person as patient, literally as a passive site for psychiatric dysfunctions (possibly rooted in the brain) that happen to affect the person in a detrimental way. Given this perspective, one is not an agent as such, but a location in a chain of causal processes. However, in other cases, the diagnostic language may also lead to the externalizations of the person's problems in a way that actually does position the person as agent, i.e., as active in relation to coping with one's problems (Brinkmann 2014, 644).

It cannot be discerned in any obvious way whether the clinicians intentionally adopt one position or other. The majority of responses we examined above suggest that clinicians – in various ways – characterize depression as something tangible, as an entity. This position was not unanimous among all informants; however, even those characterizing depression as exogenous draw links to the brain or describe it as a disease. This is perhaps unsurprising since the biopsychosocial model of medicine has increasingly attracted attention over the last half-century. The relationship between biology and psychology on this model are not viewed as two separate dimensions, but are instead taken to be recursive and mutually dependant domains that underpin conscious life.[28] However, this relationship raises several philosophical issues that have long been debated, including the nature of identity, selfhood, and the metaphysical status of mental content.

The impetus to distance patients from their depression diagnosis evinces two general outcomes. First, if the patient is held to be separate from his or her depression, it is all too easy to slide back into the biomedical model of disease: the *patient* is not the *problem*, depression is the problem. In somatic medicine, by contrast, a fractured bone is the problem; the problem is not the patient. Now, if the patient-centered or holistic approach to psychiatry is motivated by the overly generalized imperative to understand patients "as a whole," and if being a self is a complex of experiences, cognitions, and affects, is it thus desirable – or even possible – to distinguish between depressed *experience* and the person that constitutes this "whole"?

For the moment, we must unfortunately leave this question aside until the next chapter, however, one of the distinctive diagnostic differences between psychiatry and somatic diagnosis is the relative significance of explanation. As we have seen, clinicians often struggle to reconcile the DSM's categorial abstractions with the clinical realities of depression. Unlike their peers in somatic medicine, where explanations potentially provide patients with insight or understanding about their condition, psychiatric clinicians have no recourse to causally explain depression in the diagnostic situation. As some informants noted, a diagnosis gives a name to a patient's distress. Separating patients from the depression diagnosis represents a form of understanding, insofar as clinicians do not want patients to conflate diagnosis with explanation. Understanding, then, is prompted by the affective force of the diagnosis and thereby motivates clinicians to separate patients from the diagnosis. Subsequently, to avoid reducing patients to their problem (depression), clinicians convey the need to approach patients as a "whole." This diagnostic situation proves contradictory. In the unfolding of the diagnostic situation, the movement toward understanding by means of separating the patient from the diagnosis can inadvertently

—

[28] In the biological context, Damasio (2010) argues that selfhood arises out of neurological processes, namely via affective states, which leads to the conclusion that neurobiology is necessary and sufficient for the experience of selfhood.

look like an explanation. To understand the patient as a whole, the *is-ness* of depression is detached from the patient. Communicating to patients that the "problem is the problem" – thus separating the patient from the diagnosis – takes the form of a causal explanation.

By contrast, the task of the clinician in child psychiatry is to remove distance between the patient, diagnosis, and his or her constellation. What makes the constellation a central concern for psychiatry is that, as Merleau-Ponty notes, "parents are the pivots, the cardinal points of child life [...] The relations with parents are more than relationships with two people: *they are relations with the world.* The parents are the *mediators* of connections with the world" (2010a, 300, emphasis original). A diagnosis itself does not necessarily eschew the effects of a child's constellation to reveal the "true" (biological) cause of the problem. Still, a diagnostic label in child practice is significant or meaningful for the child's parents rather than the child. Whether a child is distanced from her diagnosis will depend upon the extent to which caregivers ascribe meaningfulness to the diagnosis, examples of which may be: 'this behavior is not my child's, it is the autism,' or 'my child's behavior is not due to a diagnosis, he or she simply experiences the world differently.'

Irrespective of the way in which diagnosis is signified, in child psychiatry – unlike adult psychiatry – diagnosis is expressed through the entire constellation rather than an individual. It is unnecessary to digress into theories of child development to posit – like Merleau-Ponty above – that there exists a tight connection between the sense of self and the interpersonal life constituted by caregiver and child.[29] Because a diagnosis, at least initially, is most affectively significant for the caregivers, the child will make diagnostic sense of who he or she is *via* the significance caregivers attribute to the diagnostic label. In other words, it circuits the constellational relations in lived experience. As we have seen, the coping strategy employed by clinicians in adult practice is motivated by an assumption that diagnosis interacts with patient self-interpretation. That is, clinicians tacitly recognize that the diagnosis *does* something to *who I am*. Child practice, which likewise recognizes a relation between diagnosis and self-interpretation, im-

[29] To be clear, it would be imprudent to argue that this view is held universally. In simplified terms, this is otherwise known as the nature-nurture debate, a topic that has always drawn interest from both human and natural sciences. A popularized example that runs counter to the parental influence on self and personality is the enduring work of Briggs-Meyers (1962) which developed a matrix of fixed personality types inspired by Jung's theory of archetypes.

plicitly employs a conception of self that is tightly linked to his or her situation. The distinction, then, is one of location: the adult self is inside, something one has; the child self is spread across her situation, something one is.

A plausible objection to the coping strategy described above is that, though it is practically important, the strategy is simply a strategy; it makes no conceptual claims on or about the nature of depression itself. This line of thought would further add that in the context of clinical practice, the aim is to reduce suffering and help patients cope with depression, and clinicians must accordingly adopt strategies that will facilitate patient well-being. The problem with this view is that it requires clinicians to adopt a notion of depression that may very well be at odds with how they conceptualized the "true" nature of depression. For instance, in opposition to biologically oriented psychiatrists, a clinician may eschew the brain-based or disease model of depression, while nevertheless encouraging patients to view their depression as a biological dysfunction, as opposed to a moral failing.

With this in mind, it is worth re-capitulating that when we characterize the psychiatric meeting as a discourse event, the diagnostic meaning surpasses or outlives the diagnostic event. I likewise said that the clinician's recognition of the affective force that is bestowed by the illocution and perlocution dynamic motivates their attempt to distance the patient from the diagnosis. Recall Brinkmann's contention that this intervention may follow one of two directions, namely that either patients regain a sense of agency, a sense of control over their situation, or conversely patients identify or indulge the passive sick role. The outcome cannot be predicted in advance, which means that the clinician's intention may or may not achieve the desired effect. Ultimately, at the core of this dynamic is patient self-understanding. Regardless of the strategy employed by the clinician, the entire context of meeting, diagnosing, and dialogue is integral to self-understanding, meaning that we should not take for granted that clinical attitudes concerning depression affect self-understanding.

For instance, when the interviewees characterized the relation between patient and depression diagnosis, many emphasized the following ideas: "detachment," that mind and body are "two different things," "the brain responds to our thoughts," "it is a sickness or that [it's something] people can get," and so on. If the core of the clinical encounter is predicated on meeting the patient "holistically," this imperative to see a person "as a whole" is contravened by the language of a dualist ontology, as illustrated in the examples above.[30] But if depression is ultimately characterized as a nebulous imbalance of chemicals in the brain, a person's experience of changed significance or meaning within the life-world is attributable to modifications of the brain rather than a modification of subjective experience. Yet even if the brain is a necessary condition for experience, it is an insufficient condition for experiencing something as significant. Hence, if depression is fundamentally a bio-physiological dysfunction or a serotonergic imbalance, one conclusion to be drawn is that the source of altered experience in depression arises, not through the self (as the source of all significant experience), but rather as a pathological process that is independent of who I am.

2.5.2 The tacit clinical view of selfhood

Up to this point, I have said relatively little about clinical conceptions of selfhood. One reason is simply that during the interviews, clinicians rarely, if at all, expressly referred to selfhood. This is not surprising, for although use of the term self is common in colloquial language, the ontological status of selfhood is largely an idiosyncratic topic of interest to philosophers. Still, since selfhood is a commonplace concept in Western culture, the clinicians in question undoubtedly possess some sense of what it means to be a self, even if that conception is possessed tacitly. As a consequence, we need to look beyond what the clinicians explicitly conveyed in their responses if we are to understand the extent to which selfhood influences psychiatric encounters.

Even if it is a useful strategy to detach or distance patients from depression itself, such a strategy is, in the end, artificial. Why? In anticipation of our discussion of phenomenology in Chapter 4, how should we understand the experience of depression? Is it something separate from me? Do I only think I feel depressed? These questions are overly simplistic, yet they do capture basic problems about self-experience in depression and are fundamentally connected with the experiential structures of consciousness itself.

Clinicians actively and passively participate in, and preserve, the historical institution of psychiatry. The historical vicissitudes of depression,

—

[30] Dualist ontology, put very simply, is derived from Descartes' dictum that matter and spirit, or body and mind, are distinct substances. Matter (physical world) is defined by extension in space (and consequently, in time), while mind (or spirit) is not extended in space or time. The significance of Descartes' ontology is that our experience of the world is always reduced to our thoughts about the world, which is to say: all sensuous experience is thought; to perceive is to think a perception; our body is bound to the extended world, the material world, and consequently bound by the natural laws of the material world.

which we familiarized ourselves with in Chapter 1, reflect one way that psychiatric theory permeates practice. In particular, since psychiatry became a specialized branch of medicine by adopting the medical model to disease, just as depression became a specific object of enquiry, the subjective (or lay) language patients used to report depressed experience had to be translated into the language of science. Although psychiatry has rapidly developed relative to somatic medicine, so too has the nature of its object. And while psychiatry is a profession that is explicitly concerned with the *psyche*, or better, the *self*, what is remarkable about the development of psychiatric practice is the commitment to expunge theoretical and philosophical language from its scientific foundation.

The concept of self has far less practical significance in psychiatry than concepts such as "disorder" or "anxiety." The overall claim in this investigation is that self is the phenomenal ground that makes psychiatry possible.[31] The German psychiatrist Erwin Straus recognized the centrality of subjectivity (or self-experience) in psychiatry. A contemporary of Husserl and Heidegger, Straus' work was seminal for applying phenomenology to psychology, and his legacy will be explored further in Chapter 4. For the moment, however, I simply want to highlight that, even as a physician in the 1930s, Straus was already adamant that self and world cannot be separated. This warrants an long comment from Straus in which he adamantly contends that psychiatry has strayed from its *raison d'être*:

> Since psychiatry is neither confined to the treatment of diseases of one organ nor restricted to one therapeutic technique, one may try to determine its peculiar character *not by an attempt to establish boundaries* but rather by the reverse, by *recognizing the open horizon of its thematic field*. While the activities of the physician are directed generally to a [human] as a living creature, to the organism and its function, the psychiatrist is concerned with [the human] as a citizen of the historical and social world or worlds […] The object of psychiatric action is not primarily the brain, the body, or the organism; it should be integral man in the uniqueness of his individual existence as this discloses itself – independently of the distinction between healthy and sick – in existential communication (1969, 2, emphasis added).

—

[31] In the *General Psychopathology*, Jaspers (1963) says that no concept bears more meanings or multiple applications than personality or character, and reflects a similar attitude regarding the centrality of selfhood in psychiatry. However, character and personality are not interchangeable with self.

Here, Straus contends that, while psychiatry is predicated on the standards of scientific medicine, the goal of psychiatry is not commensurate with scientific medicine. Psychiatric boundaries are not given *a priori*, but instead – if there are boundaries at all – are erected with reference to the breadth of expressive human behavior that gives rise to selfhood. The material we have explored illustrates that the clinicians have not "forgotten" the purpose of psychiatry. The clinicians' responses demonstrate fidelity to Straus' vision of psychiatry. The problem is that clinicians are constrained by psychiatric language, as well as the concepts that are established and preserved by instituting practices. As a profession dedicated to ameliorating patient suffering, there exists both a philosophical and phenomenological lacuna that inhibits the interpretive dynamic that unfolds in psychiatric *praxis*. Without phenomenological considerations, and for that matter, philosophy in general, experiences of depression as it is lived remain underappreciated.[32] Likewise, if psychiatry is in the business of treating the "troubled soul," it must jettison the Cartesian-inspired sense of a soul hidden away deep inside the patient. On the contrary, in Chapter 4 I contend that the so-called soul is anything but hidden; it is readily perceptible to clinicians through our embodied actions and intentions, expressed through the way in which we comport ourselves toward the world. For, depression is not in my brain, mind, or body: it is me. Depression is not merely in me, it is instead expressed *through* me, and thus mediated by my contact with the world.

2.6 Depression beyond internal and external causation

The way in which depression interferes with everyday life is considerably different than that of a bone fracture, gout, or infection. Depression is affectively inchoate, and all the more beguiling when we recognize that the appearance of the sufferer misleadingly suggests that the distress is qualitatively different from physical pain. What makes suffering in depression so profound is that it cannot be evaded. Few, if any, aspects of one's life remain untouched. Something is not wrong with this or that: *it is me.* Even if we could understand depression by breaking it down into smaller units of sense, whether such units are physiological or psychological patterns, such an understanding cannot ultimately make sense of depressed experience. To draw an analogy, imagine that it has become possible to identify the

—

[32] I am not claiming that clinicians are unconcerned with patient experience. What I am arguing is that "lived-experience" of depression entails more than the subjective reporting of symptoms.

physiological substrate that explains why I fear dogs. Even when equipped with this concrete explanation, it cannot explain why I fear dogs rather than cats. Likewise, I may have good reason to fear dogs, but having such a reason does not necessitate that I should in actuality be afraid of dogs. With respect to depression, causes or reasons cannot disclose meaningfulness that makes depression possible. To use another illustration, the death of an aunt, with whom I was not close, may not affect me in a significant way since she was not significant in the context of my life. Conversely, the passing of a colleague who has exerted significant influence on my work may turn out to be a source of profound grief. Even when we have good reason to do X or feel Y, without existential signification that makes something count in my life, a reason will remain empty.

When good intentioned clinicians attempt to mitigate the affective force of a depression diagnosis by distinguishing between the patient and disorder, the patient is presented with an explanation: the problem is depression, the problem is not you. In one sense, the latter is accurate insofar as the patient is not blameworthy for his or her suffering. Subsequently, however, the implication is that depression is distinct from my self-experience. Depressed experience is not really *me*; it is as if a parasite has invaded me as host. To depict depression as a "disease" process independent of the sufferer may understandably provide him or her with a sense of comfort. This has been a typical way of reducing stigma, which has long been associated with mental illness. The attempt to reduce stigma and blameworthiness are laudable aspects of practice, and indeed we see some clinicians incorporate this into their clinical repertoire, despite the fact that this characterization of depression is potentially misleading.

But what if depression is the result of neither choice nor mere biology? What if it emerges from neither outside nor from inside? In anticipation of our detailed discussion of selfhood in the next chapter, I want to suggest that common-sense views of self tend to be characterized in three vague ways: it is inside me, it is outside me, or it is a mixture of both. In the first instance, I am (broadly speaking) a rational agent in full control of my actions and behaviors within my environment, or I am at least capable of interrogating my reasons or ways of acting; in the second instance, I am carried along by my biological body whose inner states affect and determine my behaviors in the world; or last, I am an admixture of bio-psychosocial forces that converge and constrain my choices and actions in the world. A consequence of this simplistic matrix is that both selfhood and depression are conceptualized in unambiguous terms.

A phenomenological concern with the privileged epistemic status that is accorded to scientific or objective thought in modern life is that tolerance for phenomenal ambiguity is low. When we attempt to circumscribe phenomena like depression and selfhood objectively, we presuppose that phenomena are determinate. As a result, selfhood and depression are – in principle – reifiable entities, the existence of which – also in principle – may be well delineated independent of other phenomena. As a result, conceptions of self and depression are rendered simplifications of what are otherwise complex phenomena. For this reason, by applying an inside outside dichotomy to depression and selfhood, it is easily taken for granted that there is a third way to make sense of these phenomena.

Moving forward with this investigation, my contention is that, from a phenomenological perspective, depression and self are neither *in* nor *out*. In fact, I will argue that they do not have location in the geometrical sense. We need to adopt an alternative way of seeing the world, one that recognizes depression and self as "located" in the way one stands in relation to the world. And by studying this relation it will become clear that selfhood and depression are expressive behaviors that manifest the depth of our existence in lived-space.

2.7 Conclusion

The qualitative investigation we have considered in this chapter was motivated by a basic question: if depression is a disorder of the self, does it matter how psychiatric professionals understand the self? Conceptualizations of the self pervade everyday life and daily discourse so profusely that we often assume it is something with which we are well acquainted. What makes mental disorders such as depression philosophically illuminating is that they often disclose something intimate about selfhood that is otherwise taken for granted. As a cultural practice, psychiatry meets with service users whose very existence has become vulnerable. We acknowledge that the ethical psychiatric imperative, just as in any medical practice, is to reduce suffering and enhance well-being. Psychiatry is a caring profession, but it is also a profession that employs theoretical and scientific attitudes, which influence and affect those who seek care.

By asking informants about depression and their relevant psychiatric practices, the aim was not merely to elicit propositional attitudes or definitive statements regarding the concept of self. Instead, the intention was to carve out a potential point of entry that would allow us to make sense of the operative (or unreflective) way the self is conceptualised in psychiatric practice. The most salient discovery was that the psychiatric clinical encounter is permeated by ambivalent attitudes regarding clinical diagnostics. Clinicians expressed a tension at the core of their practice, a dissonance between psychiatric theory and practice. Out of this tension I identified some practical coping strategies that clinicians deploy as means to assuage ambivalence concerning the practice of diagnosis. These strategies were interpreted using Ricoeur's conception of discourse as event. We concluded that, despite practical efforts to overcome perceived problems in diagnosis, clinicians struggle to elude the residue of psychiatry's conceptual history. Consequently, clinicians are rather bound to the language of dualist ontology that subsequently permeates conceptualizations of selfhood.

The second central point of our discussion in this chapter considered the affinity between *praxis* in child psychiatry and phenomenological philosophy. The clinical encounter in child psychiatry, we noted, is markedly different from the meeting structure in adult psychiatry. Subsequently, we maintained that these respective practices draw on divergent pre-understandings of selfhood. To reiterate, the one-to-one psychiatric meetings in adult practice elicit a proclivity for demarcating the self according to inward-outward distinctions. Conversely, the meeting in child psychiatry reflects a view of the self that is distributed horizontally, or spread out among a child's constellation. As a springboard for our forthcoming philosophical analyses, our considerations concerning clinical practice provide us with a variety of points for in-depth discussion. The orientation for the remainder of our investigation may be illustrated with the help of Straus: "The separation from without refers to my world, it does not separate *the* world from *the* self, nor things from things, nor space from space" (1963, 245). Moving forward, we are working toward our goal of phenomenologically analyzing the way selfhood is implicated in depression. However, a satisfactory analysis will require that we appreciate the multifaceted notion of selfhood in a comprehensive way. With chapters one and two, the foundation for the forthcoming theoretical chapters has been established. Now that we have a historical perspective on depression, along with insights from clinical practice, we move to Chapter 3 where we will assess contemporary theories of self and the extent to which these theories are felicitous for psychiatric practice.

CHAPTER 3

Seeking the self in psychiatry: Contemporary accounts of selfhood

3. Introduction

The historical and clinical perspectives presented thus far have prepared the way for philosophical and conceptual questions concerning the nature of self and depression. The purpose of Chapter 3 is to make sense of the multifarious notion of selfhood and to contextualize its relevance – if any – for psychiatric practice. In the last chapter we concluded that, even if clinicians do not explicitly adhere to a notion of self in clinical practice, they nevertheless comport themselves according to unreflective attitudes or conceptions regarding selfhood and depression. The subsequent question is whether or not we are able to properly make sense of depression if we fail to understand the self? The central thesis of this investigation is that the best way to answer this question is by submitting depression to a phenomenological examination. However, prior to any phenomenological analysis of depression (Chapter 5), it is incumbent upon us to first familiarize ourselves with some of the divergent philosophical treatments of selfhood, as well as the way in which they are pertinent to psychiatry. The reader will find that my study of selfhood is unapologetically philosophical in nature, and non-philosophers will immediately find that the philosophical analysis in this chapter is theoretically denser than those in the preceding chapters.

Selfhood can prove to be an unruly concept since it is both culturally pervasive and semantically ambiguous. Moreover, the contemporary notion of selfhood with which we are most familiar today is the progeny of much earlier philosophical, religious, and psychological iterations (e.g. soul, psyche, ego, spirit, and so on). Justice cannot be done to the expansive idea of selfhood in a single chapter if we acknowledge that "it is an exaggeration to claim that the notion of 'self' is unequivocal and that there is widespread consensus about what, exactly it means to be a self […] it is a simple fact that the concept of self connotes different things in different disciplines" (Zahavi 2008, 103). Given this caveat, that we cannot fully exhaust the concept of selfhood, the first task in this chapter is to specify why selfhood has traditionally been viewed to be a problem related to enduring identity, a problem that broadly concerns the way in which self remains identical to itself despite the flux of world experience over time. To achieve this, I introduce two of the long-standing views of selfhood: the psychological self and the metaphysical (or material) self, both of which are intended to represent two historical conceptualizations of self that have exerted significant influence over the discourse of selfhood. Once we have established these two accounts, I will then introduce four contemporary accounts of the self that, each in its own way, attempt to remedy perceived shortcomings concerning of traditional approaches to selfhood: the Brain-based-self; the experiential-self; the situated-self, and the narrative-self. I will likewise consider the extent to which these categories may be relevant for psychiatric understanding of depression. Once we establish a foothold on these accounts of selfhood, I will subsequently argue that despite the relative merit of these accounts, in order to shed light on the self in depression, our subsequent task in Chapter four will be to propose a phenomenological notion of self. Even though my phenomenological account of selfhood departs considerably from the four models we will consider in this chapter, there are nevertheless aspects of these models that share features with the phenomenological self. Yet, the phenomenological characterization of selfhood is distinct from these accounts in ways that prevent us from simply assembling together these contemporary notions to create a new model. I will offer an account of selfhood that ultimately goes beyond the four models we are to consider below.

3.1 Psychiatry is the world of the self

A cogent discussion of such a broad notion such as selfhood faces several challenges. After all, "the self," writes Zaner, "lurks importantly in the background of thought about consciousness, politics, history, the body, and in the intriguing talk about the patient as a person, as an individual, as a particular human being" (1981, 111). Not only has the nature and constitution of *the self* been a ubiquitous preoccupation of philosophers across both Western and Eastern philosophical traditions, it has a privileged place in everyday language which is central to the way in which we understand (and refer to) ourselves as human beings. Accordingly, selfhood as it is conceived and experienced in everyday life is easily taken for granted, or as Heidegger claims, "that which is ontically closest and well known, is ontologically the farthest and not known at all" (2008, 69). In the same way that illness or injury draws attention to parts of our body that we otherwise ignore, selfhood likewise permeates lived-experience to the extent that it rarely features as the focal point of experience.

For this reason, psychiatry is always already intimately acquainted with selfhood without recognizing it, for it is in this domain where lived-world assumptions about the nature of selfhood are tested: "psychoses are, so to speak, basic experiments arranged by nature; the clinical wards are the natural laboratories where we begin to wonder about the structure of the *Lebenswelt* [...] We suddenly notice that we are beginners in a field where we deemed ourselves masters" (Straus 1966b, 257). In almost all cases of psychiatric or mental illness, something is wrong with *me*; I am not *myself* in a unique sense, and these differ from cases of somatic illness – though they do often overlap significantly, influenza being one such example. But for psychiatry, hallucinations, thought insertion, or psychosis, exemplify instances of self-disturbance that enable us to shift our attention away from common-sense assumptions of the self toward our pre-reflective – and tacit – understanding of selfhood as it is given in lived-experience.

3.2 Psychology and self-persistence

Before we address the way in which selfhood may be disturbed in chapters 5 and 6, we need to circumscribe precisely what is being referred to when we speak of the self. In addition to weighty questions such as *Who am I?* or *What am I?*, there are equally important issues to address: How does this thing we call the self remain identical over time? Is it possible for me to change without ceasing to be who I was ten years ago, or even yesterday?

Though theoretical questions regarding selfhood are central to this chapter, we need to bear in mind that the germ of such questions were anticipated in the argument established in Chapter 1, where I argued that the historical development of both depression and psychiatric practice is subtended by a bifurcated model of causal explanation: depression and mental disorder are the result of either psychological forces (analytic-inspired or Freudian) or a consequence of bio-physiological malfunctions (empirically-inspired or Kraepelinian). Subsequently, when we examined clinical practice in Chapter 2, it became evident that the "either/or" model of causation has implications for the way in which clinicians characterize selfhood and depression. When meeting patients diagnosed with depression, some clinicians felt their only recourse was to characterize the patient and the disorder as being mutually independent of one another. Other clinicians felt that depression was attributable to psychological or external social forces that constitute who the patient is. Hence, there exists, on the one hand, a tendency to causally ascribe depression to a bio-physiological dysfunction existing independent of the self, and, on the other hand, depression is manifested by virtue of the psychological forces constitutive of the person in question.

But the historical picture of depression alone cannot sufficiently account for the way in which selfhood is understood clinically in Chapter 2. There is a long philosophical tradition of treating selfhood "psychologically." It is largely recognized that the legacy of seventeenth-century philosopher John Locke remains influential for contemporary notions of selfhood, the most notable of which are predicated on a *psychological continuity* thesis. The essential feature of the self, according to Locke, is not substance or material, but rather the existence of enduring consciousness: "Nothing but consciousness," writes Locke, "can unite remote existences into the same person; the *identity of substance will not do it.* For whatever substance there is [...] without consciousness there is no person" (1998, 221, emphasis added). With respect to consciousness, Locke posits that selfhood is a psychological continuity that unites one's past and present: "For it is by the consciousness [self] has of its present thoughts and actions that it is *self to itself* now, and so will be the same self, as far as the same consciousness can extend to actions past or to come" (1998, ibid., 214, emphasis original). All that is encompassed in consciousness (for Locke) is arguably conceptually narrower when compared with contemporary discussions of consciousness. Minimally, Locke holds that consciousness denotes thinking beings who possess the capacity for reflection and recollection. It is not interrupted by changes in material or substance. To use Locke's own example, an amputated finger does not retain part of the self– that is, consciousness is not split into two substances. The upshot for Locke's notion of self is that, since I can connect my past experiences and behaviors with my current behaviors and choices, the continuity of consciousness in turn engenders self-agency. Who I am and what I choose to do is bound by self-responsibility; since it is I who did X last week, today I remain the same self and am thereby responsible for the ensuing consequences that arise with respect to my actions.

3.3 A Note on the metaphysics of self

Why does Locke's psychological-based notion of selfhood continue to exert influence centuries later? To be sure, there are a multiplicity of plausible factors. However, a simple reason is that, for a considerable length of time, the alternative option to the psychological continuity thesis was a stark version of *bodily* continuation over time. With respect to the latter, selfhood would not be defined by enduring thoughts, memories, or cognitive traits, but would instead necessitate that the *same* physical body persists over time. This thesis however, as Locke recognized, runs up against significant obstacles that render it a difficult position to retain. One immediate problem that Parfit has addressed more recently concerns the nature of *idem* identity. For some, *the* central feature of selfhood is that it must be attributable to an irreducible kernel, an unchanging, empirically verifiable entity. The basis of selfhood, when characterized this way, is characterized metaphysically. The motivation for a metaphysical notion of self is that it satisfies the putative demand for *idem* identity associated with the self. By positing the existence of an enduring and locatable entity it is subsequently possible to claim that the self remains the same over time.

If we draw upon modern biology, we know that the cellular life-cycle is an essential feature of human life. That cells continually die and reproduce over the span of our life means that there are few features of our biological body that remain identical from birth until death. Accordingly, bodily continuity does not meet the criterion for sameness at the level of biology. But Locke's objection to bodily continuation is not concerned with the macroscopic level. In the event of a finger amputation, Locke asks if the self is lost with the loss of the finger? Or conversely, is the self is split in two, one self that remains with the finger and one self that remains with the body? Locke's argument illustrates the potential spiral into absurdity.

Nevertheless, despite the fact that the Lockean psychological continuity thesis endures, some of its more modern iterations are psychological and metaphysical hybrids. For instance, were it possible to identify a brain mechanism or anatomical structure in the brain responsible for the phenomenon of selfhood, the latter would then be constituted as an *object* that remains identical to itself throughout time in the shape of the former.

It should be noted that metaphysical conceptions of self – as a homunculus or empirical entity – have fallen out of favour for most twentieth century theorists (Zahavi 2014). But the metaphysical self it is not altogether irrelevant with respect to contemporary brain sciences. Brain-bound models of the self could be loosely labelled neo-metaphysical since the aim of these models is to correlate *specific* brain systems (or brain states) with 'self-processes' that emerge from the phenomenal self (e.g. self-recognition, self-agency, etc.).

As it stands, Gallagher and Vogeley (2011) contend that brain-bound models of self are characterized by two overly broad approaches: (i) a unitary model that attributes self to a single region or consistent specialized brain function; (ii) a model that invokes multi-regional and diverse areas of brain activation. Thus, a wide spectrum of possible correlates is bookended by two equally unsatisfactory positions. Either the self is limited to one narrow region of brain activation or the interaction of brain regions and brain systems, which give rise to human action and the self, is so complex that it is near impossible to verify consistent activation that refers to self.

Having introduced two broad frameworks that have been used to conceptualize selfhood, we will now assess contemporary approaches to the self, many of which attempt to escape the confines of the traditional bifurcation of metaphysical and psychological conceptions of selfhood. It will become apparent that not all these approaches fully extract themselves from these traditions, nor do they all fit neatly under one category. Nonetheless, the models of self that we will be assessing are organized under categories that best reflect the most distinctive shared features.

3.4 Brain related models of self

3.4.1 The brain-based self

In an attempt to move away from the brain-bound or strict metaphysical approach to the self, a seminal model that links selfhood with the brain is proposed by Damasio. In so moving away from a strictly Brain-bound model, Damasio's approach is better described as brain-based. His model underscores the bi-directional relation between biological processes and conscious human life, both of which are subject to the surrounding environment. According to Damasio, selfhood is achieved by a mind that makes sense of the world at large with input from internal bodily feelings. These feelings function as a feedback loop by providing the mind with information regarding internal self-states. Consequently, affective or felt bodily perceptions give rise to *self-feeling*:

> Conscious minds begin when self comes to mind, when brains add a self-process to the mind mix [...] The self is built in distinct steps grounded on the *protoself*. The first step is the generation of primordial feelings, the

> elementary feelings of existence that spring forth spontaneously from the proto-self. Next is the *core self.* The core self is about action – specifically, about a relationship between the organism and the object. The core self unfolds in a sequence of images that describe an object engaging in the proto-self and modifying that proto-self, including its primordial feelings. Finally, there is the *autobiographical self.* This self is defined in terms of autobiographical knowledge pertaining to the past as well as the anticipated future (Damasio 2010, 22-23, emphaiss original).

Damasio's account is notable for its incorporation of both the body and feelings, a point that we will expand upon further in Chapter 4. But staying with Damasio's model for the moment, his contention is that life *qua* organism is necessarily brain-bound. The overarching feature of his account is that selfhood is couched in terms of *introspective* feelings, which are in turn explained as physical or biological sensations, or what he calls biomarkers. These sensations give rise to content in the mind in the form of *maps.* The mind is constructed by the brain's ability to mirror the sensory world, and these maps (or images) – as I understand Damasio – are integrated in the form of a feedback loop that shapes the mind. Hence, the emergent mind likewise elicits emergent levels of self.

3.4.2 Limitations of the brain-based self

The most obvious way to countenance a brain-self model is to eschew metaphysical necessity. Rather than seeking specific brain regions that correlate to selfhood, the alternative is by defining this approach to the self as brain *based.* By adopting this perspective, the self is not reducible to the brain, though the latter remains a necessary condition for selfhood. This approach, adopted by Northoff, eschews the need to posit the self as a metaphysical or empirical entity locatable in the brain. Instead it emphasizes a multi-variable relationship evinced by brain, body, and world

> results from neuroscience clearly link the self with neuronal processes related to both intraindividual experiences and interindividual interaction. There is thus a neuronal basis for the distinct aspects of the self within the context of brain, body, and environment. We therefore reject the mental characterization of the structure and organization that is supposed to define the self (Northhoff 2013, 11).

Northoff and Heinzel (2003) argue that brain models of self are confronted with the fact that scientific and philosophical inquiry are grounded by disparate epistemic points of departure, namely third-person (objective) and first-person (subjective) perspectives. To complicate matters, they contend that selfhood in psychiatry is epistemically expressed via a second-person perspective, by which they mean "drawing a relationship between content and context, i.e. the one centre of the individual self is put into the context of centres of other persons" (ibid., 50). In other words, the clinical encounter between patient and clinician is motivated by the latter's attempt to gain understanding of the former, not as an object with neural or biological states, but as another person (like herself) who experiences certain thoughts, feelings, and desires. But if we accept the epistemic position of Northoff and Heinzel *tout court*, we are confronted with a relative notion of self or a plurality of truths with respect to selfhood. For the authors, how we understand the self will ultimately depend on a context-dependent perspective from which one approaches selfhood: subjective, objective, or second-person. There is no one self, but particular selves associated with distinct observational perspectives.

Hence, an obstacle for any brain-bound model of self is that it simultaneously demands an accompanying *theoretical* notion of the self. If one is interested in identifying brain correlates of self, then one must also have a pre-conception of what behaviors or attributes are indicative of the phenomenal self. Consequently, a scientific approach to the self invariably intersects with philosophy, which calls into question the brain dependent condition of the relationship between brain and self.

Without wishing to diminish the significant inroads Damasio's work has made to remove the cognitive and neuro sciences from the Cartesian paradigm (i.e. the mind-body split), a paradigm that, historically, has elevated the status of the brain (or mind) while assigning considerably less (or no) importance to the status of the body in theories of the self.[33] Damasio's brain-based account, like that of Northoff, is simultaneously an account of consciousness that posits the necessity of the brain. But the

—

[33] For most philosophers of the twentieth century Descartes' dualist ontology has been the source of relentless criticism. As such, precisely what the "Cartesian" paradigm is intended to designate is multifarious. To clarify what is meant here is simply that, as Descartes himself says, "there is a great difference between a mind and a body in that a body, by its very nature, is always divisible. On the other hand, the mind is utterly indivisible…Although the entire mind seems to be united to the entire body, nevertheless, were a foot or an arm or any other bodily part to be amputated, I know nothing that has been taken away from the mind on that account" (1996, 101). Hence, historically, a presumption in human sciences has been that the body ought to be distinguished from the mind, insofar as the former is non-essential to the faculties of the latter.

former goes further, positing that in addition to the necessary condition of having a brain, a self simultaneously necessitates having a body. Damasio holds the body to be a passive transmitter of information. Bodily feelings or sensations are not *about* a particular object or situation in the world, but instead provide information about the state of the body itself. Consequently, Damasio's account runs afoul in light of the phenomenological facts of lived-experience. In the introduction to our investigation, we postulated that all experience is *about* something; to be someone presupposes an irrevocable relationship with the surrounding world. Because affective experience described by Damasio is strictly about one's *own* body, the *aboutness* of experience refers only to oneself. Hence, given that feelings are limited to being about oneself, his position excludes feelings that refer to (or are directed toward) the world one experiences. In other words, what we feel is some biological change or process *in* ourselves, and not the experience of the object we encounter in the world (i.e. chairs, phones, people, etc.).[34]

My reservation with Damasio's description is his contention that experience of the world is the product of representations of the external world rather than the world itself; the self is a *felt* experience of internalized biological states and cognitive maps. Why is this unsatisfactory? Though we will consider this question in depth during Chapter 4, for the moment it suffices to say that despite Damasio's attempt to shed Cartesian baggage he remains fettered by a representational model of reality inspired by Cartesian philosophy. As a consequence, his recourse is to interpret the relationship between self and the world in terms of biological (and evolutionary) processes:

> For instance, when I took my eyes off the page to think, and the dolphins that were swimming by caught my attention, I was not engaging the full scope of my autobiographical self because there would be no need for it; it would have been a waste of brain-processing activity, not to mention fuel, given the needs of the moment (Damasio 2010, 169).

The particularly notable part of Damasio's claim is found in the final phrase, "*given the needs of the moment.*" For him, *why* the self does X or Y is attributable to implicit biological considerations, which in this case, is reflected by the self's preservation of energy during a less expansive moment of consciousness. The problem is that when we describe the self, we are attempting to describe something thoroughly *personal.* To be sure, the brain

---

[34] For an extended discussion of the problems with Damasio's theory and intentionality see Ratcliffe (2008) and Bortolan (2016).

is a necessary biological feature of human life (and by extension the self). Yet, as Matthews puts it, “brains don’t think: people do (and use their brains to do so)” (2007, 116). In the previous quote taken from Damasio, when he describes the way he turns his attention toward the dolphins, he imbues this action with evolutionary meaning, namely the preservation of energy. But crucially, what I want to emphasize is that self-action is structured by meaningful situations. I do not need my “auto-biographical” self to turn my attention to the dolphins, not because it would be wasted energy, but because there is no meaningful motive for me to engage with the situation in that way. The point to be made here is that regardless of empirical self correlates, we want a notion of selfhood that will account for the way in which the self establishes a relationship with the world by personalizing it.

3.4.3 The no-self

For opponents of the Brain-bound account of the self, an appealing option is to outright reject the existence of a self. Because the Brain-bound model is unable to specify or locate a quantifiable entity to which the self may be ascribed, the no-self model argues that there cannot exist a *real* self. From a philosophical perspective, the no-self account is anti-realist, which, as Metzinger puts it, means that selves “do not subsist over time and they do not belong to the basic building blocks of reality” (2011, 280). Metzinger, who is one of the most notable no-self proponents, denies the existence of a self on the grounds that we cannot empirically identify the self in the same way we are able to identify H_2O or gold.[35] Under the auspices of this claim, the no-self argument, though opposed to all models of self, is particularly directed at models that attempt to empirically locate the self, such as the brain-based model.

The no-self alternative concedes that there may indeed be a phenomenological experience of self, but such experiences are not sufficient grounds to posit the existence of the self *per se*. Self is an illusion, or more generously, a “conceptual truth” but not an “ultimate truth” (Siderits 2011, 306). The semantic or conceptual reference to “I” does not presume an enduring, permanent, source of the self. While it may be a culturally sanctioned and

—

[35] There is an additional approach to the no-self model that is derived from the Buddhist tradition, which likewise argues that selfhood is an illusion. Of course, the Buddhist position argues from different premises and for different reasons. However, since Metzinger’s no-self model addresses Western science and Western metaphysics, the focus of my exegesis will be restricted to this particular perspective. For an overview of the no-self in the Buddhist context see Siderits (2011) and Albahari (2016).

discursive means of expressing oneself, when reduced to the most basic units of existence (matter), the self turns out to be fictitious.

3.4.4 Limitations of the no-self model

In one sense, the "no-self" alternative proposed by Metzinger is not as radical as it might seem, insofar as those of us interested in the problem of selfhood generally begin with the supposition that the self is not a metaphysical entity. Zahavi has pointed out that ontological anti-realists such as Metzinger adopt a notion of self that "by and large has been abandoned by most philosophers steeped in twentieth-century German and French philosophy, as well as by most of the empirical researchers who currently investigate the development, structure, function, and pathology of the self" (2008, 4). But then again, though Metzinger wants to deny the existence of the self, his account is limited to a narrow idea of self, namely one equivalent with (empirical) consciousness. For example, his third objection adopts a methodological anti-realist perspective, which holds that "nothing in the scientific investigation of self-consciousness commits us to assume the existence of individual selves" (Metzinger 2011, 285). In other words, because we cannot explain consciousness by empirically locating corresponding brain states that give rise to consciousness (the "hard-gap" problem), the self has no reality in the way that things exist in the world. Metzinger's "no-self" alternative is ultimately an *implicit* rejection of a specific sense of self, by which I mean, he denies existence of a self by presuming the self to be an empirical correlate of consciousness. In contrast, and as we will see soon enough, the perceived self and narrative-self models will argue that the self is a phenomenon that need not be reduced to the narrow demands of empirical correlates.

3.4.5 Psychiatric implications of brain-related models of self

The brain-based model of self is particularly relevant for psychiatric investigations that are concerned with neurobiological and empirical data, a point that Damasio himself makes explicit (2010, 19). Psychiatric research outcomes inevitably influence the development of new therapeutic interventions and even inform the revision of classificatory criteria. Consequently, it is incumbent upon us to recognize that "scientific" or brain-based approaches to selfhood cannot draw conclusions from empirical data without committing to a *particular theory* of the self.

Even though it may be the case that scientific investigations of selfhood may elicit merit worthy insights, science cannot have the final word. A robust description of selfhood will need to corroborate the phenomenology of self-experience, since even if a scientific explanation could eventually elucidate the necessary conditions for self, it would remain unable to account for *why* I do what I do, or *how* I do what I do, or *how* I understand myself as a self. In other words, *how* we experience ourselves in the world corresponds to a "meaning-explanation" (Matthews 2007) interpretive structure, which stands in stark contrast with a causal-explanation structure that characterizes the natural sciences. For example, brain-imaging may become adept enough to explain the neural correlates of depression or why some people are more predisposed to depression than others. At the same time, it is also the case that:

> Depression is a state of mind which is not merely an inner experience, but is directed toward the outside world, whether it is the world in general or some specific aspect of it. In this sense, it requires some conception of how the world is – is it seen as depressing? It cannot be identified only with inner feelings, and so cannot be explained fully by the causes of those inner feelings (Matthews 2007, 136).

Damasio's account, like most empirical investigations, makes the assumption that the phenomenon of selfhood may be understood without reference to the surrounding world. An unfortunate consequence of Damasio's assumption is that he takes for granted that self-experience – which is always antecedent to metaphysical assumptions about the world – is only intelligible against the backdrop of the surrounding world. By failing to address the fundamental connection between self and world, Damasio's analysis fails to recognize that, as the silent term of experience, it is the world that makes meaningful action and sense-making possible.

Hence, even *if* the brain is a necessary condition for selfhood, it remains an insufficient condition. To understand why a dog evokes in me an experience of anxiety while a cat does not, should prompt us to recognize that the thing about which I am anxious is not *inside* me. My anxious feelings are about the world (dog), and as a result, is meaningful for me in a way that – for whatever reason – a cat is not.

In contrast to Damasio's brain-based approach to selfhood, Metzinger's "no-self" is of considerably less practical value for psychiatric practice. Because psychiatry is a profession with deep historical connections to the phenomenon of self, patient-clinician interaction is shaped by everyday discourse and linguistic conventions that commit us to some implicit notion of it. The no-self model adopts an artificial stance toward the notion of selfhood, meaning that the coherence of the no-self perspective disintegrates outside of explicit reflection. According to Berrios and Marková, "such notions [disorders of self] can only function properly in the medium of language: they are linguistic tropes, narrative yarns, modes of talking about people and their reasons for doing things, devices to capture meaning..." (2003, 23). Like Metzinger, Berrios and Marková adopt an anti-realist conception of self; it does not exist "like a tone, a horse or a weed, nor even a concept to be considered as semantically tantamount to changes in blood flow or test scores" (2003, 10). Berrios and Marková view the putative existing self in psychiatry as a historico-political "construct" and reject the existence of self on anti-metaphysical grounds. Such a view would effecttively commit clinicians to view selfhood merely as a cultural "convention" that otherwise has no substantive existence.

Proponents of the no-self position contend that selfhood gained psychiatric relevance on account of mechanistic and psychological theories of self that became fashionable in the late nineteenth-century and early twentieth century. The chief criticism regarding the relationship between psychiatry and selfhood is that psychological models of the self are guilty of reifying a concept, the history of which is moral and metaphorical in nature. Specifically, psychiatric disorders, such as schizophrenia, became characterized as disorders of the self. On the one hand, "the anatomoclinical model of disease encouraged reification of these selves [moral and metaphysical] and soon claims started to be made as to their putative brain localization and pathology," while on the other hand, "a sort of coherence was achieved by claiming that all the disorders of self resulted from the same abstract mechanism (e.g. dissociation)" (Berrios and Marková 2003, 21). Hence, Berrios and Marková refer to the self as a consequence of the struggle for explanatory supremacy described in detail earlier in Chapter 1, where we argued that disorders are either caused by anatomical lesions (Kraepelin) or by psychological maladaptation (Freud). For Berrios and Marková, despite the non-existence or fictitious nature of the self, disorders inexorably became viewed to be either a physiological or anatomical dysfunction (e.g. amnesia), or a psychological disturbance of self as a result of defence mechanisms (e.g. self-splitting, projection etc.).

In psychiatry, the no-self model might be but one way to disavow the "realness" of self while maintaining a pragmatic attitude concerning the patient-clinician relationship. With respect to depression, however, the no-self model is considerably less compelling. Without the existence of the self, we can only describe depression causally, whether by means of a physiological dysfunction or the result of an external circumstance. This dual pathway of causation is further complicated by the fact that the no-self model cannot make causal distinctions. Whether or not depression is caused by a life circumstance or pathophysiology cannot be deduced from empirical data, for it cannot be determined whether or not the efficient cause of the physiological state, which is supposed to represent "depression", is external or internal in nature. The no-self model is perhaps appealing to clinicians who favor a biological-reductionist approach to depression, since irrespective of how depression is caused, the problem is corrected with psychopharmacological interventions.

3.5 The situated self

In addition to an emergent scientific interest in selfhood, the humanities have likewise been fertile for deepening our understanding of the self. More specifically, theories of self that champion its situated nature have added grist to the philosophical mill by broadening the constitutive scope of selfhood. Denying that the self is "a special part of a person (or of a brain)," they instead contend that it must be investigated as "a whole person considered from a particular point of view" (Neisser 2006, 4). The situated self is somewhat elusive, insofar as it is neither an explicit awareness nor is it conceptual, i.e. something we represent to ourselves or explicitly reflect upon through introspective exploration of feelings, thoughts, or desires. I will consider two different versions of the situated self, both of which share the premise that selfhood is engendered via one's relationship with the surrounding environment: the ecological-self and the enactive-self.

3.5.1 The ecological self

One of the earliest iterations of the situated self is J.J Gibson' *ecological self* (2014 [1979]), later elaborated upon by Eleanor Gibson (2006). Similar to the brain-based self, the ecological-self attempts to marry biology with perceptual experience in the context of the surrounding world. The overarching insight is that the self is dynamically coupled to the surrounding environment in a reciprocal fashion. Put another way, self is an interactive system according to which "the animal is constrained by its environmental niche and the niche is fitted to and acted upon by the animal [...] It is present potentially at birth and it develops as life goes forward" (Gibson 2006, 24). This self is characterized as a perceived self because it engenders a sense of agential capacity, to both act on the world and be acted upon by the world. The ecological self is perceived (experienced) *via* five overarching dimensions: differentiation of self from world; specification of self as a place; perception of affordances; control of environment, and representation.

Human capacity for movement ensures self-experience is dynamically opposed to (or distinguished from) the static world, which in turn leads to the recognition that I occupy a place (here) in relation to other objects (there). The experiential relation to a given environment allows us to develop our capacities for action in accordance with the layout of our surroundings, such that certain objects are experienced according to the possibilities they afford (e.g. a glass affords grasping): "if some object is to offer the affordance of a tool for an animal, it must be scaled so as to fit the animal's body and appendages and its capacities for operating the object, and it must be possible for the animal to perceive whether or not that is the case" (ibid., 32). Through a process of learning, the self *qua* human being becomes able to manage the surroundings according to his or her needs, and most crucially, in accordance with his or her capacities. Finally, unlike cognitive maps (or representations), essential to Damasio's brain-based account, the function of self-representation in the ecological self is indirect, and consequently means that the experience of oneself as represented "whether imaginal or conceptual, do[es] not underlie direct perception of the self, nor do[es] it need to" (ibid., 40). Whether experienced as a mirror or pictorial image, the self perceived in action is qualitative unique from perceptual recognition of oneself via representational form.

3.5.2 The enactive self

More recently, the situated self has been championed by proponents of situated cognition. There are numerous variations of this notion of self, the most notable of which are Enactive Cognition or 4E Cognition (Embodied, embedded, extended, and enactive cognition).[36] Though EE and 4E have developed out of cognitive science, they are inspired by Gibson's ecological psychology and the ecological self. According to Maiese, "what we call 'the self' is picked out by an essentially embodied, mental point of view, one which is an outgrowth of our animate, neurobiological dynamics and bound up with *affective framing*" (2015, 51, emphasis original). EE ap-

—

[36] There are other iterations of such theses, which both converge and diverge in minor ways. Some of these theoretical approaches include (but are not limited to) Extended-Mind, Dynamic Systems, Affective Scaffolding, and Essentially Embodied cognition. Unless otherwise stated, I refer to all such iterations as Enactive approaches.

proaches attempt to integrate sensory-motor capacities of the ecological-self with dynamic neurobiological and physiological systems in order to "offer a thoroughly non-reductionist and non-dualist form of naturalism" (de Haan 2017, 533). The premise, then, of situated cognition in general, is that neither cognition (or mind) nor self is *restricted* to the brain. Instead, a *sense of* self is "an essentially embodied point of view that is rooted in desiderative bodily-feelings and formed through engagement with the world" (Maiese 2015, 51). One way to understand the enactivist account of self is that it is a correction or modification of Damasio's brain-based model discussed above, which if you recall, emphasizes the close connection between self and affective bodily states. The crucial distinction that sets Maiese's proposal of self apart from that of Damasio is the affective "function." For enactivists like Maiese, the feelings that give rise to the self are not derived strictly from the biomarkers *in* the body, they are also elicited as sense or meaning from the surrounding world. Hence, models of the situated self recognize that selfhood is not independent from the world.

3.5.3 Limitations of the situated self

In anticipation of Chapter 4, I want to underscore that the phenomenological self we will explore in detail dovetails considerably with the situated self we are attending to here. Irrespective of notable overlaps, small but nonetheless significant philosophical differences will mean that our account will not ultimately converge with the situated-self model iterated by enactivists. What sets the situated-self apart from brain-related approaches is its fidelity to lived-experience. Specifically, the ecological self and EE self *do not* take for granted the background existence of the world (or environment). Self is consequently characterized as an active rather than a passive phenomenon. It is determined by the exchange between an agent and her surroundings. The self is not explicit recognition of interior life or the possibility of epistemic certainty. It is enmeshed with mundane life that, for the most part, goes largely unnoticed due to our capacity for unreflective activity. Crucially, unreflective life must not be construed as passive. When I speak on the phone and pace the room, it would be odd to characterize walking about the room as passive. It is no doubt active, even though it is action that need not be explicitly thematized. However, what the ecological account fails to properly specify is the bodily nature of self-perception. Gibson's description of perception utilizes anatomical and physiological descriptions, which might be of significance if we were concerned with *why* we perceive. The omission, however, is that the ecological perspective cannot account for *how* we perceive. For the ecological self, while the body and the environment are co-perceived terms, the body is experienced as an object of perception by differential reference to objects in the world.

The ensuing problem is that self-awareness for the ecological self is perceived *the same way* as objects in the world are perceived, that is, "her bodily self-awareness is indistinguishable from that of her apprehension of third-personal facts and laws of the environment" (Marratto 2012, 94). It may be true that in certain situations we do possess the ability to consider the body in an objective fashion, but crucially, this can never be absolute. The nature of embodied existence prevents this possibility by virtue of the relation between the self and body. I have privileged access to experience of myself in a way that is structurally and qualitative different to my experience of an object. On this point we defer to the next section on the Minimal self, where we will see that self-experience is necessarily not an object of experience.

A final word must be said about the overlap between the situated self and the phenomenological self that I will present in the next chapter. Having noted that the former and the latter will be tightly connected, I want to draw attention to a crucial philosophical premise that will set apart my own account of the self from the situated self. Put briefly, the concern of situated cognition may be understood to be epistemic, "a study of the way in which a perceptual system makes selective use of information about the objective world (thereby constituting for itself an environmental setting)" (Marratto 2012, 22). What is lacking, just as with the ecological self, is an account of perception itself, an ontology of perception and the way in which self is perceptually established in contact with the world. Our goal in Chapter 4 will thus be to consider the "ontological dynamics underlying the co-belonging and the difference between subjectivity and its objects" (ibid.). Thus, our investigation into the self is equally an investigation about how the world *is*.

3.5.4 Psychiatric implications of the situated self

The multifaceted nature of enactivism (and ecological approaches) has cast doubt on the legitimacy of Brain-bound models of the self. By emphasizing the multi-level dynamics between biology, the body, and perception, enactivists contend that psychiatric disorders cannot simply be reduced to brain dysfunctions. In turn, psychiatric disorders "are to be understood as shifts in sense-making that are simultaneously cognitive and affective and involve fundamental alterations in how a subject inhabits her surroundings"

(Maiese 2015, xviii). I think this characterization is apt, even though I will argue in the next chapter that the privileged role of cognition in depression obscures the significance of non-cognitive experience. That said, by emphasizing the inalienable relation between oneself and the world, the ecological and enactive approaches to the self are indeed useful for clinicians to achieve a better understanding of patient experience in depression, particularly with respect to the therapeutic context. But a limiting factor is that these approaches to selfhood have – as of yet – been unable to exert influence on empirical research in depression diagnosis.

3.6 The experiential self

3.6.1 The minimal self

An alternative model that I ascribe to the generalized category of perceived self is the *minimal self*. As the name suggests, the intention of the minimal self is to specify an aspect of selfhood, as opposed to an all-encompassing or exhaustive theory of the self. In fact, the fundamental premise of the minimal self is that it constitutes our most basic, primordial experience of the world, without which, higher order experiences of the self (e.g. cognition, reflection, imagination, etc.) would be impossible. The most influential proponent of the minimal self is Zahavi, according to whom:

> The minimal self was tentatively defined as the ubiquitous dimension of first-personal givenness *in the multitude of changing experiences*. On this reading, there is no pure experience-independent self. The minimal self is the very subjectivity of experience and not something that exists independently of the experiential flow. Moreover, the experiences in question are world-directed experiences. They present the world in a certain way, but at the same time they also involve self-presence and hence a subjective point of view. In short, they are of something other than the subject and they are like something for the subject (2009, 563, emphasis original).

Zahavi's theoretical staring point, like our own in this investigation, is inspired by a phenomenological-philosophical approach. Accordingly, it is worth reiterating that experience is held to be equivalent with consciousness (and self-consciousness). To be conscious is to have a certain type of experience, whether it is recollection, imagination, or of a particular object in the world. It is non-intentional awareness of experience. Hence, there is no-self (or homunculus) that stands above or outside of a given experience;

there is no "I" that conveys to another "I" that it is me who is having this experience.

The minimal self hinges upon the possibility of subjective experience or first-person perspective. It is an implicit awareness that whatever I experience is *my* experience: "it is a question of having first-personal access to own's own experiential life" (Zahavi 2008, 106). Unlike the ecological self, according to which self-awareness is qualitatively indistinct from awareness of an object, world experience (of objects) for the minimal self entails *pre-reflective* self-reference: it is *me* having an experience of X, not someone else, something I know without reference to propositional knowledge. The minimal self is not the grand self that common sense might associate with introspective or reflective life. When I explicitly reflect on who I am, what I desire, or what I should do, I am not "interrogating" the minimal self. In fact, such introspective acts, argues Zahavi, presuppose the minimal self, since the very possibility of reflecting on experience presupposes unreflective experience.

3.6.2 The psychologically continuous self (redux)

A neo-Lockean account of selfhood has been proposed more recently by Parfit.[37] Like Locke, Parfit contends that selfhood is not instantiated by a body that is numerically identical with itself over time. What Parfit believes is crucial to the problem of selfhood is "the *criterion* of personal identity: the relation between a person at one time, and a person at another time, which makes these one and the same person" (2011, 420, emphasis original). The desirable criterion for Parfit is not *idem identity*, which is to say, it is not essential for selfhood that our bodies be the *same* body over time. In fact, Parfit's argument is precisely that *idem* identity *qua* personal identity is ultimately unimportant. What does matter for selfhood is a particular type of relation: "the psychological continuity and connectedness that, in ordinary cases, hold between the different parts of a person's life" (ibid., 430). Importantly, this relation *could* exist in a different body (e.g. a head transplanted onto another body) on the condition that the proper part of the brain responsible for psychological continuity remains present. If this condition holds, "there will be at least one living person who will be psychologically continuous with me as I am now. And/or who has enough of my brain" (ibid., 440).

—

[37] Another neo-Lockean approach is attributed to Marya Schechtman's Narrative self, which we will address later in this chapter.

Because Parfit has developed his highly complex conception of personal identity over the course of several decades (1971, 2011), not only is his argument quite nuanced, it has also been modified over time. Ultimately, however, his characterization of selfhood is tied to past self-experience which connects me to the person I am in the present. The body is peripheral to enduring identity, save for the necessary causal parameters associated with the brain that elicit psychological connectedness.

3.6.3 Limitations of the experiential self

As I noted, Zahavi's minimal (or core) self is not intended to exhaust the notion of selfhood. His intention is to specify a basic condition of self without which other aspects of self would be incoherent (e.g. narrative self). Phenomenologically speaking, the minimal self persuasively describes the fundamental contact between self and world structuring self-experience. That said, because it is characterized by an irreducible self-presence, the minimal self does not emerge over time, it is not a developmental phenomenon and is not personalized. The minimal self, for lack of a better phrase, is pre-given, insofar as experience – whether it be early as foetal or post-natal – is predicated on the presence of the minimal self. While Zahavi would acknowledge that self is developmental, since the minimal self precedes (or is co-present with) living experience, it is always a pre-established feature of existence. However, as we will go on to argue in Chapter 4, it is entirely plausible that selfhood need not be pre-given or pre-formed. If the self is a developmental phenomenon, we need to account for the way in which it is personalized. How do I make the world my own? How did I develop this sense of myself that seems so familiar to me as an adult, yet was entirely undetermined when I was an infant? For Zahavi, one way to answer this is to compliment the minimal self with a narrative self, an account of the self that I will introduce shortly. However, in the next chapter I shall be accounting for the personalization of the self in a different way. I will thus propose a notion of the self whose personal life can be attributed to our earliest perceptual contact with the world, and whose development is evinced through expressive, bodily actions in the world.

The serious limitation to Parfit's psychological connectedness account of self is that it requires us to be unconcerned with who we will be in the future. What matters is that the psychological *relation* survives. The idea that we ought to be concerned about whether or not I will continue to exist is not rational, "it is an empty or a merely verbal question whether we shall still exist [tomorrow]" (ibid., 441). For Parfit, the question *who am I?*, is atomistic. Selfhood is reduced to rational arguments that deny the way in which we find ourselves in the world. As we will see in the next chapter, the notion that our future is unimportant (and that it is irrational even to believe the opposite) grossly underappreciates the extent to which lived-experience of depression implicates selfhood and temporality. Who we are, our desires, tastes, and so on, cannot be excised from our temporal horizons, insofar as our past and our future unfold from the present. For people who experience depression, we will soon be in a position to show that these temporal horizons, which implicitly structure our everyday experience of the world, are altered in depression.

It is also clear that Parfit's use of psychological relations ends up smuggling in certain metaphysical assumptions. His insistence that the proper part of the brain must cause psychological connectedness is a reductionist notion of selfhood that demands a particular locus for the self (i.e. the brain). Hence, though the psychological continuity model fits within the category of the experiential self, it overlaps significantly with the Brain-based self that we assessed earlier. Hence, for all of Parfit's efforts to deny the importance of identity, he remains committed (even if weakly) to the need for *idem* identity to obtain, perhaps not as a body, but as part of the brain.

3.6.4 Psychiatric implications of the experiential self

Over the last two decades the minimal self has become a significant discussion point for clinicians inspired by phenomenological-philosophical insights. It is increasingly argued that persons who report having anomalous experiences (e.g. thought insertion, psychosis, etc.) experience disturbances of the minimal self (Sass et al. 2013, Martin et al. 2018, Summa and Fuchs 2015). Because the minimal self is the most basic constituent of first-person experience, it is normally characterized as being *my* experience. By contrast, for a patient who reports that thoughts have been inserted into her mind, her implicit sense of experiential ownership is disturbed; for the patient, these "inserted" thoughts are experienced as originating outside of herself and belong to someone else. While it is true that thought insertions are still experienced *via* the patient's first-person perspective, under *normal* circumstances, we never doubt that thoughts and experiences when expounded through the first-person perspective belong to us. Yet, in this case, the nature of self-experience is transformed such that the patient no longer experiences *mineness* or *ipseity* that saturates our unreflective experiential stream of daily life. To this end, Zahavi, along with Parnas et al. (2005), has developed the *Examination of Anomalous Experience* (EASE) questionnaire, which is specifically aimed at psychiatric assessment of self-disturbances. It is a phenomenologically inspired assessment tool to better understand changes to subjective experience for schizophrenic spectrum disorders. But schizophrenia and depression are disparate phenomena with respectively unique behavioral and experiential expressions. Arguably, while the minimal-self model dovetails nicely with schizophrenic disorders, in depression it does not appear to be disturbed in the same way. Our task in Chapter 5 will be to make an explicit account of how self-disturbance is implicated in depression. This will demand an account that goes beyond the minimum requirements associated with the minimal self.

3.7 The narrative self

In recent decades the use of narrative has become a fashionable heuristic across medicine as a whole. In its most basic sense, narrative functions as a literary vehicle for storytelling. Of course, oral storytelling predates written stories we now associate with literary fiction. Indeed, as we will see, some narrative models of selfhood do indeed draw from literary theory in order to posit a close connection between fictional narrative and self-narrative. Yet, there is little doubt that the human capacity for speech has endowed us with the capacity for narrating, not only morals and myths, but stories about who we are.[38] In the context of medicine, the traction of narrativity comes from the medical humanities, which – as the name suggests – attempts to humanize patients through the lens of their stories. Rather than approaching patients as objects of investigation, clinicians have been encouraged to view patients as unique individuals for whom illness takes on various meanings and consequences in their attempts to live well.

Narratives are especially significant for clinical psychiatry (and depression) given that. in the absence of diagnostic technology, which is more widely available to specialized practices in somatic medicine, both diagnosis and psychotherapy rely on patient reporting. Likewise, for psychiatric professionals, the context of a patient's life is fundamental to any potential diagnosis, and thereby places a demand on clinicians to piece together a "portrait" of the patient in his or her attempt to achieve understanding of a patient's situation.

[38] See Walter Benjamin's (1968) excellent essay for a distinction between knowledge derived from books and oral stories.

The narrative self may also be more broadly construed as the conceptual self or socially constructed self.[39] But because these two broad labels are so expansive, they do no proper justice to the nuances comprising the narrative self. For this reason, our focus is limited to assessing the coherence of the narrative self.

One of the most notable accounts of this understanding of selfhood is formulated by Ricoeur (1992), whose work on narrativity is inspired by literary theory. Similar to the problems with which Metzinger's no-self alternative grapples, Ricoeur's main concern is how to reconcile personal identity and the problem of sameness over time without positing a metaphysical self. Ricoeur asks, "Is there a form of permanence in time that is a reply to the question 'Who am I'" (ibid., 118). Put another way, can the (numerical) sameness of identity (*idem*) be reconciled with the self (*ipseity/mineness*)? Ricoeur resolves this question by arguing that sameness and self are not mutually opposed but constitute a dialectical relationship. He suggests

> an intervention of narrative identity in the conceptual constitution of personal identity in the manner of a specific mediator between the pole of character, where *idem* and *ipse* tend to coincide, and the pole of self-maintenance, here selfhood frees itself from sameness (ibid., 118-119).

The thrust of Ricoeur's thesis is that character is developed via habits and practices, which represent a permanence or sameness of identity. Selfhood is characterized by action or events (emplotment), which roughly speaking afford the possibility of developing new and unanticipated lines of force. "The narrative," writes Ricoeur, "constructs the identity of the character, what can be called his or her narrative identity, in constructing that of the story told. It is the identity of the story that makes the identity of the character" (ibid., 147-148). Without wishing to do injustice to Ricoeur's account, we can summarize the function of the narrative self as making way for a cohesive life story that permits reconfigurations and mutations, forming a tapestry woven together by stories told by oneself (1988, 246).

---

[39] There are at least two reasons why the narrative self is equally a conceptual self and/or a social self. First, narrative entails having an idea or sense of self-knowledge about who we are. Second, narratives are shaped by language, which is both conceptually and culturally determined. Hence, any attempt at narrating one's self will always occur within a cultural context, the limits of which are linguistically pre-determined or historically delimited. See Nessier and Jopling (1997) for an overview of the conceptual self.

More recent renderings of the narrative-self share features of Ricoeur's account but raise the intricacies to a much more intelligible level. For instance, Schechtman's "Narrative Self Constitution View" holds that

> we constitute ourselves as selves by understanding our lives as narrative in form and living it accordingly. This view does not demand that we explicitly formulate our narratives...but rather that we experience and interpret our present experiences not as isolated moments but as an ongoing story (2011, 398).

The feature that underscores Schechtman's account is that events in our lives are interpreted against the larger background of a life narrative, and it is the background that influences the sense or meaningfulness of the trajectory of our lives: "The experience of winning the lottery," says Schechtman, "will, for instance, be a different experience for someone immensely wealthy, someone who has lived a life of crushing poverty, and someone who has struggled unsuccessfully with a gambling addiction (ibid.). This account, which is underscored by continuity or stable personality, is unnecessary according to Goldie, who claims that there is no need to posit narrative self- continuity. All we need, he argues, is a narrative *sense* of self: "It is the sense that one has of oneself in narrative thinking, as having a past, a present, and a future [...] a way of thinking of oneself, or of others, in narrative thinking" (2012, 118). Goldie's objection, it seems, is that narrative is a way of organizing and thinking about our lives in a structured way. What is unnecessary is that we attribute something concrete or permanent to the self. According to Goldie, it is important that we recognize a "self to which we refer when using the word 'I' in autobiographical person narratives" (ibid., 141). Thus, Goldie's narrative self designates a point around which we gather together ways of telling others and ourselves about who we are.

3.7.1 Limitations of the narrative self

The narrative self may be summarized as the way in which our desires, tastes, goals, morals, and so on, are expressed over the course of our life according to the way in which our life unfolds though actions and events. A strong objection against the narrative self is that narratives are fictions and prone to confabulation. While Descartes and Freud both believed in the possibility of accessing truthful self-knowledge, the reliance on introspection has been heavily criticized. It is often the case, for instance, that siblings have quite distinctively different recollections of shared events from childhood. Likewise, we sometimes hold on vehemently to beliefs about some particular aspect of our past, only to later find out – say, through evidence from a photograph – that we were, in fact, incorrect. Do inaccurate memories or false assertions about one's past unravel the fabric of who we say we are? Similarly, how do we reconcile explicit narrative with implicit narrative? In other words, there is most certainly a distinction between reflecting on oneself versus being a self who is unreflectively immersed in everyday life. As Zahavi helpfully points out, "it is also a question of who I am independently of what I decide" (2014, 59).

A second challenge to the narrative self is that life is not structured as a story. While narrative may be a practical way of characterizing who we are, there is a qualitatively difference between narrating a fiction and narrating one's life. If asked to "account" for oneself, to present one's life story to a listener, there is no necessary correspondence between the narrative we present and *who* we are. Specific factual events, influential moments, or traumatic experiences may indeed serve to benchmark significant moments experienced in one's life. Yet, we must always choose which parts of ourselves to narrate, those that *we* deem most worthy of mention. How these disparate events are internally related is entirely dependent upon the self we *want* to be, as well as the self we want others to perceive. The point is not to deny that we make use of narrative structure or that our life bears no resemblance to a narrative. But we can follow Goldie's account, fully acknowledging that we adopt narrative (or narrative-like) proclivities, without making the unfounded logical leap that the *use* of narrative is undifferentiated from a narrative *self* as such.

3.7.2 Psychiatric implications of the narrative self

For clinical psychiatry, the narrative self model proves to be Janus-faced. On the one hand, narrative is an invaluable means of reorienting and reconstructing what are, in many cases, broken lives (Davidson 2003). On the other hand, as we discussed at length in the second chapter, DSM diagnoses such as depression may unduly influence the way in which patients narrate *who they are* (Tekin 2011).

One crucial aspect of the narrative self in psychiatry is the emphasis on self-creation. By this I mean encouraging patients to feel a sense of agency by transmuting their illness experience into their life narrative. One such example is the rise of the "autopathography," a hybrid genre that integrates personal memoir with illness experience, entailing a "reconstruction of the experiential dimension of the condition as well as reflection on its meaning and place in the life of the author" (Radden and Varga 2013, 104).[40] Of course, the written memoir is a medium that is highly reflective and deliberative, not to mention available only to a select minority. The narrative self of autopathography is an explicit structuring of one's story. But in the clinical setting, as we argued in Chapter two, a narrative is not constituted in isolation. With a depression diagnosis comes, as clinicians reported, a "fork in the road" moment for patient self-interpretation: Is depression part of who the patient is, or is depression but a point along the patient's arching plot?

> On the one hand, it sets the subject's experience in an established classificatory system which can facilitate self- understanding by providing insight into subject's condition and giving a direction to treatment and recovery. In this sense, the DSM diagnosis may have positive ramifications on the processes of recovery and may positively affect the subject's self-perception. On the other hand, however, given DSM's symptom-based approach and its adoption of the Biomedical Disease model, a diagnosis may force the subject to make sense of her distress divorced from other elements in her life that may be affecting her mental health and may guide her to frame her experience only as a neurobiological imbalance that is unchangeable. This form of self-understanding may set limits on the subject's hopes of recovery and may bar her flourishing (Tekin 2011, 376-377).

The narrative self in the clinical setting presents a dilemma for clinicians. Tekin's characterization above suggests that the narrative self is not a *self*, but rather an ascription of identity or framework for understanding. As Goldie's account contends, the narrative self is a formal recognition that we are beings who tell stories about ourselves. But as a formal recognition (or *sense* of self), it fails to properly incorporate the pre-reflective level (or implicit narrative) of self-experience argued for by Zahavi and Gibson respectively, an aspect of which is intended to address how selfhood is *expressed* in, and toward, the world pre-cognitively. In this way, clinicians who adopt the narrative model of self, risk overlooking the fact that patients are already intimately familiar with themselves pre-reflectively prior to the story they may choose to tell about themselves. To grasp how the self is embedded in meaningful experiential structures prior to reflective thought (and narration) will require that we develop an account of the self in

---

[40] Depression memoirs (or autopathography) are numerous. For several examples, see Styron (2010), Gask (2015), Solomon (2001), Merkin (2017), and Brampton (2018).

Chapter 4 that encompasses aspects of the models we have considered without being continuous with any one of them.

3.8 Conclusion

Even though there is no general consensus on the nature of selfhood, we have attempted to narrow the conceptual spectrum by scrutinizing contemporary alternatives of selfhood against the classic psychological and metaphysical models. We considered four accounts of self that, despite certain overlaps, attempt to make sense of selfhood in unique ways: some brain-related models view the self as a phenomenon reducible to certain brain functions or systems of the brain, while at the other extreme, the no-self account claims that, not only is selfhood not in the brain, it is an illusion; the situated self, which contends that the self is dynamically embedded within its surrounding environment; the experiential self, which on the one hand, attributes the self to pre-reflective experience, and thereby a pre-condition that is implied by all higher order, reflective theories of the self, or on the other hand, might argue that selfhood is elicited by the right kind of psychologically connected relationships concerning our memories; the narrative self, which takes inspiration from literary theory to characterize selfhood by a capacity for structuring one's life according to the vicissitudes of a life narrative.

Though each model possesses certain virtues, there are likewise limitations – some more significant than others. Arguably, the strength of any theory of self should not be measured in accordance only with the theory's conceptual consistency. The accounts we have surveyed in this chapter illustrate that it is equally – if not more – important to explicitly define the limits of what the self is or is not. I contend that the desire to cash out selfhood through metaphysics by positing a stable or enduring inner substance demonstrates that attempts to reify selfhood lead us into circles. And since it has been argued extensively in the literature that selfhood, as a homunculus or a reified entity, is ultimately untenable, it is essential that we make clear the *what* and the *how* of the self: what does it do and how does it happen? In the next chapter we will address these two crucial points by drawing upon a phenomenological-philosophical framework. The intention is to introduce a notion of self that, when appropriate, draws upon some aspects of the accounts that I have outlined above. But the approach to the self I will offer in Chapter 5 is not merely a composite of the accounts we have discussed. Like many models of the self, I will emphasize the extent to which selfhood is a phenomenon that is embodied, situated, and affective. However, my approach to selfhood sets itself apart from the Brain-bound self, psychological self, experiential self and narrative self, by insisting that selfhood must be understood existentially. That is, selfhood is bound up in perceptual structures that express our existential and practical orientation toward the world. I will likewise argue that selfhood is an ambiguous phenomenon, insofar as it is experientially uncanny. It will become clear by the end of the next chapter the extent to which we are so intimately familiar with self-experience that it simultaneously proves to be foreign and elusive to us in everyday life.

CHAPTER 4

The self as expressive style: Merleau-Ponty, Straus, and existential-phenomenology

4. Introduction

The previous chapter illustrated that selfhood is not monopolized by any one model. While some accounts are more persuasive than others, the respective appeal of the brain-based self, psychological self, experiential self, or narrative self, is to a large extent dependant on how one understands the relationship between self and world. Up to this point in our investigation, we have only considered selfhood somewhat tangentially, first in the historical context of psychiatry (Chapter 1), and then in psychiatric practice (Chapter 2). The previous chapter provided the reader with an extended discussion of four influential models of the self (Chapter 3), all of which have exerted influence on the contemporary landscape of selfhood. Having only vaguely hinted at some phenomenological features of selfhood along the way, the purpose of this chapter is to introduce a novel existential-phenomenological account of the self and selfhood. If depression is indeed a disorder of the self, and if existing approaches to selfhood are not entirely satisfactory, then we must first establish an account that displays fidelity to self-experience as it is lived. Only once we have satisfied this task can we then proceed to our phenomenological analysis of depression (Chapter 5).

Here in this chapter, I develop an ontological account of the self that, while not entirely unsympathetic to the brain-based self, the situated self, the minimal self, and the narrative self, my phenomenological sketch of selfhood goes beyond anyone of these models. By employing the existential phenomenology of Maurice Merleau-Ponty, in this chapter I contend that selfhood is a developmental phenomenon that cuts across several domains of lived-experience, including embodiment, space, and perception. I further argue that selfhood is most aptly characterized as a generalized self-*style*.

The notion of self-as-a-style is not, in and of itself, completely novel. While doubtless Merleau-Ponty himself envisions selfhood as an embodied perceptual style, nowhere in his *oeuvre* are we provided with a systematic discussion of selfhood.[41] For Merleau-Ponty, selfhood is an indispensable feature of world experience, yet as I just intimated, unlike the theorists we considered in Chapter 3, Merleau-Ponty offers us no unambiguously delineated notion of the self. The challenge, then, is to piece together the way in which Merleau-Ponty understands the relationship between selfhood and the world.

Moreover, I also use this chapter to illuminate the way in which Merleau-Ponty's phenomenological philosophy is indebted to the work of the phenomenological psychiatrist Erwin Straus, specifically the way in which selfhood is underpinned by situated perception. Methodologically, their respective philosophical projects critically engage with scientific assumptions operative in the human sciences. Merleau-Ponty and Straus devote considerable attention to clinical cases to illustrate that causal explanations of pathological behavior are often erroneous. The central problem, as they see it, is that the nature of human behavior is incorrectly interpreted to be either mechanistic or representational. Accordingly, Straus and Merleau-Ponty insist that proper insight into various behavior-based pathologies is achieved only once we acknowledge that *subjectivity* – and not just biological or psychological mechanisms – is susceptible to disturbance. Turning to phenomenology and ontology, both Merleau-Ponty and Straus meditate extensively on the nature of subjectivity, with particular attention devoted to the relationship between perception and consciousness, the ultimate purpose of which is to reveal the irrecusable relationship between self and world.[42]

4.1 Objective thought

Both Merleau-Ponty and Straus were overt critics of what they perceived to be prejudices of objective thought, a pejorative phrase that is synonymous with scientific discourse. They both contend that scientific explanation is predicated on one of two overarching perspectives: empiricism or intellec-

—

[41] See also Morris and Maclaren (2015) for various ways to understand self and Merleau-Ponty's ontology, and Marratto's (2012) monograph addressing the self in Merleau-Ponty.

[42] Of course, the same could be said of Bergson, Husserl, and Heidegger to name but a few. Merleau-Ponty and Straus (perhaps less recognized) go beyond their contemporaries by positing a necessary link between perception-body-consciousness. The most obvious example is Merleau-Ponty's re-characterization of intentionality as motor-intentionality.

tualism.[43] The problem, as they see it, is that objective thought is remiss in its attempt to explain human behavior under the laws of causality or logic. The underlying point of contention for Merleau-Ponty and Straus is that empirically driven explanatory models of human behavior are derived from dubious ontological assumptions about the very world that the investigator seeks to explain. The philosopher of science Georges Canguilhem characterizes the problem in the following way:

> Physics is a science of fields, of milieus. But it has been discovered that, in order for there to be an environment, there must be a centre. It is the position of a living being, its relation to the experience it lives in as a totality, that gives the milieu meaning as conditions of existence (2009, 70).

Canguilhem's sentiment, that objective explanations of phenomena are proposed by beings for whom things matter, is echoed by Straus, who writes: "Familiarity with the existence of living creatures precedes all anatomic and physiologic investigations; it cannot be deduced from them" (1963, 51). Canguilhem and Straus both implicitly posit that phenomena are descriptively inexhaustible, which is subsequently the basic starting assumption of any phenomenological investigation. When object-thought presupposes that the natural world and that the things within it may be descriptively exhausted, the background existence of the world in all subsequent scientific investigations is taken for granted:

> [The introspective psychologist] attempted to describe the givens of consciousness, but without questioning the absolute existence of the world surrounding it. He presupposed, following the scientist and common sense, the objective world as the logical frame of all his descriptions and as the milieu of his thought (Merleau-Ponty 2012, 60)

For instance, when initiating a study of visual optics within object-thought, the scientist presupposes knowledge about *what* seeing is. The problem, for Merleau-Ponty, is that the investigator seeks knowledge about *what* seeing is while bypassing knowledge of *how* we see. By virtue of lived-experience, the investigator is *already* intimately aquatinted with the phenomenon of vision. Yet, because everyday acts of visual perception are so fundamentally woven into our experiential development (from infant to adult), the

—

[43] Intellectualism generally refers to rationalist and idealist models of thought, but Merleau-Ponty often switches rather casually between these two targets of criticism.

scientific investigator takes for granted that the act of seeing is something we do. In presuming that visual optics may causally be explicated in their totality, the scientist's investigation of vision ends up explaining the *object of perception* rather than *perception of the object.*

Straus and Merleau-Ponty's shared affinity for the use of clinical case studies in a philosophical context is indicative of a broader methodological orientation that underpins their respective philosophical projects.[44] When *Primacy of the World of Senses* was published in 1936, Straus engaged critically with classical reflex theories developed by behaviorist psychology (e.g. Pavlov). Some six years later, Merleau-Ponty's dissertation, *The Structure of Behavior,* with no explicit mention of Straus, investigates the very same problems. Similarly, Straus' conception of movement, corporeality, sensing, and perception, are all themes explicitly addressed in Merleau-Ponty's 1946 publication, *Phenomenology of Perception.* But the truly novel contribution made by both philosophers is their claim that the body (or corporeality) is the fundamental feature of consciousness. Straus and Merleau-Ponty share the same strategy to "vindicate" perceptual experience, which means calling into question the theoretical assumptions that empiricism and intellectualism employ when explaining human behavior. When the empiricist and the intellectualist attempt to explain perception, not only do their explanations lead to insurmountable contradictions concerning behavior, they likewise result in untenable philosophies regarding the nature of consciousness. Why? In short, the crux of problem lay in the classic scientific prejudice that, not only is the body an object, it is but one object among all objects.

To be clear, neither Straus nor Merleau-Ponty are anti-science. It is more accurate to say that they reject scientism. No one doubts, for example, that without the invention of corrective lenses, myopia would be a debilitating problem for many people rather than a mere nuisance. What Straus and

---

[44] This is perhaps most clear when comparing Merleau-Ponty's earlier work in *The Structure of Behavior* (1942) and *Phenomenology of Perception* (1945) –, which is often contrasted with his late work dedicated to the development of an ontology of being – and Straus' *The Primary World of Senses* (1936). Merleau-Ponty was not candid with respect to philosophical influences. Comparatively, Straus has – undeservingly – received far less scholarly attention than Merleau-Ponty, and yet there seems to be little doubt that the latter was significantly influenced by the 1936 publication of the former. Reciprocally, when the second edition of *Primary World of Senses* was published in 1956, Straus explicitly acknowledges his indebtedness to the work of Merleau-Ponty. In fact, Straus was influential for several philosophers in the second half of the 20th century, including Jan Patočka, and Gilles Deleuze, to name but a few.

Merleau-Ponty oppose is the presumption that scientific (or objective) thought not only exhausts explanations of the natural world, but likewise exhausts explanations of human activity. Merleau-Ponty is adamant that philosophy should not deign before science: "philosophy is not a particular body of knowledge; it is the vigilance which does not let us forget the source of all knowledge" (1964b, 100). Hence, the imperative is to recognize that theoretical and scientific knowledge are predicated on pre-theoretical understanding of the world, the source of which is embodied perceptual experience.

The philosophical affinity between Straus and Merleau-Ponty cannot be exhaustively catalogued here; such an endeavour would demand a dedicated study in its own right. As such, because Merleau-Ponty's philosophy of perception is considerably more systematic than that of Straus, philosophical priority in this chapter is accorded to Merleau-Ponty. Nevertheless, when appropriate, I will draw attention to points of convergence in order to buttress the overall trajectory of thought throughout the chapter, which begins by elaborating on phenomenological considerations concerning perception, culminating in a specific notion of selfhood. The diffuse nature of the self poses a challenge for selecting the best point of entry, and for this reason, we begin this chapter by picking up our line of thought developed at the conclusion of Chapter 2, where we argued that the constellation meeting model in child psychiatry is phenomenologically instructive for specifying the developmental nature of the self.

4.2 Situating the ontology of situation

In Chapter 2, my clinical informants characterized the child's familial relations as a family "system." I argued that Merleau-Ponty's term family "constellation" is a more apt (and less mechanistic) term to denote the child's world of significant interpersonal relationships. The term constellation is appropriate in the context of Merleau-Ponty's lecture, "The Child's Relation with Others" (1964a, 110), where he outlines the origins of intersubjectivity and self-awareness. Accordingly, the significance of the family constellation is essential to the way in which we understand the source of self.

Human life is a developmental phenomenon that cuts across various domains of existence (e.g. cognitive, biological, emotional, etc.). Development is not to be mistaken for "progression" or a teleological fulfilment of mental life. Broadly construed, human development denotes emergent behavior that unfolds through a dyadic self-world structure. To be sure, vital life is developmental as well. It would be remiss to deny that physiological changes to the body have no effect on behavior. Arthritis, muscle atrophy, and diminished cognitive capacities, will all impinge upon our experience of the world. Importantly, however, our behavior is not servile to the causal realm of bio-physiology. The source of behavior – as an expressive relation to the world – is always *someone*; whether the biological body is in early development or beginning to fail, it is not a source of expressive behavior.

As an expressive relation to the world, human behavior emerges out of our primordial experience of the world according to the structuring logic of *situation*. Ontologically, situation is the founding or establishment of "an immediate non-presence, but perspective understood as opening its beyond, leading to it by its very thickness, [which presupposes] relief, obstacles, configuration" (Merleau-Ponty 2010c, 6). In other words, things matter to us because they demand some sort of action or resolution.

Unlike the minimal self discussed in Chapter 3, Merleau-Ponty takes the position that infants do not initially possess a strict distinction between themselves and others. Importantly, this does not mean, as William James contended (1918), that the infant is simply bombarded by confused and chaotic sensations. The infant's first perception of the world initiates an inexorable opening onto being that is perceptually articulated in a generalized and impersonal fashion. But even this nascent stage of perception is saturated with meaning (or sense), which is ultimately the source according to which situations are established: "the confrontation of the self with the world is originally very general [...] Experience as such can, in turn, only be understood as so many constrictions, consolidations, and definitions of this [relation of self and world]" (1963, 87). One way to characterize the notion of situation is that it is a movement from pre-personal to personal experience, an opening onto a future self: "I experience sensation as a modality of general existence, already destined to a physical world, which *flows through me without being its author*" (Merleau-Ponty 2012, 224, emphasis added). Perception establishes contact with Being, initially as highly generalized perceptions that will eventually develop into highly specific ones. When Merleau-Ponty claims that Being (or existence) flows through us as, and has, sense for us, it is because we are endowed with a body that is perceptually sensitive – inexorably and irrevocably – to sense. Our first perception opens us onto a field that surrounds our mortal lives and from which our contact can never be severed.

A child's nascent perceptions become more articulated over time by "laying down" perceptual levels that subtend all future perceptions. Merleau-Ponty's phenomenological investigation of perception leads him to posit that all perception is a prolongation of our first perceptions: "The first contact, the first pleasure, there is initiation [...] the opening of a dimension that can never be closed, the establishment of a level in terms of which *every other experience will henceforth be situated*" (Merleau-Ponty 1968, 151, emphasis added). To illustrate by analogy, the second floor of a house is accessed from the first floor via a staircase. The first step opens onto the second, the second onto the third, and so on. The final step connects to the second floor, and yet the *entire* staircase is indirectly connected to the second floor as an extension of the very first step; the final step refers to the previous steps by necessity. In a sense, the first step, which is most distal from the top, is subsumed by the final step. This comparison attempts to clarify the basic developmental character of perception as an experiential process that is never fully exhausted due the indeterminate nature of phenomena. Our earliest contact with the world is not shed like the skin of a snake; quite the opposite, a "thickness" of perception becomes sedimented as increasingly complex perceptual capacities that structure our entire manner of relating to the world.

Being situated does not constitute a spatial position (i.e. situated in the center of the city) or a point in geometrical space. To be sure, all experience presupposes that it takes place from *somewhere*. How is it possible to be in a non-positional somewhere? To remedy this, we have recourse to Merleau-Ponty's assertion that "our body is not *in* space, nor for that matter *in* time. It *inhabits* space and time" (2012, 140). Space formulated this way is the rejection of space according to objective thought. If we are *in* the world the way a cookie is contained *in* a jar, then we are ultimately but one entity among others comprising the totality of things "present-to-hand" within the world (Heidegger 2008, 93). By contrast, to be situated is to say we are *of* the world. For Straus, "one might as well say, 'to find oneself in a situation' – this is exactly what experiencing signifies" (1966c, 247). Situations are structured *a priori* by the body and its perceptual capacities that put us in direct contact with the world, a world that is not of my making, yet contingent upon the way in which we take it up. Hence:

> What counts for the orientation of the spectacle is not my body, such as it in fact exists, as a thing in objective space, but rather my body as a system of possible actions, a virtual body whose "phenomenal" place is defined by its

> task and by its situation. My body is wherever it has something to do (Merleau-Ponty 2012, 260).

The body is a pivot around which the world of practical significance is organized. By virtue of being a body, the world appears as a multifarious field of possible actions, some of which solicit behavior that is specific to the demands of a given situation. A solicitation to act belongs to an entirely different species than the decision to act; this is especially evident when we consider the nature of what we perceive: "By opening up to the structure of the thing, the senses communicate among themselves. We see the rigidity and the fragility of the glass, and when it breaks with a crystal-clear sound, this sound is borne by the visible glass" (ibid., 238). If objects presented to a consciousness are perceived as possessing individual and distinct qualities, it is because we dissect them analytically by removing ourselves (and the objects) from the perceptual milieu. Similarly, a glass is graspable because the body is disposed (or sensitive) to grasping; there is no need to deliberate about how to grasp the glass on the counter; the *glass is graspable.* Likewise, the glass is not encountered as being three meters away, rather it is in reach, out of reach, near, far, graspable, moveable, and so on. What is more, the glass is not only perceived as a manipulandum for me but is likewise perceived as something *one* is able to grasp (an object that is perceptually available to *others*). And it is this what Merleau-Ponty has in mind with respect to the virtual body, it is a power or capacity to immediately grasp what can or cannot be done in accordance with bodily sensitivity to a world of knowledge that is non-conceptual. Situations elicit non-thematic lines of force through sense or meaning. Decisions, by contrast, are reserved for limit situations which are initiated when we are confronted with an inability to deal with a situation.

4.3 The perceptual something

The philosophical significance of situation is comparable to that of being-in-the-world (Heidegger 2008), both of which are variations that express the same theme: *intentional consciousness.*[45] Unlike traditional attitudes toward consciousness, which often attribute consciousness to a brain state or function of the mind, intentional-consciousness is neither an object nor is it epiphenomenal. Intentionality *is experience itself* and is characterized by

---

[45] Unless otherwise specified, intentional consciousness and consciousness are used interchangeably.

directedness. Directed experience further implies an anchored perspective that orients us *toward* otherness, which is nothing other than the world of sense.

As I have already noted, the first perception of the world establishes a level upon which all future perceptions will develop from.[46] At this stage of life an infant indeed perceives the world, but only in a generalized way. Just as the body develops over time, so too does perception. The trajectory of perceptual development begins with vague distinctions, highly generalized visual perceptions (shapes, colours, outlines), tactile feelings, and attunement to sounds, all which become with experience increasingly more specified articulations of the world. Development of highly refined perceptions, according to Merleau-Ponty, is made possible by establishing perceptual structures. Perception of otherness (the world) is not disclosed as ready-made, and it certainly does not emerge with the clarity that is so familiar to adult life: "Perception is like a net whose knots progressively appear more clearly" (Merleau-Ponty 2012, 12). Likewise, perceptual development is not concomitant with the development of conceptual knowledge; the child's identification of objects is not obtained through judgment or concepts, nor does she associate previous perceptions with current perceptions:

> Although research shows that when awake, new-borns can discriminate objects as discrete three-dimensional objects, they do not do so systematically. Most of the time they do not pay much attention to objects and do not seem to engage in much learning about them. *If their eyes are open they seem to see something rather than look at objects.* If they do look at objects – and we know they do – it is rather fleeting as opposed to frequent and systematic (2009, 69, emphasis added).

—

[46] Merleau-Ponty does not address the plausibility of in uterine perception. We will proceed following Merleau-Ponty's position since the issue cannot be unpacked here. Likewise, it will later become clear that this topic is inherent to selfhood, and we cannot evade an either-or decision about the origins of perceptual experience. What makes this topic complicated is the relationship between self-awareness and development, which, simply put, falls under how to interpret the status of the "body schema," a concept we will address later in the discussion. With respect to body schema, opinions are split as to whether or not the body is an innate structure that is developed prior to birth. Gallagher (2005) and Zahavi (2008) are two notable proponents of this view that challenge Merleau-Ponty's position. What makes this ongoing debate philosophically significant is that the way in which one understands the body schema necessarily influences one's conceptualization of the self.

Rochat's contemporary account of perceptual development is in line with what Merleau-Ponty proposes. Perceptual attention is not directed at qualities or even well-defined objects (including people). The influence of Gestalt psychology on Merleau-Ponty is witnessed in his insistence that perception is structured. But perceptual structures are not simply relics of early life. They are constitutive of perceptual life itself, such that even mature perception does not exhaust phenomena in their entirety. The error of objective thought is the assumption that we perceive individual qualities and that objects may be empirically validated by enumerating its qualities. But qualities or *qualia* are not given to perception as atomistic sensations. Otherness is able to appear because we actively grasp things in the world according to general outlines or physiognomies. In order for something to appear, something must disappear, which is but one way to express the perceptual relationship between foreground and background. I do not need to perceive individual parts of a face (eyes, nose, ears, mouth) to understand that the person across the street is a friend. To separate the individual parts of the face into parts would destroy the relations that first made it possible to recognize the friend. What we grasp is neither the form nor content, but rather the relations of sense that express the whole prior to an artificial distinction between content and form. Perceptions cannot be adequately described as individual sense impressions or as objects delivered by a perceptual act, since perceptions can only belong to a field by virtue of being related to a background, against which perceiving is made possible. Merleau-Ponty uses the example of a white dot on a black background to illustrate that the dot is perceived only because of its relationship to the background. The meaningfulness of perception is not instantiated *after* an agent's act of perceiving. The black is perceived because of its relationship to the white. This perception is given in perceptual experience. One apprehends the significance bound up in this relation using the eye rather than the mind. The meaningfulness of the perception arises from the internally related figure-background relationship.

4.4 Putting the self in perspective

Phenomenology, for Merleau-Ponty, is not directed at knowledge of objects but rather knowledge of Being, that is, the nature of existence that makes objects possible. That we are always in contact with sense proves fundamental for Merleau-Ponty's account of selfhood. Because perception *qua* body is the *a priori* for sense, perception must be actively taken up as our own, or better, we are inexorably situated in a world that is not of our own making, which we nevertheless must make our own *because* we are situated. In between these two poles of necessity and contingency is the nebulous space that will give rise to the self, the locus of which is "grounded" by situated perspective.

Perceptual structures organize our perceptual field through sense. When the infant begins to perceive red, she establishes a general physiognomic structure of red – not as red in-itself – but in terms of physiognomic "distinctions, such as between 'warm' shades and 'cool' shades, or between 'colored' and 'non-colored'" (Merleau-Ponty 2012, 32). It is likewise the case that sensing is "directed to the physiognomic characteristics of the alluring and the frightening," (Straus 1963, 201), which underscore the global nature of perceptual experience. Perception is indicative of our communication with otherness (or the world), such that "we direct ourselves to the world and the world directs itself toward us" (Straus 1963, 201). Perceptual development is a dynamic – but ambiguous – relation that builds increasingly upon perceptual sense of the surrounding world: it is both passive and active. This ambiguous dynamic is what motivates Straus and Merleau-Ponty to characterize perception as a movement from the indeterminate to the determinate: "To experience the color, we must turn toward it, look at it, actively master it" (Straus 1966a, 15). Being 'situated-in-the-world' or 'finding-oneself-in-the-world' are variations of the same point: to be perceptually sensitive to the sensible world, as beings capable of affecting and being affected, of being committed to and committing to our situation. But if an infant's first perceptions are structured merely as inchoate or general outlines, in what way can we say they are situated?

If empirical or scientific descriptions attempt to explain perceptual experience by way of internal sensations, brain processes, or representations, perception itself is treated as a quantifiable object *in* the body. Merleau-Ponty's reply to this is that "*beneath* objective and detached knowledge of the body, there is this other knowledge that we have of it because it is always with us and because we are bodies" (ibid., 213, emphasis added). Here is an essential distinction that points to the ontological priority of situation; if the ideal end of objective thought is a description of the totality of natural phenomena – without concealed sides – it does so on the presumption that it is possible to suspend perspective. For instance, increasingly sophisticated brain imaging technologies ostensibly produce various representations of the brain that, when considered together, elicit a picture of the whole *partes extra partes* (e.g. 3D modelling, MRIs, fMRIs, etc.). The observer, who stands out over and above the object – in this case the brain – consequently takes the brain to be one entity among all entities of a world which thus becomes "an ontical concept, [which] signifies the totality of those entitles which can be present-at-hand [...] entities as 'belonging to the world', or 'within-in the world' [weltzugehöring oder innerweltlich]" (Heidegger 2008, 93). The problem for objective thought, as I indicated at the outset of this chapter, is presupposing the existence of the world, meaning that the object of study is not located in the world but is instead inserted into consciousness as content.

All activity of human life takes place against the backdrop of the world. We always experience from *somewhere*, and thus always perceive things in the world prespectivally. "As particular beings," writes Straus, "we live in perspective. Human existence has a perspectival character [...] it is not only an optical phenomenon" (1963, 322). The same sentiment is expressed by Merleau-Ponty: "for my window to impose on me a perspective on the church, my body must first impose on me a perspective on the world, and the former necessity can only be a purely physical one because the latter necessity is metaphysical" (2012, 93). The possibility of having a perspective is a condition of being situated in the world, an anchorage point that precedes conceptual knowledge and is instituted as perceptual experience of Being which stands out for us because it has *sense*. Merleau-Ponty's confidence in perspective is predicated on the nature of self, insofar as the phenomenal field is the originary opening onto the world as a pre-personal self (as a perspective), which "guarantees" that the personal self will actively be expressed by a perceiving body. As we move to the next section, we will further explore the pre-personal and personal distinction by looking at the way in which infants discover themselves in the world.

4.5 Becoming aware

Infant life is both a source of insight and vexation with respect to the nature of selfhood. Infants undoubtedly experience the world but are unable to convey the "what it is like" quality. The infant's initially limited capacity for unsupported movement restricts self-awareness or self-recognition. Consequently, the world of the child can appear baffling: incessant crying; inability to move from here to there; and a proclivity for erratic moods. Language and increasingly complex behavior will eventually bridge the communication gap to the other. However, even once achieved, the nature of experience for the young child is not yet like that of the adult:

> The perception of others and the intersubjective world are only problematic for adults. The child lives in a world that he believes is immediately accessible to everyone. He is unaware of himself and, for that matter, of others as private subjectivities (2012, 371).

Merleau-Ponty's point, that intersubjectivity is only a problem for adults, refers to the putative problem of "other minds." That we will never directly know what others think or feel is only a problem for objective thought. There are two ostensible consequences: first, the adult world is one in which subjects are bound by subjective experience that is impenetrable by others, and thus only permits inferential knowledge of others; second, in the absence of a theory of mind, a child cannot transcend themselves, and experience, devoid of reflection, is subsequently rendered blind adherence to desire and to impulse.

However, as we have repeatedly iterated, even in its most nascent state experience is not a passive reception of meaningless sensations. Contra the objective attitude, infants and children are not mere slaves to biological processes. Instead, they "simply reflect that they behav[e] directly on the basis of their sense-experience with no conception that sense-experience is something that one possesses" (Welsh 2013, 11). Put otherwise, conscious experience for infants and children manifests primarily at the level of operative-intentionality (non-thetic), where causal explanations of phenomena have yet to efface unreflective experience. Adults, on the other hand, possess the ability to reverse or shift experiential aspects, between thetic consciousness (reflective) and operative consciousness of world engagement. It is imperative that the ability to shift between reflective and pre-reflective attitudes is not to be mistaken for a cognitive achievement, since these perspectives are two sides of the same coin; the structure of intentional consciousness in everyday experience is characteristically directed toward the world and away from ourselves, which is another way to say that intentional consciousness is situational. The possibility of thetic consciousness itself is predicated on operative intentionality, which is the source of our foremost contact with the world through the body. Only when a situation breaks down or fails to achieve resolution are we turned back toward ourselves when thematizing (or isolating) a specific aspect of experience.

As Merleau-Ponty makes clear, the self cannot coincide with itself, preventing the possibility of fully disclosing the self to oneself with absolute clarity. On the contrary, the self is structured by an obverse relation that implies distance from oneself, a self that is initially unaware of itself "in its absolute difference. Consciousness of oneself as a unique individual, whose place can be taken by no one else, comes later and is not, primitive" (Merleau-Ponty 2010b, 119). Until the child differentiates herself from others, she is experientially indistinct from others. Having said this, self-recognition (and, or, awareness) is not an achievement of identifying *myself*. Even once a child has come to recognize her bodily boundaries, self-recognition is not obtained in the full sense; a perspective on oneself remains incomplete. The child perceives others and their behaviors without yet having perceived herself. The lack of self-perspective consequently assigns a substantial role to the specular image. Unlike adults who see themselves in the mirror, when the child first "encounters" herself in the mirror image, what takes place is not the comprehension that she is distinct from her parent (or other), rather the child recognizes that the parent is some*one* other than her, a self situated *there,* not here. To say "self-recognition," in some sense, is misleading, for we become aware not of ourselves but of ourselves as a perspective for others, and it is this conclusion that reveals to the child that she *has a perspective* on others.

4.5.1 Self-distinction and the minimal self

Until an unambiguous distinction between bodily boundaries and self-recognition is acquired, the infant does not discern between *mine* and *yours*. Bodily boundaries are the condition of experiencing perspective because the body anchors us to a place, which at the same time ensures that aspects of the world remain hidden from us. Without distinct corporeal boundaries, the child adopts the perspectives of others since she lacks her own:

> The perception of others cannot be accounted for if one begins by supposing an ego and another that are *absolutely* conscious of themselves, each of which lays claim, as a result, to an absolute originality in relation to the other that confronts it. On the contrary, the perception of others is made comprehensible if one supposes that psychogenesis begins in a state where the child is unaware of himself and the other as different beings. We cannot say that in such a state the child has a genuine communication with others. In order that there be a genuine communication, there must be a sharp distinction between the one who communicates and the one with whom he communicates. But there is initially a state of pre-communication (Max Scheler), wherein the other's intentions somehow play *across* my body while my intentions play across his (Merleau-Ponty 1964a, 118, emphasis original).

If, as Merleau-Ponty insists, early life is characterized by an indistinction between the infant and others, it follows that our relationship with others is not given to us immediately. Consequently, Merleau-Ponty contends that intersubjectivity *precedes* subjectivity, an ontological argument that is likewise espoused by Jan Patočka. (Strandberg 2018). What does this mean? Intersubjective life is not accomplished by a meeting of two wholly individuated subjects who then (somehow) traverse their respective boundaries of subjectivity. Genuine communication – and thus genuine intersubjectivity – emerges out of "syncretic sociability". We can compare this to the structure of a "zipper." Before achieving self-distinction from others, the infant is initially intertwined with others in the way the teeth of a zipper interlock when a jacket is zipped up. Unable to fully discriminate herself from others at first, the beginning and end of the infant's undeveloped bodily boundaries become further specified over time and cleave the subject-side of existence from the object-side, just as the teeth of a zipper pull away from one another when one pulls down on its tag. The child's initial experiences, then, are a "feel[ing] that he is in the other's body" (ibid., 134), and consequently, "cannot separate what *he* lives from what others live, as well as what he sees them living" (ibid., 135, emphasis original). This characterization of experience lacks *ipseity* or *mineness*. However, the claim is not that the infant does not experience; we are claiming instead that her experiences are undifferentiated from those of others.

By taking this position, that we initially do not distinguish ourselves from others, we must consequently reject the basic premises associated with the minimal self. When we considered the minimal self in Chapter 3, there were two crucial components: (i) infants are born with an already developed body schema, and (ii) they subsequently experience themselves as having stark bodily boundaries. Proponents of the minimal self, such as Zahavi, Gallagher, and Nessier, support their arguments by appealing to more recent studies in empirical psychology than those referred to by Merleau-Ponty. On this point, it must be acknowledged that aspects of Merleau-Ponty's essay "The Child's Relation with Others" draws on knowledge that has subsequently proven to be inaccurate. For instance, his claims about the myelinization process and the specific stages of infant development – which admittedly appear almost arbitrary – are incorrect. Having said this, the specific developmental timeline (in weeks and months) is not relevant to this particular discussion; when certain developmental phases occur is a secondary issue, what matters is simply that the phases do occur. More importantly though, consensus regarding the premises of the minimal self is not unanimous.

While it is true that there exists some affinity between Zahavi's minimal self and the account I am proposing here in this chapter, these two conceptions of self are fundamentally unique in their constitution. The minimal self, for instance, is an immanent phenomenon that is the basis for any and all experience. In other words, proponents of the minimal self argue that any type of experience is self-experience and that all experience begins with well demarcated boundaries between the self and other people. Consequently, since the minimal self is not developmental, the distinction between self and other is presupposed by intentional world experience. So, although I concur with its proponents that experience is always characterized by *someone* who experiences, my criticism of the minimal self model is that it is perhaps not minimal *enough*. That is, the sense of self ascribed to the minimal self is conceptually loaded. For instance, Rochat (2001, 44), like Zahavi, contends that empirical evidence supports the claim that infants distinguish self-touching from the touch of others. However, we must wonder if there is not a significant epistemic leap made in this interpretation. If an adult touches the infant with a finger, on what basis can we say that the infant *knows* she is being touched rather than the one touching? Such an achievement would require a fairly intact sense of agency, which is arguably incompatible with the infant's significantly underdeveloped capacity for self-movement – not to mention reflective awareness – at three months old.

With this in mind, I think Maclaren is right to argue that the differentiation between oneself and the other is "a relative sense of indeterminacy or ambiguity" (2008, 65) and that it is "an ongoing negotiation of boundaries, a process of *coming to make sense of* and thus *coming to master* the perceptual situation by gradually determining what it is that moves one, and thereby establishing oneself as an agent in relation to it" (ibid., 68, emphasis original). Part of this process includes perceptual differentiation between inanimate objects and humans. Maclaren herself also draws on empirical research to support the non-distinction argument, the most salient of which draw a distinction between an infant's perception of humans and inanimate things. This sensed difference between things and persons reinforces the notion that the development of the self is intersubjective:

> Confirmed by the other [through recognition], consolidated in her sense of herself as an embodied intentionality at grips with the world, the infant is able to experience a sense of agency or mastery, a beginning sense of self-

> possession or self-identity, that is not present initially in her encounter with an inanimate thing. Whereas the inanimate thing *tears her away from herself, dispossess her*, leaves her perplexed in the face of an alien being she cannot yet make good perceptual sense of, *the recognitive other returns her to herself.* This sense of mastery and relative self-possession is expressed in the smoothness and organization of her bodily movements, in the expressiveness and mobility of her face, and in the normalization of her heart rate, none of which are present in the face of the inanimate thing (Maclaren 2008, 86 emphasis added).

The infant's perception of inanimate things evokes heightened physiological and visibly disorganized behavior that, according to Maclaren, is not witnessed in the infant's perception of a person. With respect to the former, the "frustrated" ability to perceptually master an object – due to undeveloped motor skills and vision – also supports the phenomenological argument that our perceptions only become more determinate as we learn to "master" our situations. In the case of perceiving others, the physiological and behavioral equilibrium of the infant are indicative of Merleau-Ponty's claim that the infant "perceives his intentions in his body, perceives my body with his own, and thereby perceives my intentions in his body" (2012, 368). Recognized in the other is a certain conduct rather than a specific person, and it is the conduct of others that refer us back to our own intentional lives. And now that we have considered the role of intersubjectivity and development of self-awareness, we can put aside the discussion of the minimal self by further addressing the development of the self.

4.6 Becoming aware of the body

As we have suggested, a fundamental change in the child's relation with others occurs as the child discovers that she has her own body. Increased ability for self-movement and diminished reliance on bodily support (e.g. holding, carrying) from others is indicative of a fundamental intentionality that subtends conscious life in the world: *motor-intentionality.* Our relationship to the world, insofar as it is directed at something, is expressed through possibilities for action. This allows us to further characterize consciousness as *bodily*-consciousness, which is "originarily not an 'I think' that, but rather an 'I can'" (Merleau-Ponty 2012, 139). Put another way, bodily capacity to do things in the world is not a deliberative achievement, rather it is already a *doing* prior to reflecting on what is being done.

Motor-intentionality – which is to say embodied consciousness – is structured by two poles: body and world. Discovery of the bodily p0le is simultaneously the discovery of one's place in the world. Merleau-Ponty follows Lacan by identifying infant experience of the mirror image as a definitive phase of development:

> From this moment on, the child is also drawn from his immediate reality; the specular image has a de-realizing function in the sense that it turns the child away from what he affectively is, in order to orient himself toward what he sees and imagines himself to be (ibid., 137).

Recognizing the existence of others is not a secondary outcome due to self-recognition, but is instead the first realization that others have a perspective on us:

> [it is an] understanding that the image in the mirror is [*the child's*] image, that it is what others see of him, the appearance he presents to other subjects; and the synthesis is less a synthesis of intellection than it is a synthesis of coexistence with others (ibid., 140).

The recognition of body ownership in the specular image is not a "synthesis" of the body as seen and the body as experienced. It is a reckoning that *I* am one that is not *you*. This polarization is simultaneously the emergence of the child's concrete situation since "the other's look tells me, as does the image of the mirror, that I am *also* that being who is limited to a point in space" (ibid., 153, emphasis original). Initially, without body distinction, the child only identifies *her* situation; she *is* her situation. With time, as the child discovers that she has a perspective – because she is a perspective for others – she comes to know that she may be placed in different situations. The infant finds herself in a world by virtue of a body that anchors here to *some* place.

Until bodily boundaries become articulated, the child is not anchored to a perspective. Instead, the child's constellation is so many ways of living through others. Perspective, we noted earlier, is characterized by a body anchored to *some* place, and to have a perspective is to discover the possibility of being placed in different situations. Then again, a self does not magically materialize with the achievement of self-recognition. In a certain sense, the pre-personal self is older than the personal self that is destined to be a project of the world. What could we possibly mean by this? How can the self be older than itself? Let us, then, re-formulate: the self is expressed as a movement that is traced from a pre-personal self to a personal self.

In the most general sense, the relation between pre-personal and personal is one of both contingency and necessity. We are inexorably caught up in a world through perception, a sense-laden world that is not the result of a constituting consciousness. In its most primordial form, perception is initially structured as *one who perceives*: "Sensing gives us the world in perspective; it becomes, as it were, our own. Which is to say that in sensing, we have an environment, but not yet the world" (Straus 1963, 201). Personal perception, which is actively accomplished, is built upon pre-personal experience. The world prior to existence is the necessary term beyond our control; we are not authors of the world, rather we are ensnared in a cultural and historical world anterior to our existence. Being-in-the-world is constrained by this world, and yet it is not constrained absolutely. The constraints of the "necessary world" must nevertheless be lived according to contingent possibilities that give rise to the personal self: "personal existence is the taking up and the manifestation of a being in a given situation" (Merleau-Ponty 2012, 169). Existence is thus a project taken up and *personalized,* not because we are absolutely free to choose ourselves, but "because we are in the world, we are *condemned to sense*, and there is nothing we can do or say that does not acquire a name in history" (ibid., xxxiv). We see now why Merleau-Ponty's phenomenology is an *existential-phenomenology.* The dialectics of pre-personal and personal, sedimentation and spontaneity, or the determinate and indeterminate, are various ways of saying that existence is an inexhaustible project characterized by the passing from contingency to necessity:

> My personal existence must be the taking up of a pre-personal tradition. There is, then, another subject beneath me, for whom a world exists before I am there, and who marks out my place in that world. This captive or natural mind is my body, not the momentary body that is the instrument of my personal choices and that focuses upon some world, but rather the system of anonymous "functions" that wraps each particular focusing into a general project (ibid., 265).

Let us parse this difficult passage by considering the notion of the pre-personal, since we have yet to fully specify its relevance. Pre-personal signifies our basic perceptual contact with Being, which can be neither renounced nor chosen. It is a tradition insofar as the sense of Being precedes us and will (presumably) pass into history after us. The pre-personal level of experience precedes our capacity for reflection, which is traditionally the hallmark of subjectivity. Moreover, in contrast to reflective subjectivity (or thetic consciousness), pre-personal experience is the guarantee for reflective subjectivity, or as Merleau-Ponty says, reflective consciousness attempts to recover the unreflective. That there exists "another subject *beneath* me" is not the body-subject or personal self characterized as a project of the world; this subject is an "anonymous self," the perceiving being who with time specifies more elaborate perceptual structures that permit things to appear from the indeterminate to the determinate. In short, "if one perceives with his body, the body is a natural self, as it were, the body is the subject of perception" (ibid., 213). The anonymous or pre-personal self is the body through which the sense of the world moves through because we are perceptually sensitive beings.

Note that the passage in question concludes with a crucial qualification. How is the pre-personal or anonymous self "started over at each moment"? Earlier in the chapter I claimed that our first perception sediments a perceptual level upon which all future perceptual experience refers to:

> With the first vision, the first contact, the first pleasure, there is initiation, that is, not the positing of a content, but the opening of a dimension that can never be closed again, the establishment of a level in terms of which every other experience will henceforth be situated (Merleau-Ponty 1968, 151).

The body's sensory regions (vision, touch, sound, etc.) actively – but non-thetically – structure behavior, insofar we *use* our eyes, ears, and hands, as a certain expressive style of meeting the world. By style we mean something akin to personality, but devoid of psychological concepts and content. Style is not specific in the way behavioral traits are classified in behavioral science. It is a entire manner of comporting ourselves toward the world that affects us according to the perceptual significance of things, soliciting our sensitive bodies for certain actions: "Sensing is, therefore, a sympathetic experiencing. It is directed to the physiognomic characteristics [, for example] of the alluring and the frightening" (Straus 1963, 201). The significance of a book is not realized in its individual chapters but through its totality. Nor is it a matter of parts constituting the whole. The first chapter is not merely a passage to the second. A novel unfolds as a trajectory, the style of which cannot be explicitly specified. An individual chapter reaches across the totality that is the book. Similarly, I come to know and recognize people by their style, not as individual features, but in their entire manner of comporting themselves. From my office I am able to recognize colleagues in the corridor by the sound of their footfalls; I recognize a friend at a distance according to a perceptual physiognomy that is general yet recognized in its particularity. But style cannot be decomposed. I can no more specify the writing style of Virginia Woolf than I can specify the bodily style of a close friend.

It may be objected that individuals are physiologically or physically pre-disposed to a diverse range of personality or character traits. But the burden of proof remains with the objection to explain how pre-disposition *determines* behavior. Without a particular milieu or situation, what would elicit putative pre-disposed behaviors? Behavior manifests as responses to situational demands. It is important here to appreciate that situations are *affective*, to move or be moved by something, which is but another way to say that behavior is indicative of situational significance. Thus, on the one hand, certain dispositions – in principle – would remain latent in the absence of necessary and sufficient conditions. On the other, what makes the characterization of expressive behavior as a style an attractive way to understand selfhood is that it is developmental, particularly that it is a manner of dealing with the world that cannot be anticipated in advance. To state that someone is pre-disposed to anger, shyness, or other types of traits, presupposes that such traits are pre-ordained with meaning independent of a situation.

4.6.1 Pre-personal becomes personal: Self and body schema

Thus far I have sketched a picture of perception that is fairly abstract. To recapitulate, perception reveals our fundamental contact with existence through a developmental process that involves acquisition of perceptual structures, permitting things to appear. Arguing that we are not mere receptacles that are passively bombarded with sensations, perception has instead been characterized as an active trait of existence. In order for things in the world to have sense, a foreground-background structuration of the perceptual field is organized according to the significance determined by our perceptual structures (e.g. why one thing stands out over another). That things are significant to us is tied to our situatedness. Because I can perceive and have a perspective that necessarily orients me toward the world, there is always a "perceptual something." This perceptual something is initially indeterminate or limited by our underdeveloped perceptual capacities. I noted that there is an impersonal (or pre-personal) aspect to perception that is the basis for the "personal self", the active project of subjective life.

Having hinted that there is a relationship between perceptual style and the personal self, this section threads together this connection more concretely by illuminating the essential role of embodiment.

Recall from Chapter 3 that the main characteristic of Zahavi's minimal self is that it is experientially pre-reflective. The emergence of a higher-order expression of selfhood (i.e. representational, narrative, conceptual, etc.) depends on the first-order or "non-intellectual" experience of self. The minimal self is modelled on – though not entirely – Merleau-Ponty's well-known account of "the body schema," which highlights an overlap with the portrait of selfhood being sketched in this chapter.

In order to make sense of pre-reflective experience it is imperative that we understand why motor-intentionality and corporeality are essential to a notion of self that is internally related to perception. The body schema is not grasped in thematic experience: "a subject who is absorbed in the act of reading is not explicitly conscious of the body's adjustments, which may include squinting and moving closer to the text" (Gallagher 2005, 139). The body schema reveals our relationship to the world as a "posture toward a certain task, actual, or possible [...] it is a *situational spatiality*" (Merleau-Ponty 2012, 102, emphasis added), making it possible to "forget" ourselves in our everyday dealings with the world. My body cannot be the object of my experience if world-directed action is to be possible. For this reason, the body schema is "not merely an experience of my body, but rather an experience of my body in the world" (ibid.), which is the ultimate precondition for something we call the self.

The body schema expresses a certain manner or style of meeting things in the world. On the one hand, our bodies are determinate, insofar as we do not choose them or create them, fleshy masses that impose practical and physical limits due to anatomical and biological structures. On the other hand, our abilities and capacities for action develop and may be refined. As we learn to perceive the world, we simultaneously begin to comport ourselves according to the things perceived. The body becomes a point around which the world coalesces. The practical significance of the world saturates perception; objects are experienced as near, far, graspable, climbable, and so on. Perception and motor-intentionality define subjective life as a project of the world, a project that is never fully complete, but is nonetheless always the horizon of our life.

The continuity of this "project" is achieved through perceptual habit. Habits permit us the possibility of dealing with situations (and the world as such) by retaining non-conceptual knowledge that develops out of our earliest contact with the world:

> Situations are mastered (though never finally) through a process of articulation and patterning which at one and the same time is the formulation of actions and of dispositions. These creative situations are then retained as sedimented structures which are repeatedly actualized whenever they are appropriate to the present setting (Mallin 1979, 16).

Habits, broadly construed, are practiced or repeated acts that we enact without having to mentally represent them (that is, consciously to think about them). Since bodies are developmental, we become sensitive to, and at ease with, situations and the corresponding affective solicitation that a given scenario elicits. As adults we have grasped the ways in which certain entities or situations in the world are manipulated or engaged with on account of having incorporated them non-cognitively into our body as habits. Our capacity to cope with situations begins with our initial (perceptual) contact with the world and is further articulated through our embodied world experience. Our general awareness of, and readiness for, a situation is shaped by bodily knowledge from past experiences that remain deployable in the present and future.

Habits at the same time express a dialectical movement from prepersonal to personal, from indeterminate to determinate: "The acquisition of a habit," says Straus, "is a transition from less to more determinate behaviour [...] *we* are a kind of plastic material which itself is modified in the process of habit formation" (1963, 193, emphasis original). Because perception is an active – but non-thetic – accomplishment of the self, our earliest perceptions in infancy gradually develop the way in which we perceptually contact the world, as personalized or stylized perceptual habits.

Consequently, our perceptual contact with the world means that the self is an instituted project of existence, such that its transformation both preserves itself and surpasses itself (Merleau-Ponty 2010c). Hence, through "the first vision, the first contact, the first pleasure, there is initiation, that is, not the positing of a content, but the opening of a dimension that can never again be closed, the establishment of a level in terms of which every other experience will henceforth be situated" (Merleau-Ponty 1968, 151). The way in which my body establishes contacts with the world is an ongoing reorganization of the body schema, an unending establishment of perceptual scaffolding that expresses the self as body and by the body.

4.7 Ambiguity of the self

At this point, we have explored some fundamental aspects of a phenomenological or ontologically inspired self. We are now in a position to say that selfhood is the development of a certain style or manner that is expressed through bodily habit. A problem with this characterization is that it eschews the paradigm of the self that is predicated on reason, where self-knowledge and well-delineated "boundaries" are indispensable to the constitution of selfhood. For instance, the narrative self and the Lockean self, discussed in Chapter 3, are presumed to be circumscribed by explicit self-referencing. In the case of the former, the self is something I convey to others according to *who* I believe myself to be; I refer to my goals, desires, beliefs, even habits, which come to define the story of who I am. In the case of the latter, who I am is expressed through the continuity of my life history; my memories and past experiences permit me to refer to previous times, which accordingly confirm that it is *me* who existed then and who continues to exist now. These two accounts of the self entail a substantial sense of self-determination or self-identification, a sense that we knowingly decide who or what we are.

By contrast, the description I have offered of the self as a bodily-style ultimately calls into question the extent to which it is possible for us to articulate the selves that we are. Note that I am not suggesting that we lack experience of self-sameness over time. On the contrary, I am arguing that this experience of self is one of which we are intimately aware, yet at the same time eludes articulation: "My identity, then, is a way of having a world, and, accordingly, it is an identity that 'I' do not primarily possess; it is thrust throughout my world – in my way of interacting with things about me" (Jacobson 2015, 35). As Kirsten Jacobson indicates, full possession of myself would mean that my body's operative-intentional grasp on the world would be effaced. The self is a style by virtue of our body schema through which we are perceptually geared into the world of sense. Mazis shares Jacobson's sentiment, saying that "the self, then, is not something we possess or that appears with clarity, but in its enmeshment with the world is difficult to discern" (2015, 50). Hence, selfhood is structured by an ambiguity. We are anchored by our body to some place *here* and yet are oriented toward some place over there.

For this reason, Merleau-Ponty goes on to say that "if we are situated, then we are surrounded and cannot be transparent to ourselves, and thus our contact with ourselves must only be accomplished in ambiguity" (2012,

401). Since the operative intentional structure of the body schema is enmeshed with a perceptual field (or transcendental, for Husserl), the sense (*sens*) of the world inexorably solicits our attention away from *here* to *there*.[47] Selfhood is punctuated by an obverse relation that precludes self-coincidence, which is why Merleau-Ponty contends that contact with ourselves may only be achieved in ambiguity. This ambiguity may be expressed in various ways. A classic example employed in the phenomenological tradition is the phenomenon of touch: "the impressions of touching, and of being-touched," says Straus, "can most easily be exchanged with one another. Every touching is also a being touched" (1982, 59). In Merleau-Ponty's later philosophy he characterizes the touching-touched relationship in countless ways, one of which is that "it would be better to say that the body sensed and the body sentient are as the obverse and the reverse, or again, as two segments of one sole singular course [...]" (1968, 138). To illustrate more concretely, the relationship between self (or the body) and world is comparable to a piece of paper, one side marked with an X, the other marked with a Y. The two sides comprise one inseparable entity, yet to see side X precludes seeing side Y, and vice versa.

The same metaphor, when applied to the self as an expressive style, represents bodily habits as one side of the paper and situations as the other side. Put in phenomenological terms, the self meets the world with given (determinate) capacities, as well as sedimented habits, yet remains capable of spontaneous (indeterminate) action that permits the creation of new habits. Hence, the self is ultimately the "double movement of sedimentation and spontaneity" (Merleau-Ponty 2012, 132). A key point to highlight is that changes to the body schema can alter thetic consciousness. This will have implications for the analysis of depression in Chapter 5, with particular relevance for the relationship between strong feelings and the altered existential dimension of *depth* that structures our action in the world. We will pay close attention to the relationship between depth, self, and depression, in the next chapter. In anticipation of this discussion, it is worth noting that the style of self may very well include altered modes of inhabiting space through the dimensions of motility, perception, affectivity or temporality

---

[47] I have included the French *sens*, whose double meaning has been extensively noted in the literature, to emphasize that sense (for Merleau-Ponty) indicates *meaning* but also *direction* (or towardness).

> changes or distortions introduced at the level of the prenoetic body or body schema result in changes or distortions in perceptual consciousness or motor behaviour. But this simply reflects the general rule. In all cases, prenoetic performances of the body schema influence intentionality. They operate as constraining and enabling factors that limit and define the possibilities of intentional consciousness (Gallagher 2005, 146).

This passage illustrates that the body schema, as the sedimented source of self-style, is an intertwining of the pre-personal and personal dimensions of self-experience, which may constrict or dilate the way in which the self is expressed.

Before we reflect further on the phenomenology of depression, it is imperative that we briefly address the relationship between self and time. There are minimally two reasons for addressing the temporal nature of selfhood. First, the "double movement" between sedimentation and spontaneity is itself temporal. The establishment of habits is subtended by the horizons of situations. Self is the locus around which the past (determinate) and future possibilities (indeterminate) coalesce. Many phenomenological accounts of depression emphasize how patients describe anomalous experiences of temporality, and thus it is necessary that we make some cursory remarks on selfhood and time. Second, as Merleau-Ponty sees it, "we must recognize a sort of sedimentation of our life: when an attitude toward the world has been confirmed often enough, it becomes privileged for us" (2012, 466). Accordingly, he goes on to say that, "so long as we are alive, our situation is open, which implies both that it *calls forth privileged modes of resolution* and that it, by itself, lacks the power to procure any of them" (ibid., 467, emphasis added). Hence, the self is stylized in direct relation to the way in which situations are engaged with over the course of our lives. The account of selfhood that I have outlined here will enable us to consider depression beyond psychological and biological explanatory frameworks whose historical influence on psychiatric practice was outlined in Chapter 1. I will consider a third way to approach depression by employing a phenomenological framework to describe depression in terms of *style*.

4.8 Self-as-a-style and time

Using the philosophy of Merleau-Ponty and shared insights from Straus, I have proposed a notion of self that is embodied, perceptual, and habitual. From Merleau-Ponty's perspective these three characteristics are perhaps redundant since each one is reducible to the other. Gathering these themes under one succinct description has led us to the point where we can argue that the self is more accurately described as an expressive style. That is, the *self-as-a-style*. However, until now we have not considered the way in which the body, perception, and habit, dovetail together to elicit a style. This connection is to be attributed to temporality.

Merleau-Ponty's discussion of time is somewhat challenging and lengthy, which means we must limit ourselves to a primitive sketch. True to the phenomenological tradition (e.g. Husserl, Heidegger), Merleau-Ponty eschews an objective notion of time (or "clock" time).[48] "Time," he writes, "must not merely be, it must come into being" (2012, 438). In other words, time is not independent of consciousness or subjectivity: "there must be another time, a true time, where I learn what passage or transition is in itself [...] not an object of knowledge, but rather a dimension of our being" (ibid., 438). I emphasized earlier that the body schema is the locus of sedimented bodily habits. This is also but one way to say that our body schema is sensitive to the world according to capacities for action: "I reckon with what is around me, I depend on my tools, and I am caught up in my task rather than standing before it" (ibid., 439). The body schema does not stand before its task because it usurps representational action. Rather, what is or is not possible in a given situation is understood anterior to any intellectual deliberation, given that "my world is carried along by intentional lines that trace out in advance at least the style of what is about to arrive" (ibid.). Here Merleau-Ponty is alluding to Husserl's "protention" and "retention" structure that constitutes temporal horizons, that is, the relationship between our past and our future subtending the present. Based on this notion of time, the present is not isolated from the past or the future, but rather the present (and subjectivity) "entails" both past and future.

The notion of time as a present that carries both past and future is what permits Merleau-Ponty to characterize existence as the double movement between sedimentation and spontaneity. There is an obvious tension

---

[48] Kelly (2015) argues that Merleau-Ponty's "Temporality" chapter in the *Phenomenology of Perception* anticipates his later ontology. But he also suggests that while Merleau-Ponty initially follows Husserl's intrinsic self-awareness theory, the account of temporality moves toward adopting Heidegger's immanentist theory of self-awareness. The nuances of this discussion lay outside the purview of this chapter. However, to avoid confusion or perceived inconsistencies in Merleau-Ponty's language, I want to make clear that only a close reading of the chapter will make it possible to fully discern the nuanced linguistic differences applied by Merleau-Ponty. The task here in this chapter is, as far as this is possible, to provide a general outline of the role played by temporality in selfhood.

between these two poles: on the one hand, sedimentation prefigures and structures the future possibilities of the self. On the other hand, future possibilities always remain open to reorganization. Sedimented perceptual habits of the self are the past retained in the present, but they also aim us toward the future:

A past and a future spring forth when I reach out toward them. I am not, for

> myself, directed toward the present time; I am just as much directed toward this morning or toward the night that is about to arrive, and although my present is surely this present instant, it is also just as much today, this year, or even my entire life (Merleau-Ponty 2012, 444).

If our days or lives often conform to our anticipations of what is to come, it is because operative intentionality is both prospective and retrospective. More simply, embodied perception is not only directed to something, it pre-reflectively prepares the body for the perception that is to come. Through the body schema, the self is able to deal with similar situations by calling forth sedimented capacities in response to the demands of the situation. Crucially, however, habits are not mechanisms or reflexes, insofar as the self is capable of not only establishing new habits, but of reorganizing and incorporating sense into new habitual structures via spontaneous behavior: "the body, then, has understood and the habit has been acquired when the body allows itself to be penetrated by a new signification, when it has assimilate a new meaningful core" (Merleau-Ponty 2012, 148). The relation between understanding and signification is tied to meaning (or sense). The former is achieved when an intention is fulfilled, and the latter is the establishment of new sense. In other words, new possibilities emerge for the self once the body has incorporated a new habit.

Our final word on the self and time concerns expressive style and change. I have emphasized that there is a plasticity to selfhood, such that "thanks to time, [I have] an interlocking and a taking up of previous experiences in later experiences, but I never have an absolute possession of myself by myself, since the hollow of the future is always filled by a new present" (ibid., 250). Self, as a style, though it is not fixed, must nevertheless retain an enduring trace of recognition, since style, by definition, is implicitly recognizable according to a *generalized* physiognomy. In this way, the self reflects an existential project, the values of which are subtly articulated as perceptual values in the form of *sense* or *meaning*. I want to briefly draw attention back to Ricoeur's narrative self, which I outlined in the previous chapter, since the description of self I have provided thus far shares a certain fidelity with that proposed by Ricoeur. Like Merleau-Ponty, Ricoeur employs habits as a fundamental component of the self. To overcome the problem of *idem* and *ipseity* over time, Ricoeur contends that the temporal nature of selfhood is attributed to habits, which "gives history to character, but this is a history in which sedimentation tends to cover over the innovation which preceded it" (1992, 121). Character, as conceived by Ricoeur, is precisely what Merleau-Ponty characterizes as the double movement between sedimentation and spontaneity; a determinate set of capacities that may be deformed or re-specified as habits in accordance with intentional experience. For Ricoeur, the self is temporal insofar as habits are dispositions or traits that are stabilized as *character*. Hence what I have described as *style* is what Ricoeur identifies as character. But for Ricoeur (borrowing from Aristotle) character is also the habituation of moral dispositions. By belonging to a community, character is also acquired through the internalization of ideals, values, norms, and so on. In this way, selfhood is predicated on a quasi-commitment, what Ricoeur calls *self-constancy* or "keeping one's word" (1992, 123).[49] Consequently, Ricoeur's eventual positing of the self as narrative is a transition toward language.

It may seem curious that little has been said about the relationship between self-as-a-style and language. On the one hand, the complexity of Merleau-Ponty's philosophy of language and speech demands a protracted discussion that is beyond the purview of this investigation. On the other hand, we have remained taciturn since the notion of self-as-a-style does not ascribe primacy to the domain of language in the way that is necessary for the narrative self. That Merleau-Ponty says little – if anything – about narrative is, *in part*, owing to the simple the fact that narrative theories of identity have only become rather fashionable during the last quarter of the twentieth century. One could even argue that Ricoeur's introduction of narrative rectifies a lacuna in Merleau-Ponty's work regarding selfhood. While there may be a kernel of merit to this claim, I want to suggest that had Merleau-Ponty been alive during narrative "turn," he would not have assigned absolute priority to narrativity. Similarly, I think one should be cautious about attributing narrative to Merleau-Ponty's notion of self when

[49] A similar line of thought can be found in Judith Butler's (2001) work where she employs the phrase 'giving an account of oneself.'

there is no evidence to support such an attribution.[50] But if self-as-a-style does not correspond to the narrative self, we need to specify why the latter is not ultimately an elaboration of the former, as well as why little emphasis has been placed on self-as-a-style and speech.

Until now I have characterized self-as-a-style almost exclusively in terms of perception and embodiment. Merleau-Ponty wants to outline a notion of self that does not begin from the primacy of cognition. Cognition and language are indeed one region of embodied life, but it has no priority over other regions, which are the regions of perception, affectivity, and motility. Self-as-a-style directly opposes *reflective* theories of the self by recovering the pre-reflective aspect of existence. Narrative selfhood requires speech, which for some theorists, likewise necessitates reflective deliberation about who or what one is. Of course, the self-as-a-style regularly employs speech, yet Merleau-Ponty is concerned with the way in which expressive behavior is tied to our most primary contact with the world. Like all perception, speech is but one way to express the relation between self and world. But speech is tied to perception, which is to say the body, and accordingly first belongs to the realm of gestures rather than reflection:

> When I know [a word], it is not an object that I recognize through a synthesis of identification, it is a certain use of my phonatory apparatus and a certain modulation of my body as being in the world; its generality is not the generality of an idea, but rather that of a *style of behaviour* that my body 'understands' insofar as my body is a power of producing behaviours [...] The word has never been inspected, analysed, known, and constituted, but rather caught and taken up by a speaking power, and ultimately, by *a motor power that is given to me along with the very first experience of my body* and of its perceptual and practical fields. As for the sense of the word, I learn it just as I learn the use of a tool – by seeing it *employed in the context of a certain situation* (Merleau-Ponty 2012, 425, emphasis added).

Speech is expressive behavior that germinates out of pre-personal contact with the world. Our capacity for language is but *one* way of "taking up" the world, but it is not isolated from the bodily specification of the perceptual world. As Merleau-Ponty suggests, speech coalesces around perceptual signification revealed by and through the demands placed on us by our

---

[50] For instance, Antich (2018) argues that Merleau-Ponty's distinction between pre-personal and personal life permits one to characterize the self as narrative. Even though his account is not uninteresting, he nevertheless ascribes a role to narrative in selfhood that Merleau-Ponty simply does not make explicit.

situation. Because speech is gestural, it too is an expressive behavior that is not limited to the content of propositions. In addition to speech content, the aural "quality" of speaking is conveyed by aspects such as facial expressions, movements of the body, intonation, and volume. Hence, self-narration will always express more than we *say*. So, if we do not hold that self-as-a-style is narrative, how is it possible to retain a communicable sense of a cohesive life?

One appeal of the narrative self is that it is expressly temporal. Who I am now simultaneously reflects the history that has brought me to the present, as well as the possible future. But the self-as-a-style satisfies the temporal dimension of selfhood by carrying the past forward through sedimented habits rather than in the form of a narrative. What permits the communicability of self-as-a-style without any reliance on an explicit narrative is Merleau-Ponty's notion of *institution*.[51] In order to extricate himself from the traditional strictures of consciousness discourse, Merleau-Ponty's "mature" philosophy of ontology turns away from the Husserlian constituting consciousness by supplanting it with instituting consciousness.[52] For the sake of clarity, the sense of institution – at least for our immediate purposes in this chapter – is not a physical institute (e.g. the institute for Urban research).[53] For Merleau-Ponty, the solution was to articulate consciousness as a pre-reflective (or non-conscious) productive organization of the sense-laden world, a perceptual organization that is established according situational "values," that is, the way in which things are experienced as being significant in a given situation. Over time, such values engender an inertia of preferential embodied behaviors that "initia[te] a present, which is productive after it" (Merleau-Ponty 2010c, 6). This is in line with our previous characterization of the self as a movement from determinate to indeterminate, a stabilizing prolongation of "who we are" that carries the past forward to the present, and toward an open future.

Institution thus has the character of an existential project. Importantly, though, it is

—

[51] Institution is the English rendering of the German word *Stiftung* employed by Husserl, and appropriated by Merleau-Ponty (1973, 68).

[52] Constituting consciousness is the process of consciousness that builds up, and makes possible, the presentation of objects to consciousness.

[53] Merleau-Ponty's analysis exploits the various senses associated with institution. On the one hand, he is indeed interested in institution as a community (e.g. institution of psychiatry), under which physical institutions that house communities are also subsumed. However, I am focusing on Merleau-Ponty's treatment of human institution, which is characteristically productive or active in nature.

> a non-decisionary project, not chosen, [an] intention without a subject: living. The project [implies the] existence of norms or levels, uncrossable mountain, upright objects or not, paths. This does not mean that what I am doing is determined: I can learn to cross these "obstacles" or not. But it is on the basis of the given obstacle that I will learn. I can learn to know the surroundings better through science, but this will always be the re-working of the perceived world, the employment of its structures (Merleau-Ponty 2010c, 6).

There are several points to draw out here. Earlier in the chapter I drew attention to the way in which infants learn to distinguish themselves from others by learning bodily boundaries. Prior to this distinction, the infant is a-subjective, she has yet to be situated, the condition for perceptual articulation of self and world. Once situated, our perceptual contact with the world, which is initially generalized, develops into clearer and better articulated structures according to the situations we encounter. Importantly, the later development of reflective thought or "scientific" thinking, as Merleau-Ponty notes, will become available to the personalized self, but only by virtue of a reorganization of our initial perceptual contact upon which reflective life is made possible.

To say that the self-as-a-style is synonymous with the narrative self would belie the significance of operative intentionality that underscores human life. As soon as we attempt to present ourselves with words we simultaneously slip away from ourselves: "When I am actually speaking I do not first *figure* the *movements* involved. My whole bodily system concentrates on finding and saying the word… furthermore, it is not even the word or phrase that I have in mind but the person" (Merleau-Ponty 1973, 19, emphasis original). Since we always find ourselves situated, the body is "saturated" with motor-significations motivated by otherness. That is, the significance of a situation affects our comportment toward the world and toward intersubjective life. Communication with others is not achieved solely through propositional meaning. In fact, even if one prepares in advance what one intends to express, our speech will ultimately create and convey thoughts successfully if we find the proper expressive manner that will "gear" into our listener.

By substituting institution for narrative, the intention is to underscore that linguistic meaning is accorded neither primacy nor priority. Even a comprehensive list of traits, qualities, or thoughts, could not account for the way in which the nuances of practical and non-conceptual experience shape the self. Rather than looking for specific qualities or traits, selfhood is expressed in a general way: as an outline or silhouette, such that the self is recognized, not as a sum total of its parts, but instead as that which transcends simple qualities in favour of a global (indeterminate) whole. In the same way that we recognize a face without having to explicitly identify its individual features, self-as-a-style expresses a cohesive yet generalized outline that we can recognize according to the way in which self-as-style is *done;* that is, self-as-style is accomplished in and through world-oriented and embodied action.

Hence, the function of narrative, which is to convey a broad story about who we are, only captures an aspect of the embodied and practical totality expressed by selfhood. When I claim that self-as-a-style institutes (rather than narrates), I am drawing attention to the dynamic tension between sedimentation and spontaneity, an ambiguous tension that represents the double movement of situated life. Put otherwise, the self is a phenomenon that is simultaneously determinate yet inexhaustibly indeterminate. Characterizing self-as-style in this way underscores that selfhood is a phenomenon the promise of which is always *en-route*; it is an emergent expression of the intersection between personal life and pre-personal life that entails "those events in an experience which endow the experience with durable dimensions, in relation to which a whole set of series of other experiences will make sense [...] events which deposit a sense in me [...] as the call to follow, the demand of a future" (Merleau-Ponty 2010c, 77). Selfhood, as I have characterized it, reflects both our past and future, such that the former is prolonged in the latter. In other words, the sense or meaning established by the body with the world carries forward into the open future.

But sense and meaning are not fixed, as evidenced by our ability to adopt new habits or skills. Sense may be reorganized according to our situations. New parents, for example, may find that their home takes on the sense of danger when it was previously a source of comfort. Electrical outlets, stairs, and sharp edges, the significance of which had hitherto proven to be innocuous, take on new significance as potential sources of danger to their infant. But what if it is not just the house, but the entire world that becomes a source of danger or threat? To a certain degree, we can acknowledge that the world is indeed threatening or dangerous. However, for many people, only some aspects of the threat stand out as significant, enabling them to live what we might call a "care-free" life. Meaning or sense associated with our sedimented lives may be re-organized by virtue of our open future. The way in which we find ourselves in the world cannot be determined or planned by virtue of how we want it to appear. The same applies to the way in which we establish our self-as-a-style that expresses our relationship to the world: "in this exchange between the situation and the one who takes it up, it is impossible to determine the 'contribution of the situation' and the 'contribution of freedom'" (Merleau-Ponty 2012, 480). Consequently, if depression affects the self, how should we understand this dynamic between situation and spontaneity?

On the one hand, I have already suggested it is dubious to assume that depression is causally reducible to *biological* dysfunction. Conversely, I have likewise challenged the logic that depression is causally attributable to *psychological* mechanisms, the history of which I explored in considerable detail during Chapter 1. The outcome, the reader will recall, left us with a less than desirable causal dichotomy: is depression determined by the laws of biological nature? Or is depression an outcome of adopted cognitive attitudes concerning the world? In order to extract ourselves from this dilemma, we need to consider depression within the framework of lived-experience, which means a framework that will enable us to describe depression according to the way in which the self establishes a relation to the world. As I have reiterated throughout this investigation, neither biological nor psychological explanations of depression are exhaustive of the ontological aspects of selfhood considered here in this chapter. To properly grasp depression beyond simple signs and symptoms of the DSM-5, the task of the next chapter is to reconsider the implications of depression within a context of situatedness and selfhood.

4.9 Conclusion

At the outset of this chapter we were already acquainted with several contemporary notions of selfhood. My intention was to introduce an account of the self that contained aspects of contemporary approaches while going beyond each one of them in isolation. By drawing on Merleau-Ponty's existential phenomenology, along with insights from Straus' phenomenological psychiatry, I emphasized the central role played by perception in the development of selfhood. Drawing on Merleau-Ponty's ontology of situation, I argued that perception is bodily, and therefore situated. Accordingly, selfhood was described as a developmental phenomenon, the origins of which are a-subjective. An infant discovers that her bodily boundaries distinguish her from others insofar as the body is anchored to a perspective, which in turn permits others to have a perspective on her.

In addition to learning bodily boundaries, infants actively articulate perceptual structures that permit otherness (or the world) to appear. The structuration of perception is established according to the sense (or meaningfulness) of the world. What counts as perceptually significant for the infant is revealed through the practical demands of her situation. Accordingly, the "mature" self acquires bodily habits that endow her with various capacities for intentional action without invoking representational maps for decision-making. By highlighting the perceptual development of the self, I have further illustrated how perception actively "takes up" the world as an original motor-intentionality, the uniqueness of which is expressed as a perceptual style. This led us to propose a notion of self that is not tethered to material or psychological explanations by characterizing selfhood as a style: expressive behavior that is readily recognizable yet simultaneously resistant to propositional knowledge.

A central characteristic of the self-as-a-style is that its cohesion is ambiguous; it is both determinate and indeterminate, what Merleau-Ponty calls a double movement between sedimentation and spontaneity. This ambiguity reveals the development of selfhood from pre-personal to personal life. Hence, temporality is an essential component of self-as-a-style, since it preserves itself (its style) over time by carrying forward past habits and yet is always turned toward an open future wherein habits (or motor-significations) may be deformed or established through a reorganization of sense. For this reason, we spent time distinguishing self-as-a-style from the narrative self, since the latter makes sense of the self-totality *via* stories, while the totality of the former is concretely manifested through the body and proves to be rather resistant to linguistic expression.

Even though we now have a grasp of the self-as-a-style, we have yet to consider the potential implications that depression poses for selfhood. I have stressed that psychiatric illnesses like depression are not detached from intentional life. Even though somatic illnesses, like chronic pain syndrome, can invade the entirety of a person's life, they often begin from a particular bodily location. Depression, on the other hand, is experienced as being everywhere and nowhere, that is, as something uncanny – completely alien yet familiar. In the next chapter our aim will be to describe the phenomenological implications of depression from the perspective of the self-as-a-style, by addressing the relationship between self, space, and our grip on the world.

CHAPTER 5

Depression *in-depth:* Self-style and lived-space in depressed experience

5. Introduction

In order to offer a rich phenomenological analysis of depression it was incumbent upon us first to situate depression in its historical context (Chapter 1). From there we considered the way in which selfhood is conceptually operative in clinical practice (Chapter 2). The next step of our inquiry was to make sense of the contemporary theoretical landscape of selfhood (Chapter 3), a task that then permitted us to establish a phenomenological account of the self (Chapter 4) using the notion of self-as-a-style. The underlying goal of the preceding chapters has been to illustrate that medical knowledge alone cannot exhaust our understanding of depression, particularly if depression is a disorder of the self. Assuming that the latter is correct, it follows that selfhood is by no means an esoteric theme that is restricted to philosophy. Even though psychiatric medicine is not explicitly invested in the nature of selfhood, I argued in Chapter 2 that the ostensible absence of an explicit theoretical stance regarding the self in psychiatry in no way precludes individual clinicians from having implicit conceptual commitments about selfhood. Hence, one conclusion to be drawn from this investigation is that, even if psychiatry is (theoretically) silent regarding the phenomenon of selfhood, it does not follow that selfhood is silent in psychiatry; the qualitative study presented in Chapter 2 made it clear that the concept of self circulates within psychiatry through the attitudes of individual clinicians.

The task in this chapter is twofold. The first task is to assess several of the recent influential phenomenological investigations of depression. I argue that phenomenological accounts of depression are all but unanimous in characterizing depression as an affective change to one's relationship with the world. I will show that, even though these influential approaches to depression tend to draw similar conclusions about the nature of depression as I do, none of these approaches account for the way in which depression is manifested via selfhood.[54]

The second task in this penultimate chapter is dedicated to a phenomenological analysis of depression, one that incorporates the notion of self that I sketched in Chapter 4. I will likewise continue to draw from the philosophy of Merleau-Ponty, with which we also familiarized ourselves during the same chapter. What makes my phenomenological investigation of depression distinct from those we will consider in this chapter is that I trace essential structures of depressed experience through spatial experience, specifically, existential-space. Drawing on Merleau-Ponty's phenomenological description of lived-space, I posit that depression is fundamentally marked by an experiential-modification of space. While this will initially seem counter-intuitive, my intention is to illustrate that an analysis of lived-space and the experience of depth not only compliments other phenomenological approaches, it likewise satisfies the need for a perception-based description of the change between self and world currently absent from the literature.

5.1 The affective turn in depression

The most influential phenomenological accounts of depression arrive at similar conclusions regarding depressed experience, namely that depression may be characterized by affective change to the relation between oneself and the world. Yet, despite this consensus, not only are these treatments of affective change theoretically disparate, they fail to specify the constitution of selfhood that comprises one half of the relationship between self and world. For instance, Ratcliffe's seminal account of depression characterizes the affective change in depression as a loss of practical possibilities (Ratcliffe 2015, Ratcliffe and Broome 2012), while Fuchs and Svenaeus both accord emphasis to the lived-body, arguing that the affective change in depression involves bodily attunement (Svenaeus 2014a) or bodily resonance (Fuchs 2005). Moreover, Fuchs (2001) and Wyllie address a connection between time and altered affective experience by examining the putative loss of temporal horizons. These accounts share the overarching argument that depression renders everyday actions otherwise unproblematic and effort-

—

[54] More recently, Ratcliffe (2018) has taken up the question of selfhood and depression. However, Ratcliffe's interest in selfhood is not to develop a notion of self but instead to trace selfhood (in depression) through interpersonal, affective regulation.

less, explicit and obstacle-like. To illustrate, a respondent from David Karp's influential study of depression characterized the loss of possibilities by saying, "if you're in your bedroom and someone said there's a million dollars on the other side of the room and all you have to do is swing your feet over the edge of the bed, and walk over and get the million, you couldn't get the million. I mean you literally couldn't" (Karp 1996, 30). Even though this description seems somewhat stark, it underscores how basic motivations for something seemingly simple as getting out of bed in the morning become insurmountable obstacles in depression.

5.1.1 Possibility space: Ratcliffe

Monographs dedicated solely to the phenomenology of depression are scant.[55] Ratcliffe's recent contribution is arguably the most expansive and detailed account to date.[56] His investigation characterizes the lived-experience of depression as the transformation of a possibility-space. The notion of possibility space is an elaboration of his earlier work where he developed the notion of existential feelings, an appropriation of Heidegger's (2008) study of mood (*Stimmung*). Ratcliffe argues that existential-feelings, which are not always explicit yet ever present, disclose a background sense (implicit) of belonging to the world. They "constitute the general *space* of possibilities that shapes ongoing experience and activity. In addition to changes in specific possibilities, the overall possibility space can be heightened or diminished, open or constrained" (Ratcliffe 2008, 122, emphasis orignal). These feelings extend beyond the relatively limited linguistic repertoire used to describe various affective attunements to the world, which might include feelings that the world is "'overwhelming' or 'suffocating'" (ibid., 38), or feelings of being vulnerable or isolated. Existential feelings are notable insofar as they provide a vocabulary that articulates affective experience beyond the common-sense conception of feelings that are internal states, epiphenomena, or a physical manifestation of emotions.

In contrast with the common-sense or everyday understanding of moods as something subjective and internal to oneself, Ratcliffe follows Heidegger by characterizing moods (and existential feelings) as experientially ir-

—

[55] The other monographs that engage with the phenomenology of depression belong to Herbertus Tellenbach (1980) and Jill Gilbert (2014). However, Tellenbach's work should be qualified as a clinical and historical study regarding the vicissitudes of melancholy pre-DSM III.

[56] To appreciate the scope of his study, we must allocate this discussion considerably more space than what is required for the other accounts.

reducible to internal subjective mental states. Moods are neither inside nor outside; they are *felt* or affective modes of experience that, like operative-intentionality, they dispose us toward world significance anterior to conceptual thought as

> background orientations through which experience as a whole is structured. Second, they are *bodily feelings*. As these feelings constitute the basic structure of 'being there', a 'hold on things' that functions as a presupposed context for all intellectual and practical activity, I refer to them as *existential feelings* (Ratcliffe 2008, 38, emphasis original).

The notable point in this passage is that feelings reveal our hold on things in the world by virtue of what appears enticing to the conscious body. Rather than internal states-of-mind that constitute the world, existential feelings are the affective experience of what "weighs on us, that to which we are subjected" (Lingis 1996, 13).

The function of existential feelings, then, is that they constitute a "possibility space" (Ratcliffe 2015, 59) whereby one's overall felt sense of the world discloses the extent to which something appears as a possibility for action. From a phenomenological perspective, Ratcliffe argues that in depression a person's possibility space is transformed; possibilities for action no longer appear enticing.

What qualifies as a "possibility"? A possibility not only reflects a person's "physical capacity or disposition to find *p* significant in context *c*, but whether she can find anything significant in that way in any context" (Ratcliffe 2015, 62). As I understand it, possibility loss is not merely the loss of one thing among many, that is, the loss of interest in playing tennis while remaining enticed by other possibilities (e.g. reading, going to the gym). The loss of possibilities means one can no longer conceive that *anything* will be enticing. Then again, I may still experience things as being significant without being enticed, and consequently "a drive towards action is gone from experience and [one] feels unable to respond to significant possibilities, even though [one] still cares" (ibid., 166). The relationship between enticement, significance, and possibilities, may be experientially organized through a variety of permutations. Things may be less enticing then they once were, they may also be experienced as offering no enticement, despite the fact that a certain action remains something significant, something I want to undertake yet cannot be drawn in by it. Ultimately, the main characteristic that subtends the above considerations is that depression discloses changes to the kind of possibilities available to me.[57]

Ratcliffe employs six distinctions with respect to the kinds of experiential possibilities: (1) perceptual modality; (2) content; (3) mode of anticipation; (4) relationship to agency; (5) significance, and (6) interpersonal accessibility. Clearly, the various ways Ratcliffe believes possibilities are transformed in depression is a nuanced issue. While a detailed overview of each kind of possibility is beyond the scope of this chapter, I will say something about these possibilities as a whole. Ratcliffe's notion of "possibility space" is compelling, and I generally agree with his analysis. Yet, what remains unaccounted for is *how* significance and enticement are perceptually discerned. The kind of possibility associated with (1) perceptual modality is merely a distinction between the way in which a certain possibility solicits a particular sense (i.e. touch, vision, taste, etc.). In light of the substantial role played by existential feelings (non-operative world disclosure), it is somewhat curious that Ratcliffe does not specify the way in which *any* of these six possibilities come to appear at all.

As I argued in Chapter 4, embodied perception is the irreducible foundation upon which we discover the sense of the world. Accordingly, significance or enticement is, first and foremost, *perceptual* significance or *perceptual enticement.* Moreover, because our relation to the world is "deeper than every explicit perception and deeper than every judgement" (Merleau-Ponty 2012, 378), perceptual significance and perceptual enticement can only appear by virtue of operative-intentional situatedness that permits world sense to appear. For this reason, all six kinds of possibility presented by Ratcliffe must be derived from perceptual experience. Hence, what Ratcliffe's account does not provide is a phenomenological description of how embodied perception structures the sensible world that springs forth from our situatedness. This does not diminish the strength of his account of depression. What it does mean is that his analysis of possibilities does not spell out the practical and perceptual origin of possibilities.

—

[57] Ratcliffe's focus on "possibilities" is – much like existential feelings – deeply indebted to Heidegger's ontology of time. For this reason, depression is always situated in the perspective of the future. As a consequence, depression is taken to be a phenomenon that is rooted in "disturbed" becoming. This is, in part, why I believe that the philosophy of Merleau-Ponty is useful for understanding depression, given that his understanding of temporality does not limit us to situating depression solely in terms of future possibilities. Merleau-Ponty's emphasis on the relationship between past, present, and future, permits us to classify "loss of possibilities" as but one aspect of depressed experience rather than the dominant theme.

An additional gap in Ratcliffe's study is how *selfhood* is implicated in the loss of practical significance and enticement, and more generally, how selfhood is implicated in depression. According to Ratcliffe, practical significance and enticement are potentially modified in three ways in depression: a loss of both enticement and significance, a loss of enticement but not significance, or a loss of significance but not enticement (2015, 181). The crucial question is whether loss of both significance *and* enticement is compatible with the basic premises of intentional consciousness. Why? Recall from Chapter 4 that for the self-as-a-style, practical significance and enticement co-emerge with perceptual self-development within the logic of situations. In the absence of both enticement *and* significance, being-situated becomes incomprehensible. Without enticement and significance, how might one thing in the world stand out over another? Moreover, how should we understand the experience of transformed significance or enticement? We can agree with Ratcliffe that it is undoubtedly an affective experience, but how is this broad category of experience to be described? I will return to this question shortly (in section 5.3) to suggest that the relationship between practical significance and affective experience in depression is rooted in lived-space. But for the moment, now that we have become familiarized with Ratcliffe's approach to depression, I want to consider two additional studies of depression that are essential to the literature.

5.1.2 Does this resonate with you? Depression according to Fuchs and Svenaeus

Prior to the publication of Ratcliffe's seminal work in 2015, both Thomas Fuchs and Fredrik Svenaeus had developed (article-length) phenomenological accounts of depression that share considerable overlap. In their respective attempts to understand the affective change in depression, both Fuchs and Svenaeus conduct embodied analyses that characterize altered lived-experience in depression as a disruption between body and world. In spite of certain affinities, there are of course subtle differences between the approaches of Fuchs and Svenaeus, thereby warranting that we consider each account in its own right. I begin by addressing Fuchs' notion of affective atmospheres before I then move on to consider Svenaeus' account of depression and bodily attunement.

Like Ratcliffe, Fuchs' scholarship has exerted considerable influence over the way philosophers of psychiatry understand the phenomenology of depression. The most salient contribution made by Fuchs is his analysis of atmospheric moods, a concept that incorporates – but also goes beyond –

Heidegger's discussion of mood. For Fuchs, the idea of atmospheric moods accentuates the way in which our world-orientation is rooted in embodied consciousness. Like moods (*Stimmungen*), affective atmospheres should not be misinterpreted for something inside the self. Fuchs posits that the bodily incapacity to be affected by the world is exemplified by melancholia: "the corporealized and frozen body loses this capacity of emotional resonance" (2001, p. 98). One's affective orientation toward the world is disturbed as the body itself becomes an obstacle, thereby inhibiting one's ability to act unreflectively. In phenomenological terms, the unreflective structure of action is attributed to operative intentionality. In other words, it denotes our ability to be directed toward the world in such a way that our intentions are fulfilled without explicit awareness of the body's fulfilment of these intentions (e.g. walking, talking). Operative intentionality, then, permits us to act and fulfil intentions without the explicit need to think about the act itself (e.g. grasping a cup, walking, having a conversation). In depressive experience, Fuchs contends that the body becomes thing-like, reified, or "corporealized"

> the body loses the lightness, fluidity, and mobility of a medium and turns into a heavy, solid body that puts up resistance to the subject's intentions and impulses. Its materiality, density, and weight, otherwise suspended and unnoticed in everyday performance, now come to the fore and are felt painfully (ibid., p. 99).

The "force" of embodied intentions, which normally spread centrifugally across the world, no longer "gear into" or find anchorage (Merleau-Ponty, 2012, 272) in the things that populate our perceptual field. Fuchs rightly points out that the experience of depression is centripetal and thus renders self-awareness explicit. The body no longer resides in the background of experience but instead becomes the experiential foreground.

As a consequence, the self no longer recedes into the background, and as a result, becomes focally oriented toward the reflective (or thetic) mode of experience. Everyday tasks now require explicit effort; one must think or will oneself to do basic tasks, and the extent to which a task is experienced as obstacle-like is commensurate with the severity of the depression symptoms. In a severe case of major depression, just putting one's feet on the floor demands a level of effort that may seem impossible.

Fuchs' account outlined above is quite helpful in understanding the affective transformation in depression, however there are two issues that need to be addressed. The first, and perhaps, less critical point is that Fuchs' analysis is explicitly concerned with melancholia rather than depression itself. As I argued in Chapter 1, the historical debate regarding the continuity (or discontinuity) of depression and melancholia remains – and will likely remain – unresolved. Whether depression and melancholia are the same phenomenon remains a contested question. Fuchs refers to depression and melancholia interchangeably, which consequently means we must assume the phenomena to be continuous. Of course, that melancholia and depression are continuous is a valid position to hold. But as Ratcliffe has pointed out, depression is a heterogeneous phenomenon (2015, 234). Thus, a failure to properly delimit what is meant by depression leaves Fuchs susceptible to the objection that it will be unclear whether the analysis describes depression, or melancholia, or both.

A feature of Fuchs' approach that is open to challenge is his claim that depressive experience indicates a loss of bodily resonance. This premise raises an immediate question: does loss of resonance – and subsequently corporealization of the body – accurately depict depressed experience? For instance, in severe cases of depression, where a person has lost all (or nearly all) functional or practical abilities (e.g. unable to get out of bed), a total loss of bodily resonance may very well be an apt description of depressed experience. But just as I earlier questioned whether or not it is tenable to claim that depressed experience entails the loss of both enticement and significance, we must likewise question whether it is ontologically permissible to posit the total loss of bodily resonance? In the absence of bodily "resonance," is it viable to say that one even "has" a world any longer? Interestingly, Fuchs elaborates the notion of resonance by analyzing Cotard's delusion, a disorder in which one believes oneself to be dead. The main experiential feature of Cotard's is the decay of both world and things. If a total loss of resonance is, indeed, experientially possible, I believe that Cotard's delusion best exemplifies this transformation rather than depression. A person with Cotard's delusion is no longer perceptually geared into her situation; instead, rather than being turned toward the world, the absence of resonance elicits a fictional milieu in which a person extricates herself from shared reality in favor of a private one. Cotard's delusion is unique insofar as the sufferer believes herself to be dead yet remains capable of communicating this belief to others. She will insist she is dead despite residing among other living persons. The significant experiential loss for the

Cotard sufferer is the inability to recognize the unique phenomenal character of others through whom we come to recognize ourselves.[58]

As I noted at the beginning of the chapter, Fuchs' analysis of depression overlaps considerably with the analysis found in the work of Svenaeus. Svenaeus proposes a notion of bodily attunement, which like both Ratcliffe and Fuchs, is inspired by Heidegger's discourse on moods. Svenaeus elaborates on how *Befindlichkeit* (how one finds oneself in the world) discloses mood attunement to the world *through the lived-body*. Similar to the way Ratcliffe's existential feelings reveal our affective relation to the world, bodily attunement prefigures the way in which the self is open to the world, whereby what "matters" to us is contingent upon bodily dispositions (or bodily attitudes) of being-in-the-world. Thus, in depression, Svenaeus claims that the body may become differently attuned, and as a consequence, discloses the world as "painful, unrelenting unhomelike-ness" (2014, 14). Unlike Fuchs who posits loss of resonance, Svenaeus rightly contends that resonance may diminish rather than disappear altogether. However, how or why embodied consciousness – or motor-intentionality – is implicated in diminished resonance remains unspecified.

For Svenaeus, bodily attunement is undoubtedly affective, but it is less clear according to which perceptual modality a "painful" bodily disposition is manifested. If I am correct in presuming that bodily attunement emerges from tactile perception, then perceptual experience remains quite germane to making sense of the way in which we are sensitive to, or "attuned" to, the world.

I argued in Chapter 4 that all perception is fundamentally affective, which is why this investigation argues that we need an analysis of *embodied perception* to understand the nature of the affective changes that arise from the relationship between self and world in depression. For instance, if affective attunement (Svenaeus), or affective resonance (Fuchs), is predicated on embodied feelings, these feelings – which disclose something to us about the world – must always be indicative of the way we relate to things around us. The affective dimension of experience should therefore not be considered in isolation from other dimensions of experience, namely the dimensions of perception and motility, both of which enable the structuring of lived-space. It is also important to question how we understand the scope of bodily attunement. For example, a person may remain

[58] Both Ratcliffe (2008) and Svenaeus (2018) have also discussed elsewhere the phenomenology of Cotard's delusion.

capable of performing basic functions or daily activities (e.g. getting out of bed, going to work, cooking dinner, etc.) despite being clinically depressed. How should we understand the quality, or disabling effect of altered attunement? In my analysis of depression that will be presented later, I propose that the spatial experience of depth not only compliments the accounts we have discussed thus far but will deepen our understanding of the nuanced way affective experience is interwoven with perception, movement, and embodiment.

5.1.3 Depressed time: Accounts of Fuchs and Wyllie

The last phenomenological account of depression I want to consider is explicitly concerned with temporal experience in depression. In Chapter 4, I made some brief remarks regarding the reciprocal relation between temporality and the self. Unlike the clock-time of objective thought, which is punctuated by a series of "nows," the phenomenological approach insists that time is predicated on intentional-consciousness. Temporal horizons that subtend self-experience are disclosed by what we do, insofar as what concerns us at a given moment is imbued with perceptual significance. In addition to his analysis of bodily resonance in depression, Fuchs also considers depressed experience from the perspective of disturbed temporality. Along with Fuchs, Martin Wyllie has also proposed an account of distorted temporal experience that has been well received in the literature.

Since there is significant overlap between the analyses offered by Fuchs and Wyllie, I shall consider these two accounts interchangeably. Broadly speaking, phenomenological descriptions of temporality in depression underscore how temporal horizons preclude the many possibilities for practical action that normally appear to the self. In certain cases, even the possibility of change itself over time is rendered inconceivable; the future is experienced as closed off, where one's relationship with the world and time is experienced centripetally. This characterization of temporal experience in depression prompts Wyllie to claim that depression evokes a sense of being condemned to "an unchanging past and an unchanging future" (2005, 176). For Wyllie and Fuchs, this experience of time is why people with depression often describe being trapped in an unending present with no prospect of being well again.

Disturbed temporal experience in depression is intimately connected with the self's loss of practical possibilities, the intimacy of which is often cashed out in terms of how the body is affected by the loss of possibilities. Fuchs and Wyllie, who both focus exclusively on melancholy, suggest that distorted experience of time is a pronounced symptom typifying melancholy. In fact, for Fuchs, changed temporality is *the* primary symptom of melancholic experience. Even if melancholia is marked by a fundamental change in temporality, it is not obvious that the same holds for depression, even if it is nevertheless *a symptom* of depression. The connection between time and depression is commonly couched in terms of "closed of horizons" and "closed future", thereby denoting disturbed temporality. To illustrate, Wyllie writes: "with the future 'closed,' the sufferer's experience of the past also becomes disordered because the past can no longer be experienced as a horizon" (2005, 183). In a similar vein, Fuchs suggests that "the future loses the character of openness, novelty, surprise, and becomes reified as inevitable fate or calamity, at least to a rigid continuation of the past or a recurrence of the same" (2001, 98). With this conception of temporal horizons in depression, Wyllie then posits that "the sufferer cannot project themselves into a future of events and there is therefore no sense of 'things getting better.' The sufferer is biologically living, but the future appears dead in terms of fulfillment" (2005, 182). Though important, this portrayal of time in depression is perhaps too stark, and I believe warrants closer phenomenological consideration.

The standard view of altered temporality accompanying depression I have sketched out here emphasizes the sense of being trapped in the present, that it seems impossible one's situation will change. Consider the two following descriptions of time-experience in depression:

> When you are depressed, time becomes an enemy [...] Each second holds an exorbitant amount of pain. It traps you. You feel each beat. Minutes are full and long as the crawl toward the new hour, and you do nothing but try to hold still and live through them. Time is wasted because you concentrate on living through each moment (Marchenko 2016, 40-41).

> When you are depressed, the past and future are absorbed entirely by the present moment [...] You cannot remember a time when you felt better, at least not clearly; and you certainly cannot imagine a time when you will feel better. Being upset, even profoundly upset is a temporal experience, while depression is atemporal (Solomon 2001, 55).

Now, let us juxtapose these self-reports with Wyllie's account of distorted temporality in melancholia

> if the future is closed, the possibility of change is denied because there is no possibility of change without a future in which to make that change. The

> future gets blocked in some melancholic states by the negative attribution that things will not get any better. This conviction dominates the person's outlook, rendering it deterministic (Wyllie 2005, 180).

I want to draw out two issues relevant to our phenomenological investigation. While Wyllie's description of a blocked future seems to corroborate the experiences of Marchenko and Solomon, from a phenomenological perspective, it is imperative that we employ caution when using absolutist terms with respect to existential issues such as temporality and consciousness. Both Marchenko and Solomon convey how depression interferes with otherwise ordinary experiences of time, and which Wyllie characterizes as a "blocked" future. It should, however, be made clear that the experiential *absence* of future horizons would render intentional consciousness non-existent. We can (and should) acknowledge that altered temporal experience is consistent with depression, but we must still do justice to phenomenological principles that characterize temporality and consciousness in the first place.

If we understand temporal horizons in the context of our ubiquitous and irrevocable experience of perception, then it is a mistake to suggest that the future disappears or is closed off. We have already indicated (section 4.6.1) that self-experience unfolds according to the way in which various concerns or things disclose practical significance, some of which are more proximal while others are held at a distance on the horizon of one's life. The world itself is the horizon that unifies the various dimensions of our life, not just a single dimension (e.g. temporality), but all dimensions. As a project of existence, the self is not assembled *partes extra partes*: it is always sketched out on the horizon as a whole. Our involvement with our life may at times feel distant. Certain concerns are held at a distance, as vague outlines of meaning that trace the landscape of one's life. With respect to temporal horizons here, it is remiss to claim that they become closed off, and that they are *only* potentialities-for-being. Horizons background our situational predicaments. The successful resolution of a new situation establishes a new significance or new sense, around which we organize our world. Once we have learned, for example, to ride a bike, a new layer of knowledge is sedimented in the body. Having "mastered" the situation, we become intentionally oriented toward the world with a re-organized signification or meaning that now entails a manifold, non-conceptual reference, to cycling.

The sense of what is to come in the future is not anticipated according to horizontal or flat time as a successive series of punctuated *nows*. Temporal experience is always a field of presence, insofar as our hold on the future implies that: “I know only that there will be something to see in general. I possess no more than the abstract style of these distant landscapes [...] My possession of the distant landscape and of the past, like my possession of the future, it is only a possession in principle” (Merleau-Ponty 2012, 346). Here, the relevance of lived-space becomes an especially pertinent feature of depression in the context of temporality. While I have not yet introduced the full significance of lived space in depression, a salient aspect of the relationship between temporality and space is the contrast between the verticality of lived-space and the horizontal conception of “objective” time. The latter traditionally imagines our past to be a succession of events causing or leading to certain possible futures.

When space (and particularly depth) is implicated in time, our past is no longer a horizontal succession of events but instead an experiential matrix organized according to the sense or significance attributed to particular events. The “vertical” character of depth in time is comparable to the collision of tectonic plates in the earth’s crust. When the boundaries of large slabs of the earth’s crust meet, they exert force upon one another such that they become enjambed and envelope one another in a vertical fashion, thus creating mountainous landscapes due to the dynamism of the tectonic plates that engender a vertical “pile up” of sediment, a process that we witness as the seabed rises up out of the water to form spinous mountain peaks: “recollection can never be a mere recollection, since it is both a present act and a welling up from within time’s unfolding itself that holds within itself that past” (Mazis 2015, 49). Hence, so-called gaps in one’s memory are not simply empty spaces between certain events; some memories are more salient than others by virtue of the significance those events have exerted on our sense of who we are, nor are they isolated or atomized pockets of experience. We do not endure or undergo time as a linear compilation of memories that, if added together across a horizontal plane, would concretely depict the trajectory of one’s life.

Instead, just like existence itself, time is “taken up” but only as a general outline or sketch: “‘physiognomy [or outline] of all events, objects, and beings of the world is introduced [by Merleau-Ponty] to show how memory is elicited by *meaning encountered* in the perception of any being” (ibid., 55, emphasis in original). When selfhood was characterized in Chapter 4, we said: “Time exists for me because I am situated in it, because I discover myself already engaged in it” (Merleau-Ponty 2012, ibid., 447). Thus, our sedimented past gives shape to the future, which both preserves and prolongs the intentional project characterized by the relationship of self and world: "my world is carried along by intentional lines that trace out in advance at least the style of what is about to arrive" (ibid., 439). But what does this mean for depression? How should we make sense of the relation between depressed experience and disturbance of time? The implication is that time is perceptually significant, meaning that time is interwoven with our bodily capacities that habitually carry us toward the world. Likewise, if we accept Merleau-Ponty's claim that subjectivity (and by implication, the self) *is* time, then my contention is that we will need to appreciate how the changed relation between self and world in depression manifests through our habitual comportment toward the world according to the experience of lived-space.

But before fully specifying the relationship between depression and space in section 5.3, we must first still make sense of why the descriptions of temporality offered by Fuchs and Wyllie *overstate* the temporal dissolution of time in depression. One way to understand the claim that depression is experientially marked by a closed future is that the description is simply figurative; rather than literally describing *what it is like* to experience depression, the description merely captures its seeming sense, that is, *as if* one's horizon is closed. The literal closure of a future horizon, as I have repeatedly noted, would render sense or significance non-existent. For instance, with the exception of extremely severe cases of depression, practical abilities for most people remain intact in spite of suffering and despair. The most basic act of getting out of bed in the morning presupposes an intact future horizon, which further implies intact meaning structures.

What the literature often fails to distinguish between, I argue, is the difference between embodied meaning structures and transcendent meaning. That is, loss of meaning associated with depression is *not primarily* the loss of "subjective" meaning, but rather a *loss of the sense* that life is bereft of meaning – that life is pointless, or that nothing matters. There is no question that nihilistic attitudes are a commonly reported aspect of depressed experience, and this is undoubtedly a source of suffering. But it is crucial to note that transcendent meaning is always proceeded by primary (or primordial) meaning structures that are instituted (*Stiftung*) by virtue of being perceptually situated in the world. A disturbance to primary significance or meaning is more indicative of catatonic states, witnessed in persons with severe schizophrenia or atypical cases of severe depression. Just as I have argued we should resist characterizing temporality as "absent," "disappeared," "or static," the same applies to possibilities for action, which do not altogether disappear from experience. And while the experience of diminished possibilities is certainly indicative of depression, diminished possibilities alone do not descriptively exhaust its essential structure. Though certain possibilities may *seem* unavailable to oneself, we will soon see in section 5.3 that this apparent unavailability or impossibility is more accurately characterized as a *change in lived-distance* to the world, the origin of which is derivative of the perceptual relation between self-style and the world.

We will soon turn our focus to the way in which existential-space is affectively organized according to perceptual sense, subsequently making it possible to interpret the notion of attunement, resonance, and possibility, as experiential aspects of depth. But before we do this, it is imperative that first we clarify how our phenomenological analysis will proceed.

5.2 The phenomenological Scope

Recall from Chapter 2 (section 2.3.1) that I considered some of the limitations and uses of phenomenological methodology in qualitative research. while phenomenologically-inspired research is currently fashionable, it is often the case that the application of phenomenological concepts errs on the side of superficiality. It is often (incorrectly) assumed that the purpose of a phenomenological analysis is to merely describe lived-experience. Unfortunately, detailed descriptions from the first-person perspective alone do not necessarily secure phenomenological insights. To be sure, first-person reports are invaluable resources for phenomenological analysis. At the same time, even though individual experiences of depression are undoubtedly unique, we should not presume that first-person reports necessarily reveal unique truths about depression. The phenomenological relevance of subjective reports is not limited to their uniqueness, *per se*. On the contrary, the purpose of analyzing first-person reports is to seek out experiential structures that are common to depression in general, or as Ratcliffe suggests in his phenomenological study of depression, the aim is to "distinguish the *types* of existential change associated with diagnoses such as 'major depression'" (2015, 30).

Since the phenomenological impetus is to disclose fundamental experiential structures of first-person experience, the task is not only to consider reports about "what it is like" to be depressed, but if the goal is to access homogenous structures of experience then we must also attend to what lies beyond *what is said* (i.e. what is implicit). Another caveat with respect to first-person reports is that, because "objective thought" has a privileged place in Western culture, it is quite common that personal descriptions of experience often attempt to *explain* experience (principally through cause-effect accounts) rather than describe it (i.e. *how* it is). For this reason, the phenomenological task in this chapter is to "return to this world prior to knowledge, this world of which knowledge always *speaks*, and this world with regard to which every scientific determination is abstract, signitive, and dependent" (Merleau-Ponty 2012, lxxii). Because our intention is to let depression *speak*, positive knowledge of depression is complemented by pre-conceptual knowledge, the taken for granted aspects of experience that, as Merleau-Ponty says above, is the very condition of all possible knowledge.

5.2.1 Where to find depression

There are two obvious ways of sourcing experiential reports about depression: qualitative studies and autobiographical literature. The qualitative study that I presented in Chapter 2 investigated psychiatric professionals – rather than patients – for the simple reason that this sample group is underrepresented in the philosophical literature concerning depression.[59] Likewise, I also claimed in the second chapter that depression is more than a category of illness: it is also something that *is done* (an event) *by* and *with* clinicians, which makes it all the more important to recognize that our phenomenological findings concerning depression will have implications for professional knowledge, something I will explore in the sixth, and final, chapter. By attending to clinical perspectives of depression, it became clear that professional knowledge is considerably more practical in nature than it is strictly theoretical. However, I also illustrated that practical knowledge – much like everyday experience – is largely pre-reflective, and therefore, is taken for granted. We have an abundance of depression narratives (including qualitative studies and autobiography/memoir) at our disposal and this existing depression literature will sufficiently serve to elicit phenomenological insights regarding depression in this study.

Before we move to the analysis itself, I want to draw out two possible criticisms that may be leveled against the use of narratives written from the first-person perspective. First, it has been argued that the criteria-based category of depression is far too heterogeneous to allow for veracious phenomenological insight (Fernandez 2019). According to this objection,

—

[59] A feasible qualitative study involving both clinical and patient populations would have required resources that were practically and logistically unavailable to this investigation.

the DSM-5 category of depression is overly inclusive, meaning that the likelihood of false-positive diagnoses is high. If our investigation relies on clinically diagnosed cases, so the objection goes, we cannot ensure that the phenomenon under investigation is depression. This objection rightly reflects the general sense of discomfort with the operationalization of psychiatric diagnoses (see Chapter 2), which in recent years has led to calls for the categorical diagnostic model to be replaced with a dimensional model (Cuthbert and Insel 2010). How should this objection be handled?

On the one hand, the criteriological and dimensional models of diagnosis face the same problem of establishing boundaries or thresholds for a given disorder. Ultimately, neither approach will conclusively ensure valid diagnosis. A dimensional approach has the positive benefit of tolerating fuzzy boundaries. Furthermore, it makes room for degrees of severity, and can acknowledge the possibility that there may exist a variety of depression types (e.g. existential, melancholic, endogenous, etc.). On the other hand, the current categorical model of diagnosis employed in DSM-5 gathers together a substantial grouping of persons who exhibit common symptoms that point to the presence of depression. Despite the well-documented shortcomings of criteria-based diagnosis (see Chapter 1), phenomenology can conceivably make sub-category distinctions or even help to rule out depression. Phenomenology alone cannot resolve the theoretical limitations of psychiatric diagnosis, yet our investigation can draw from the current depression category (broadly construed) to assess the extent to which changes to fundamental experiential structures in depression implicate and involve changes in self-experience. Accordingly, the purpose of our phenomenological analysis is not to delineate sub-types of depression or to redefine the boundaries of depression. Following Ratcliffe, our endeavor simply recognizes that "the ability to make more refined phenomenological distinctions surely has the potential to inform classification" (2015, 8). How these distinctions may be incorporated into practice will be the focus of the sixth and final chapter, but for the moment I want to address the second limitation of depression narratives.

A significant objection to the use of first-person accounts of depression is the epistemic legitimacy of these texts. Radden and Varga (2013) argue that the veracity of descriptions conveyed by depression memoirs should be treated with caution. Their worry is that experiential content captured by harnessing first-person perspectives is constrained and modified by the conventions that govern the memoir genre. Pursuant to this, Radden and Varga contend that the nature of depression "affects autobiographical memory and writing style in ways that will influence the structure and content of the narrative" itself (ibid., 100). Importantly, not all authors of this genre fail to recognize the "extra" constraints Radden and Varga impute to depression life-writing or narratives. When Daphne Merkin attempts to make sense of her life-long struggle with depression by reflecting on her past, she does so with an ambivalence about the value of what she might discover:

> Still, we are left largely in the dark as to the whys and the wherefores of our own emotional development except as we can fathom them through a process of retrospection, which is unreliable at best. I suppose why I harbor a documentarian's curiosity about my childhood, as though I might unearth some crucial piece of evidence if only dig deeply enough or duck my head into the right cave, and thereby prove that what I believe to be true about my own history is not merely a subjective narrative but the definitive text, immutable Scripture (2017, 54).

Merkin's own worry over the authenticity of her depression narrative points to a general anxiety that applies to the subjective nature of narrative in general. Whether or not depression narratives are less reliable than "non-pathological" narratives is a question that cannot be answered by this investigation – and in fact it is a question that may ultimately remain contested among narrative theorists themselves. Still, our task is not to assess the validity of narratives or of narrative theories as such. Ultimately, the epistemic value of the memoir content cannot be discerned unambiguously, since it resides somewhere in between being a literary genre and a personal narrative, which is further complicated by the self-reflective position an author adopts when re-presenting herself as the protagonist of her own story.

Indeed, it is clear that the nature of narratives and self-reports lead to worries about authenticity. But we have at least two reasons to justify the use of depression memoirs as a source of insight into depression. First, as I already noted above, reliance on first-person reports to gain insight into depression need not be strictly limited to an author's descriptions *prima facie*. Of course, we should initially approach the experience-based descriptions on their own terms. Outright rejection of the admissibility of a person's narrative invites potential objections over epistemic injustice, meaning that a person's subjective position unfairly renders his or her "testimony" unreliable or untrustworthy. We can acknowledge the importance of *explicit* descriptions expressed in a depression memoir while at the same time recognizing that we have considerable interest in what remains unexpressed in the memoir itself. That is, in addition to considering the narrative as it is, there are likewise valuable insights to be gained from what is *implicitly* expressed in the narrative's background; we allow the descriptive particulars to open onto more general aspects that characterize all self-experience.

The second reason to feel confident about drawing from depression memoirs is that, even though genre conventions may negatively constrain and exert influence on a narrative, these conventions may positively contribute to a person's ability to articulate what he or she might otherwise struggle to express. For instance, Anna Bortolan writes, "the existence of narrative models may provide patients with the linguistic and conceptual scaffolding necessary to describe experiences which could otherwise be very difficult to report" (2019, 1056). This is a problem faced by most qualitative investigations of depression. Those who suffer from or have suffered from depression are often exasperated by its ineffable nature: "Eventually, there's a threshold in which depression cannot be fully articulated, no matter how much you try. It is a dark matter, swirling in dead space, pushing on orbits without a trace" (Park 2017, 18). Since the experience of depression can prove too elusive to linguistic articulation, authors often find that the only suitable recourse is metaphorical language. Should we hold reservations about metaphorical flourishes when our task is to gain sound insight into the nature of depression? In his novel *Strange Bodies*, Marcel Theroux resoundingly answers we should not: "tears, heartbreak, pathetic fallacies of weeping skies and bleeding sunsets: these aren't lousy approximations of lived experience, they're the nerves and fibre of human life itself" (2013, 124). Regardless of the expressive medium, the only satisfactory way forward is to assess first-person reports of depression (or any kind) in a balanced way.

5.3 In the space of depression

In order to understand depression phenomenologically, a primary point of reference is necessary if we want to establish a foothold on the phenomenon, of which the most salient point of reference, I have argued, is lived-experience rather than third-person observation.[60] Accordingly, to inves-

---

[60] I do not wish to suggest that third-person observation is of no value. However, a serious shortcoming with the third-person perspective is that the resultant observations may belie what is occurring in lived-experience. For instance, a clinician may report that a person exhibits lethargy and flattened affect. Yet, as we will see later in this chapter, affect is anything but "flattened" when examined from the phenomenological perspec-

tigate depression we will draw on polymorphic first-person reports in order to disclose monomorphic structures of lived-experience, all the while being mindful of the limitations associated with narrative, self-knowledge, and subjective reporting.

Despite consensus among other phenomenological studies that depression is fundamentally characterized by an affective disruption (Aho 2013, Fernandez 2014, Fuchs 2001, Jacobs 2013, Svenaeus 2014, Ratcliffe 2015, Smith 2013, Bortolan 2017) associated with the lived-body, little has been said regarding the centrality of both perception and self in depressed experience. The main purpose of this investigation is to fill this gap with a comprehensive analysis of embodied perception in depression that specifies how we ought to understand the affective change between self and world. Going forward, I contend that if we want to appreciate the relationship between self and depression, our analysis must address *lived-space*. This approach not only contributes with a much-needed perspective on depressed experience and selfhood, it both compliments the existing analyses of depression and further refines the way we understand affective changes in depression.

Since depression is clinically characterized as a disorder of mood, it may sound somewhat counterintuitive to posit a relationship between depression and *space*. It becomes less curious, however, if we follow the phenomenological critique that Merleau-Ponty and Straus level against "objective thought", which I outlined in Chapter 4. According to "objective thought," the perception of space "is the knowledge that a disinterested subject could have of spatial relations between objects and of their geometrical characteristics" (Merleau-Ponty 2012, 293), whereas perception of lived-space "is a structural phenomenon and is only understood from within a perceptual field that, as a whole, contributes to motivating it by proposing to the concrete subject a possible anchorage" (ibid.). In lived-space, the body is not merely one object among others, according to which spatial relations are deduced via geometric positionality. Our bodily anchorage in situations precedes the possibility of geometric or abstract space, which is what permits us to say we are of space rather than in space.

tive. It is worth recalling that our brief survey of the *standard* theories of self in Chapter 3 suggested that the narrative self is the most relevant for psychiatry. And though we addressed shortcomings associated with the narrative model, we also acknowledged that the nature of psychiatry is discursive. The only way to approach depression is through self-reporting, which means that third-person observation is impotent without first-person insight.

Recall from Chapter 4 that the body-schema grounds our pre-cognitive perception of the world due to the body's ability to reach across the world with our capacity for movement. We likewise said that the self is the source of temporality, and this equally holds true for spatiality; the experienced space is simultaneously the creation of space, a milieu that we *in-habit* (or establish) and "take up" *vis-à-vis* our existential project. Just as the self is the source of temporality (see section 4.8), the self is likewise the creative (or organizational) source of space. The quintessential character of spatial experience is the sense of depth – not depth given objectively, but as an organization of space in light of practical significance. Perception of depth is not a geometrically constituted operation of thetic consciousness. In depth we perceive what Ratcliffe refers to as enticement and significance; or, using Merleau-Ponty's phrasing, in depth we are solicited to act by the world and things in the world. But most importantly, depth enables and motivates the spatial orientation of the self.

Because we are sensitive to the sensible world unreflectively, our everyday experience of lived-space is seemingly banal. As Morris points out, this banality may be interrupted when things appear out of place; in normal experience, things in the world solicit us to act or do things in certain ways without our explicit awareness of the solicitation. A table has sense insofar as it demands that I move around it in a certain way to be able to reach the kitchen counter; the table motivates the movement, just as the coffee mug on the kitchen counter motivates my goal of getting around the table to grasp it. Hence, motivation is dialogically structured by solicitation and intentionality. A motive solicits our attention without recognizing it as a motive; it is something that ordinarily escapes our reflective awareness. However, with respect to depression, this relationship is fundamental to understanding the way in which selfhood is affected in depression.

Bodily perception puts us "in touch" with a world that is voluminous or "thick," wherein we find "a certain indissoluble link between the things and me by which I am situated in *front of them*" (Merleau-Ponty 2012, 267, emphasis added). The perceived distance between here and there emerges from an anchored (and thus embodied) perspective that is "geared first of all to thing-place relations [...] Our attention is grabbed by things that are 'out of place.' Things that are in place fit so well that we do not even notice their dependence of place except, perhaps, in the moment when something that vanishes into background place becomes apparent as a thing" (Morris 2004, 113). In everyday life perceptual thickness – my contact with the world from here to there – is rendered inconspicuous when our anticipated intentions are perceptually fulfilled. That which is apperceived "silently" fills our perceptual field in such a way that it is invisible to thetic consciousness. But this invisible thickness is not only the sensed world at the level of operative-intentionality. The perceptual thickness of lived-space is perceived as, and *motivated* by, spatial depth.

The perceived distance or volume between self and world is what Merleau-Ponty designates as *the existential dimension of depth*. For both Merleau-Ponty and Straus, depth is pivotal to their respective phenomenological descriptions of space. Classical conceptions of depth (most notably that associated with Berkeley) held that depth cannot be seen, that it is simply breadth transposed onto a vertical axis. Moreover, the argument that depth cannot be seen relies on the assumption that the visible world is represented via two-dimensional retinal images, which in turn precludes the possibility of perceiving more than two-dimensions. For Straus, the premises on which this classical explanation of depth is based are remiss: "to be sure, we can *think of* the plane as two-dimensional form. But can we actually *see* a plane as such – without any depth?" (1963, 342, emphasis original). Put another way, denial of depth's visibility is only possible if perception were to supervene on rational thought. However, I emphasized in Chapter 4 that Straus and Merleau-Ponty refute this conditional proposition by arguing that perception is not subsequent but anterior to rational thought. Straus' sentiment that vision necessarily entails experience of depth tacitly informs Merleau-Ponty's motivation for characterizing depth as an existential dimension. Simply put, for Merleau-Ponty, depth presupposes a perspective, which is to say, embodied subjects or selves are situated in front of things. Hence, when a person is walking away from us, "the increasing distance merely expresses that the thing begins to slip away from the hold of our gaze, and that it joins up with it less succinctly [...] [so distance is defined] through the situation of the object with regard to the power of our hold on it" (Merleau-Ponty 2012, 273). For the sake of simplicity, we can simply characterize depth as a relation between the self and things. For Straus, this means that "in depth, I have things as they are for myself, from my point of view" (1963, 345). To be clear, the spatial relationship to motivation is not strictly dependent on the sense of near or far. Merleau-Ponty employs an example of the death of a family member when living abroad. The death itself neither *causes* one to return home nor is it the *reason* to return:

> Motive and decision are but two elements of a situation: the first is the situation as a fact; the second is the situation taken up. Thus, a death motivates my journey *because* it is a situation in which my presence is required, whether to comfort a grieving family or to pay my "final respects" to the departed; and by deciding to undertake this journey, I validate this motive that I proposed and I take up this situation. The relation between motivated and motivating is reciprocal (2012, 270, emphasis original).

Motivations cannot manifest without the experience of depth. In the passage above, distance is not a measurement between two distal points. It indicates that motivation serves to structure situations in such a way that our concerns, or what counts as significant for us, need not be close to hand: "a lived distance links me to things that count for me and exist for me, and links them to each other. At each moment, this distance measures the 'scope' of my life" (Merleau-Ponty 2012, 299). Unlike reasons or causes, motivations resist thematization. One way to appreciate what Merleau-Ponty means by motive is to draw a comparison with Hume's well-known critique of the role played by reason in moral philosophy. Succinctly put, while reason may well be capable of telling us what to do in a given circumstance, reason alone cannot compel us to act in a given circumstance (Hume 2007). Motives affect the self by way of solicitations, the sense or significance of which is expressed in a given situation that need not necessarily be unfolding here and now

> were it possible to unfold at each moment all of the presuppositions in what I call my "reason" or my "ideas," then I would always be discovering experiences that have not been made explicit, weighty contributions of past and of the present, and an entire "sedimented history" that does not merely concern the *genesis* of my thought, but that determines its *sense* [or significance] (Merleau-Ponty 2012, 416, emphasis original).

It is indeed possible that a reason for X may also be a motive for X, but what prevents us from identifying a *motive* as a *reason* is that motives are not given to the explicit awareness of thetic consciousness. A motive cannot be expressed in propositional form the way a reason is conveyed as a proposition. Because Merleau-Ponty follows Edith Stein in adopting a broader notion of motive (Wrathall 2004), a motive is not a reason since we do not explicitly experience the motive; it does not amend itself to the explicit experience of deliberation.

By contrast, in order to understand why one thing may stand out as a motive over and above another, it is not that "one phenomenon triggers another, through some objective causality, such as the one linking together the events of nature, *but through the sense it offers – there is a sort of operative reason, or a raison d'être that orients the flow of phenomena without being explicitly posited by any of them*" (ibid., 51, emphasis added). Thus, when our focal awareness shifts from one aspect to another, from a tree to a house for example, the perceptual field is organized according to sense that is internally related to the previous aspect. As I focus on the house, the house does not succeed the tree; the two phenomena are internally related, such that their respective indeterminacy results in a motivated-motivating structure. Or alternatively, the motivated-motivating structure expresses the way in which the foreground-background structure organizes our perceptual field. The experience of space, and especially depth, coincides with the experience of time.

Merleau-Ponty prioritizes motivation to characterize our relationship with things because scientific study of perception *objectifies perception* rather than recognizing its contingent and active nature: "[if] we prematurely locate in perception a science that is in fact constructed upon perception [...] *we lose sight of the original relation of motivation*" (Merleau-Ponty 2012, 51, emphasis added). In other words, when perceptual experience is subjected to scientific study, our primordial or immediate experience of the world is explained by seeking causes or reasons that give rise to that experience. However, as Merleau-Ponty rightly notes, when we explain perception either causally or by giving reasons, we do so by abstracting from lived-experience. For example, a loud bang outside my window *caused* me to turn my head; or the reason I turned my head is due to the loud bang. The problem with these two avenues of explanation is that they do not bear fidelity to the actual experience of perceiving. Merleau-Ponty's point is ultimately that scientists who engage in the "objective" study of perception fail to recognize that they are already acquainted with perceptual experience of the thing to be studied. Hence, if our explanations of natural phenomenon are restricted to reasons or causes, we take for granted that world experience is predicated, first and foremost, on non-conceptual knowledge of worldly phenomenon. Because motivations elude explicit awareness, they may seem almost ethereal. But crucially, motivation – unlike cause or reason – does not explain why I chose X instead of Y; our relationship with things in the world *motivates* my response to do X or Y; objects of perception motivate us to grasp, to hold, to touch, and so on.

Causal explanations and reasons for action operate on the assumption that my most recent past will provide reasons for choosing X. Or, if we trace our experience far enough back in time, we would eventually – in principle – disclose the cause or reason for this decision. But I have argued to the contrary, that our sedimented bodily habits from the past, which are imbued by preferences for certain actions or dispositions, are *motivated* (or solicited) by meaningful significations; to be pulled in by, or repelled by, things in the world is to be perceptually geared into the world in a way scientific thought takes for granted.

The relevance of motivation for understanding depression is exemplified by Benedict Smith's (2012) cogent treatment of the relationship between depression and affectivity. Smith's account nicely illustrates how motivation is phenomenologically central to understanding depression. He contends that physiological and psychological perspectives alone cannot adequately make sense of embodied experiences of depression. These two perspectives fail to grasp that, in depression, the relationship between self and world is marked by practical changes to what an agent can *do*, particularly with respect to what appears *possible.*

One main limitation of Smith's account is that he fails to fully articulate the scope of motivation, which is admittedly a difficult task. Still, without linking motivation to depth, what Smith reveals about depression does not go beyond the basic finding that has already been recognized by those phenomenological accounts of depression we considered earlier, namely that depression expresses an altered relationship between the body and sense of the world. Having said this, Smith is right to point out that the structures of practical life do not simply vanish: "subjectivity," he says, "may still be structured by essentially practical orientations, although the bodily changes experienced as part of depression articulate that orientation more in terms of 'I cannot' rather than 'I can'" (2013, 632). Husserl's well-known description of consciousness as 'I can'– and later adopted by Merleau-Ponty – should, however, be employed in the context of depression with caution. In this case, if the structures of practical life permit a sense of agency, is it ever permissible to characterize experience as "I cannot"? While it may be accurate to claim that one can no longer do *some* things, the nature of intentional consciousness retains – and must retain – its primary form in the "I can." Why? As Merleau-Ponty expresses it, the condition of possibility for operative intentionality (or embodied consciousness) is an *a priori* capacity to *do* something in the form of *I can*. For this reason, I believe we must insist that in depression the "I can" of embodied consciousness is not *lost;* instead, our capacity for action is *re-structured*, and this re-structuring not only involves our practical possibilities, it similarly refers to a reorganization of the way in which the self-as-a-style comports itself toward the world.

5.4 The depth of de-pression

When the word depression is employed as a noun in psychiatry, it denotes a specific thing: a disorder that we call depression. Outside of the context of psychiatry, the word depression typically refers to low spots (as in meteorology or economics), or the act of depressing itself. Taken literally, to depress means to press down on something. However, in the context of our discussion of lived-space, the prefix *de* is not insignificant. Interestingly, *de-* signifies separation in space and indicates being "away from." The word "press" is indicative of exerting force or pushing against.

In the context of psychiatric illness, depression colloquially expresses the feeling of being pressed down upon or the feeling of heaviness or weighted burden that often accompanies depression. Having said this, according to our analysis of space and depth, the lived-experience of depression more appositely captures *de*-pression as a pulling away from the world. Moreover, if we take the opposite of de-press to be *im*-press, we are in a position to characterize normal lived-experience between self and world as *impressing.* In normal experience, non-thematic experience is an ongoing tension evinced between self and world, and is revealed through our intentional behavior as the coupling of our intentions with the perceptual resistance of things in the world. Through the structure of operative-intentionality – our most basic mode of perceptual contact with the world – we actively impress upon, and touch things, in the world while reciprocally remaining open to being impressed upon and touched by the world. Thus, depth is realized through embodied perception as a tension:

> Each complex of signification that manages to emerge is the outcome of a *mutual* solicitation of what the *thing itself recommends* and *what the perceiver intends* […] Depth makes something seen or heard coexist with other sights or sounds by allowing some to be concealed as background, while this background as a certain absence sustains the very prominence of another (Steinbock 1987, 340, emphasis added).

In normal everyday life, the thickness between me and the world is apperceived or co-perceived such that things need not be explicitly present to my immediate awareness. Likewise, the various possibilities and motives of action that are open to me need not be thematized, since my body is sensitive to the depth of things in the perceptual field. Put another way, in normal experience, self-as-a-style dilates its surroundings or situations as a field of possible actions through embodied perception. Conversely, in depressed experience, I am arguing that, as possibilities for action, surroundings or situations are *contracted*. Hence, normal self-experience is centrifugal (expansive) while depressed self-experience is centripetal (constrictive).

Since a contraction of lived-space – like all human experience – is dependent on our situated perception, that is, a self who is *perceptually* "at work" in the world, I will spend the rest of the chapter articulating the way in which depression and the experience of depth implicate the self as an expressive sedimented style.

5.5 The depth of depression: World organization

We are now in a suitable position to fully articulate the implications of an existential-phenomenological description of depression characterized by the relationship between self and space. And this relationship as we have seen is far from straightforward. Phenomenological accounts of depression generally agree that depressed experience is predominantly characterized by a change in how things in the world stand out as being meaningful for us. Phenomenologically speaking, world significance (or salience) refers to the variety of ways that the body-subject may be affected by virtue of how he or she contacts the world. But what remains less clear is how salience is transformed.

This transformation of world salience or significance is best described as a reorganization of sense. To avoid disambiguation, this reorganization is not a conscious or explicit decision. The changed significance that defines the experience of depression is not constituted, rather it is instituted, which is to say: "the establishment in an experience (or in a constructed apparatus) of dimensions […] in relation to which a whole series of other experiences will make sense and will make a history or a *sequel*" (Merleau-Ponty 2010c, 9). Our past experiences always remain past, and yet the significance we derive from the past is not preserved forever like a fossil encased in amber. For instance, we may have seemingly distinct and unrelated experiences from the past that initially appear insignificant or unrelated. However, these disparate moments may be brought together in such a way they establish new sense, that is, an entirely new signification. Merleau-Ponty often invokes romantic love to illustrate this point:

> I discover that I am in love. Perhaps nothing of the facts that I now take as proof escape me: not that quickened movement from my present toward my future, nor this emotion that left me speechless, not this impatience for the day of our date to arrive. But alas, had I not brought these facts together or, even if I had, I did not think it involved such a strong emotion. But now I discover that I can no longer conceive of my life without this love (2012, 399).

Additionally, love "is not a thing that one could outline and designate [...] it is rather the way the lover establishes his relations with the world; it is an existential signification" (ibid., 401). Of course, our interest is not love but depression. Nonetheless, we can highlight from this example the way in which significations take on new sense. In depression, just as love, the body-subject *establishes* specific relations with the world. Once the lover arranges what were previously held to be unrelated or individual experiences, the sense of the past *and* future is entirely reorganized.

It is commonly noted that depressed people retrospectively report that they have always been depressed. A similar feature of depressed experience is the inconceivability that depression will ever end:

> From the outside in, her life might strike others as good, if not enviable. She knows this on some level but the knowledge dries up as the wind howls through her, reminding her that she feels barren and lost and quite without hope [...] The condition that envelops her respects no calendar; it arrives precisely when it feels like it. To the woman, it seems as if she has felt this way, in one form or another, for what feels like forever (Merkin 2017, 9-10).
>
> As much as I wind my mind back in time, I'm unable to locate the start of a downward spiral (Mehler Paperny 2019, 37).
>
> Doubtless depression had hovered near me for years, waiting to swoop down (Styron 2010).

The notion that one's situation is immutable is indicative of the overall structure of depression. Cognitive models of depression (Beck et al. 1979, Disner et al. 2011, Ellis 1987) have long insisted that the proclivity for depressed people to be pessimistic about the future is elicited by negative cognitive biases. My contention, however, is that the phenomenological perspective provides a different conclusion, namely that the sense of depression's intractability is an affective (or felt) experience rather than cognitive. The pervasive feeling associated with depression may be experienced as one of engulfment, suffocation, or envelopment, terms that underscore the way in which depression is a ubiquitous self-experience. We are no more "in" depression than we are "in" the world; we inhabit or live depression just as we inhabit the world. Consequently, it is not entirely unsurprising that depression narratives often indicate a sense of having been depressed in the past and will likewise continue to be depressed in the future. Rather than attributing this observation to cognitive bias, we should re-interpret this observation as reflecting a non-thetic reorganization of one's situation. More precisely, the hitherto stable sense of worldly significance, expressed through one's stylized comportment toward the world, becomes "silently" re-established in a *new* habitual style.

The acquisition of a new style is organized around new existential structures of meaning and expressed through the motor-intentional habits of the self. This acquisition of style is instituted by the self, an active and passive synthesis of worldly significance: "human institution is not only the utilization of the past or the utilization of an experience as a substitute […] [it is] the integration of this past into a new signification […] It is the past becoming a symbolic matrix" (Merleau-Ponty 2010c, 19). Because we are situated, we are open to a future by virtue of our past experiences. But the past is not carried into the present as a mere "trace"; the past is expressed through one's preferred bodily ways of dealing with situations that are similar in kind. By way of analogy, just as a palimpsest retains the indentations of written words that have been erased, the sedimented past of the sensing and sensible body retains "imprints" of the way we deal with our worldly concerns.

The onset of depression typically follows no logical or predictable pathway. On the one hand, and just like a light switch, there are cases of depression that manifest spontaneously. On the other hand, for many, depression subtly pervades the self without awareness. A depressive style is engendered by past experiences that push forward into the present, yet simultaneously recede into the extant series of retentions. There is "a certain inertia […] an activity *en route*, an event, the initiation of the present, which is productive after it" (Merleau-Ponty 2010c, 7). This inertia is evident in simple actions such as grasping a cup. Our initially limited motor-capacity for grasping is eventually developed to the point that we are able to effortlessly deal with a grasping situation. But even with highly refined motor-capacities, the act of grasping for an adult is a prolongation of early attempts to deal with a grasping situation.

We should not lose sight of the existential dimensionality that constitutes the backdrop of self-situatedness. Our habitual ways of coping with the world are not mechanisms or reflexes. We meet the world through our preferential ways of dealing with it: "this does not mean that I am determined: I can learn to cross these 'obstacles' or not. But it is on the basis of the given obstacle that I will learn" (ibid., 6). Just as the earlier example of love illustrated how the lover expresses an entirely new way of moving toward the world, with depression, once I have explicit awareness of being depressed my embodied relationship with the world has already been reorganized. Hence, the thickness of "lived distance [which] links me to things that count and exist for me, and links them to each other" is modified (Merleau-Ponty 2012, 229). With this in mind, when a person reports it is inconceivable that he or she will ever be free of depression, the description is not so much that he or she is "stuck" in the present; it is rather a description of a change in depth.

Clinical depression is notorious for presenting symptoms such as physical sluggishness, languor, heaviness, and in general, a lack of spontaneous expressiveness. In some cases of depression, these putative symptoms may not necessarily be symptoms of depression as much as they are existential significations reflected by structured embodied habits. I want to provide an example of how the significance of our situatedness permeates our lives from infancy until death. In the aptly titled "The Depressed Person," David Foster Wallace offers a portrait of a young adult woman whose childhood experience was marked by inter-parental conflict: "[Her parents] had displayed far more interest and passion and emotional availability in their hatred of each other than either of them had shown toward the depressed person herself, as a child, the depressed person confessed to feeling, sometimes, still" (2007, 39). As an adult, the woman "who was agonizingly sensitive [...] she admitted, to the possibility that anyone she was trying to reach out and share with was secretly bored or repelled or desperate to get away from her as quickly as possible [...] and never once failed to notice when the therapist glanced ever so quickly either up at the clock" (ibid., 53).

This example illustrates how the depressed woman's parents, unaware of their own habituated proclivity to be self-interested, repeatedly put their own interests above those of the child. The parent's failure to recognize their daughter, whether it be her grades at school, her appearance, or as a person whose well-being takes precedent over their own, is anything but innocuous. Her parent's interpersonal dynamic, which is characterized almost exclusively by personal conflict, consequently (and understandably) structures the way in which interpersonal relationships are negotiated. As an adult, the young woman's ability to cope with her interpersonal situations is structured by coping skills she developed as a young child in response to the demands of the situation. To be sure, we cannot predict in advance how a situation will solicit the child to act one way over another. Still, it is plausible to conceive that the child's continued inability to master this interpersonal situation will mean that subsequent encounters with situations similar in kind will be affectively imbued with a sense of ambivalence; that is, her parents have significance as a source of care and love, but they are simultaneously also a source of stultification. Understandably, because the style of her "family situation" was repeatedly enacted, as a child the young woman learned to *inhabit* behavior that was best suited to coping with this type situation. The ambivalent sense of the situation may elicit a particular motor-habit or postural schema against a background sense of guilt; that is, guilt as an existential-feeling or affective stance toward the world simply by virtue of her very presence, as a source of disappointment, or as someone who is uninteresting, all which is continually re-confirmed through her relation with her self-involved parents.

Recall from Chapter 2 and Chapter 4 that self-development is fundamentally interwoven with the family constellation. Learning how to navigate the world of objects simultaneously requires that we learn to navigate intersubjective relations. A crucial difference is that in the case of the latter, those who belong to the family constellation already possess established habits for dealing with both world and others. Hence, our developed way of comporting ourselves toward both world and others is always constrained by virtue of our close ties to others. The inability to skillfully cope or deal with situations is indeed a stultification. It prevents the spontaneous establishment of new motor-habits possible in other dimensions of our lives.

Subsequently, in nascent interpersonal situations like the one described here, the self establishes motor-habits or a style that become reified. And even in "normal" everyday life, one's situational coping will ultimately be expressed in our preferred ways of meeting the world: "we must recognize a sort of sedimentation of our life: when an attitude toward the world has been confirmed often enough, it becomes privileged for us" (Merleau-Ponty 2012, 466). To be situated is to put questions to the world that in turn answers with resistance, and over time, these answers become embodied as an expression of one's own relation to the world. As a result, the successful resolution of previous situations affords us with a repertoire of sedimented capacities that may be adopted when similar situations are encountered in the future. Because situated space is fundamentally perceptual depth, the self possesses a "general power of adhering to different milieus, of determining himself through different experiences, and of acquiring structures of behavior" (Merleau-Ponty 2012, 161). The conclusion to be drawn from the example of the young child is that our preferred ways of meeting the world may be established according to significations that are independent of anything related to depression. If one's repeated inability to master certain milieus (or situations) eventually coincides with the emergence of depression then this is not due to a lack of resilience, since the notion of resilience implies returning to a previous state or form. A particular situation that repeatedly appears in one's life and cannot be adequately managed will remain resistant to spontaneous resolution.

5.6 Depressive style: Time and others

All experiences structure our future experiences. This consequently means that there can be no return to a previous state of "self" or "normal self." The depressive situation is one in which the plasticity of one's situation shrinks to the extent that future horizons are experienced as being diminished or closed off. Hence the common feeling that one is trapped in an immutable present. Yet, earlier I contended that describing horizons as closed off was an oversimplification (section 5.1.4), insofar that such a description is incompatible with the structure of intentional consciousness. Instead of characterizing depressed experience as temporally closed or absent, I believe we should understand the relationship between time and depression using the metaphor of a diaphragm, insofar as its expansion and contraction constitute the implicit movement of existence. Thus, temporal experience in depression should likewise be understood precisely in these terms of expansion and contraction, such that our hold on the world is always a temporal hold. However, this experiential hold, like the diaphragm, can be more or less expansive, and it is the implicit rhythm that backgrounds all intentional experience. In depression, temporal horizons are not "closed" off or absent, since this would necessarily imply a break with existence itself. Instead, I want to emphasize once more that self-style is concomitant with temporality (as the upsurge of time).I In the context of depressed experience, this means that temporality is literally visible on the body; in other words, when we observe affective expressions of languor, flattened affect, indolence, or corporealization, we witness depression as expressed temporally through the body.

Returning to the example of the "depressed person" that I borrowed from Foster-Wallace, as a consequence of living through the ambivalent interpersonal situation with her parents, while able to cope "successfully" as a young child, as an adult her habitual self-style which developed in response to the demands of her situation, prevents her from transcending this instituted level of coping; we witness what Merleau-Ponty calls a prolongation of her past, which "if not a destiny, has at least a specific weight, and that it is not a sum of events over there far away from me, but rather the atmosphere of [her] present" (ibid., 467). The significations of certain interpersonal behaviors and relations may eventually be organized in such a way that the self adopts a depressive style or behavior that is in notions such as "this situation will not change," "I'm guilty of disappointing and boring other people," "I dislike myself."

Importantly though, the above self-referential propositions (or evaluations) are not only epistemically dependent on linguistic expression. These sentiments are also revealed tacitly through one's habitual way of situational coping.[61] Arguably, then, depressive style carries forward previously established structures of sense or meaning from one's past experiences and overflows into the present (and future): "[space] and its modalities always express the total life of the subject, the energy with which he tends toward a future through his body and world" (2012, 296). Therefore, we have good reason to characterize self-experience in depression as simultaneously entailing a modification of lived-space as well as time. Because space and time are co-implied, and because both space and time are phenomenologically characterized by dilation (or contraction) and expansion, "the perception of space is not a particular class of 'states of consciousness' or of acts, and its modalities always express the total life of the subject, the energy with which

---

[61] Some readers might suggest that the account of depressive-style being proposed dovetails with psychoanalytic theory. In the example of the young child we employed in this chapter, the psychoanalytic approach would insist that the source of depression must be sought in the vicissitudes of one's personal history. Acknowledging that the phenomenological account I have outlined, like analysis, suggests a quasi-archeological methodology to disclose the source of one's affliction, the likeness between these two perspectives is apparent only. The phenomenological framework is crucially dissimilar to psychoanalysis insofar as the former not only rejects unconscious mechanisms, but the existence of the unconscious itself.

[we] tend toward the future through [our] body and [our] world" (Merleau-Ponty 2012, 296). We must understand depressive self-style, then, as that which reveals a particular spatio-temporal hold on the world. Thus, the altered experience of existential-depth reveals to us the extent in which depression affects our hold on the world. Importantly, the self is not constituted by physiological or psychical sequences of events, it is rather the source of time and space springing forth. Hence, the perceptual experience of depth is simultaneously an experience of time, and in depression, these otherwise expansive (centrifugal) experiences are contracted. Lived-space and lived-time, for the depressed person, are not mundane experiences; on the contrary, things and others can prove to be stumbling blocks to mundane experience, the nature of which are characterized by feelings of affective distance and the loss of one's future.

Unsurprisingly, the organization of sense or significance also affects the way in which we establish intersubjective relations. The development of a depressive style likewise implicates the way we deal with others. The example of the ambivalent child illustrates that self-development is not only derived from a dialectic between self and perceptual objects, self-development is simultaneously born out of a dialectic between self and others: "not only do I have a physical world and live surrounded by soil, air, and water, I have around me roads, plantations, villages, streets, churches, a bell, utensils, a spoon, a pipe. Each of these objects bears an imprint the mark of the human action it serves" (Merleau-Ponty 2012, 363). Hence, the way we establish our relations with the world is indicative of how we establish our relations with others and *vice versa*: "our relation to the social, like our relation to the world, is deeper than every explicit perception and deeper than every judgement" (ibid., 378). Accordingly, what we have said thus far concerning the development of a self-style with respect to the perceptual world applies equally to our relationship with others. Subsequently, a depressive style is invariably *informed* (but not necessarily determined) by our contact with others.

However, the case of the "depressed person" we have been employing illustrates why interpersonal situations are inherently structured by two or more selves that possess their own respective will and style. As a young child, the woman's repeated encounter with self-involved parents reveals the extent to which her situation is affected by the convergence of conflicting preferential habits or attitudes expressed by her parents. Her parents also carry forward their own sedimented behaviors that are prolonged or instituted expressions of their own situational (in)ability to cope with the child-parent relation. Thus, as an adult, the woman's preferred way of dealing with situations involving interpersonal conflict or a lack of recognition will be organized in such a way that her preferred style hinges on past habits that overflow into her adult relations with others. The child's sense of being a burden, which spills over into adult life, finds its expression in her inability to cope with interpersonal situations; intimate relations with others may be held at a distance, or conversely, she may learn to resolve this type of situation by comporting herself in such a way that she tries to remain inconspicuous, trying to avoid becoming a burden to those who are supposed to care for her unconditionally. In whatever way she – as a child – came to cope with her situation, the overall way in which the self comports itself in the world is ultimately fashioned according to this inability to resolve affectively demanding situations. And while her coping style may have been both necessary and successful in this situation, as an adult this woman finds that her self-style of coping elicits conflict in her adult relationships with others.

John Russon, who draws upon Merleau-Ponty, has persuasively argued that our inability to master a situation as children can reappear in adult life in the form of "neurotic" embodied habits.[62] However we ultimately wish to characterize embodied habits that are engendered by frustrated development – be it neurosis, stultification, trauma, and so on – the source of frustrated self-development is anchored in "some sector of a person's life [that] cannot function compatibly with the demands of intersubjective life as developed in other sectors of that person's life" (Russon 2003, 81). Situations that, for whatever reason, cannot be mastered, will accordingly engender embodied habits that, if repeatedly enacted, may lead to a privileged or preferred coping (self) style ill-suited to the demands of that situation. With respect to the case of the "depressed person", which I have adopted from Foster-Wallace, I want to supplement it with a long quote from Russon to illustrate how our inability to master a situation structures our non-conceptual, expressive behavior:

> As a child, a woman encountered an arbitrary and authoritarian father and a mother of unpredictable mood and behavior. The household was a site of consistent discomfort, being characterized by frequent outbursts of anger from her father that included threats, humiliation, hitting, and various

---

[62] When Russon uses the term neurosis he is referring to embodied habits that have a neurotic character, meaning that they are the result of "traumas" and manifest themselves when we encounter situations that we were unable to cope with as a child.

> forms of invasion of privacy [...] psychological "survival" in this context required habits for coping with such pressures. As a child, this woman was motivated by her situation to develop a habit of being constantly alert to the explosion of violence [...] [Here parents] induced in her a contradictory experience of other persons, and this motivated her to develop self-defence habits of suspicion and retaliation [...] In her adult life, however, these habits of human interaction fit poorly with the demands of her important personal relationships. What was wise circumspection in her dealings with her parents is unjustified distrust when turned on her non-oppressive friends and companions (ibid., 881-82).

By repeatedly adopting this anticipatory and embodied stance toward similar intersubjective situations in her adult life, the young woman's situational coping as a child becomes sedimented in her self-style. In adult life, the repeated conflict between her self-style and intersubjective situations effectively becomes a depressive style, insofar as her comportment toward the world and others is organized according to the habitual meaning or significance that was structured in her youth.

5.7 Interrupted self-style: Isolation from the world and others

The relevance of intersubjectivity in the context of depression is perhaps more noteworthy when a depressive style is not the primary feature of depressed experience. Due to depression's heterogeneity, not all instances of depression may involve a depressive style, *per se*. To illustrate what I mean, consider a parent who by her own account, leads a generally satisfying life. Yet, when her teenage child leaves home for university in another city or country, she inexplicably finds herself seeking help from the doctor, reporting symptoms of depression. Until now, she reports an otherwise "healthy" life free of depression: "I've never been subject to anything awful enough to warrant this mind-swallowing badness. I have a supportive, loving family, had a happy childhood" (Mehler Paperny 2019, 36). The crucial point to draw from this example is not to speculate whether the child's departure caused her depression. What I want to underscore is that, until this experience of depression, self-experience for her was relatively stable and "well-adjusted." However, what distinguishes her experience from that of the child who develops a depressive style is that the manifestation of depression is acute rather than a consequence of chronic, repetitive habit; every-day life, which otherwise unfolded without explicit disruption, abruptly becomes obstacle-like. Self-experience is interrupted such that she is unable to "be herself."

In contrast to a depressive style, which is a certain way of establishing relations with the world, the parent who unexpectedly finds herself depressed is no longer able to effortlessly enact her self-style. Not only is it the case that world solicitation no longer affects the self "normally", things – and people – are encountered as obstacles: "depression starts out insipid, fogs the days into dull colour, weakens ordinary actions until their clear shapes are obscured by the effort they require" (Solomon 2001, 17). The perceptual thickness that ordinarily marks out significance in lived-experience is affectively diminished: "depth makes something seen or heard co-exist with other sights or sounds by allowing some to be concealed as background, while this background as a certain absence sustains the very prominence of another" (Steinbock 1987, 340). In normal experience, the self spreads out across the perceptual field without the interplay of foreground and background being expressly thematized.

Conversely, in depression, at the level of pre-operative consciousness, the self is no longer "grabbed by" world salience in quite the same way, and the foreground-background structuration that ordinarily permits one to "forget" oneself is inverted. The experience of diminished salience is therefore a constraint of one's ability to *feel* disposed toward one action over another, which is a simplified way to say that the anticipatory character of the protention structure constituting future horizons is disjointed.

Diminished salience or significance is not experienced as a lack, or as an absence of something. It is likewise not a perceptual dysfunction. Instead, the modified capacity to affect or be affected by things in the world is, in part, associated with the way intentional consciousness is oriented toward the world. In particular, thematic (reflective) self-awareness, which is not ordinarily our primary mode of encountering the world, shifts from the experiential background to the foreground of self-experience. Broadly speaking, the diminished ability to be moved by the world consequently renders one painfully self-aware of this inability. By way of example, Gillian Marchenko says that she "focused on the depression alone while everything else in my life dulled to the point where people started to look blurry to me" (2016, 38). A similar sentiment is noted by a respondent in Ratcliffe's qualitative study of depression: "[it] is the worst feeling in the world and when you're absorbed in its depths you just don't even want to be there, anything to stop the numbness and pain" (2015, 111). Both descriptions express two essential components of depressed experience: first, depression envelops the self to the extent that it stands out over and above any other aspects of experience. Yet, this change in focal awareness is not aimed at depression as an object-in-itself; rather, the focus is thematically directed at oneself.

The second component captured by the above description of depressed experience emerges out of this "new" thematic self-awareness, namely that the world of significance recedes in favor of explicitly painful feelings. As the second passage above intimates, depression is often associated with feeling numb or an inability to feel anything, which presents us with a contradiction: the feeling of numbness and the inability to feel, are in fact, both *feelings*, very often overwhelming feelings. Hence the sense of being unaffected remains a thoroughly affective form of experience.

The altered capacity to be affected by one's situation does not represent a gap between oneself and the world inasmuch as it denotes an interruption to the self's pre-reflective stylization. As a result, when persons with depression describe being unable to feel, what they are in fact describing is a heightened feeling, that is to say, the inability to feel is itself a strong feeling. This further leads to a shift in embodied world orientation, such that self-experience is no longer directed away from oneself toward the world, but is instead centripetally turned toward the body. Keeping in mind that the embodied structure of the self is reversible – between the sensing body and sensible body – ordinary, everyday self-experience is predominantly oriented toward the world through the sensing body. Yet, as I have already indicated, in depression, the feeling of numbness or the painful feeling of *not feeling*, denotes a focal experience shift toward the *sensible* body; that is, the body as I experience it explicitly.[63]

On this view, world significance, to which the sensing body (lived-body) is normally attuned, is subordinated to the overwhelming affective discomfort of depression that *invisibly* saturates the body: "depression thrives on its unrelenting invisibility…it thrives by hiding" (Park 2017, 11). To experience depression then, is to experience it as being *everywhere*, an unfortunate consequence of which is that depression is simultaneously experienced as being *nowhere*. Had our investigation of depression been limited to the historical dimensions discussed in Chapter one, we would only be able

—

[63] Drew Leder (1990) characterizes this intentional focal shift toward the body as a dys-appearance. His main argument is that, in illness, one becomes painfully aware of the body. Dis-appearance, on the other hand, is the basic pre-reflective awareness of the body that permits us to conduct practical activities such that the body "dis-appears" from our focal awareness.

to explain the heightened affective experience in depression by appealing to one of two explanatory models: these numb or ubiquitous feelings in depression are a consequence of either an underlying bio-physiological pathology (Kraepelin) or psychic defense mechanisms that are intended to "protect" the depressed person from unresolved, latent psychic conflicts (Freud). We now know, however, that these two polarized explanations of depression do not bear fidelity to lived-experience. The legacy of Kraepelin and Freud, which I argued remain operative in contemporary clinical psychiatric practice (see Chapter 2), cannot accommodate the affective experience of depression I have described since both explanations of depression are abstractions of our being-in-the-world. Had we elected to investigate depression solely from its historical context, as either physio-pathology or psychic conflict, we could only explain depression as something *internal* to the self; that is, as a physical pathology or as psychic mechanisms, both of which are physically located *in* the person. By now, however, it has become clear that this historical dichotomy is based on the ontological assumption that we are *in* the world empirically in the same way that a cookie tin contains cookies. This faulty assumption effaces the obverse structure of intentional experience, which is why it was critical for us to examine the aspects of depression that psychiatry has generally failed to recognize, namely that the self and world form an originary, reciprocal relationship that may only be undone if we adopt an artificial attitude (i.e. objective thought) toward the world.

When we adopt a phenomenological attitude, as we have, the overwhelming affective experience of depression, whereby experience is re-oriented toward one's sensible body, is intelligible as an impediment to establishing or maintaining interpersonal relationships. No one dimension of existence alone can provide us with a complete picture of depression, since each domain is implicated in all other domains; in addition to the perceptual dimension, affective dimension, and linguistic dimension, which are implicated in all conscious experience, we must also address the intersubjective dimension to appreciate why depression is only intelligible against the backdrop of otherness.

What stands out as significant among the shared world with others may fail to affect the person with depression. Slaby has remarked that depression is "marked by profound inability to interactively connect to other people, depressed patients come to feel removed, detached, and alienated from others" (2014, 27). Others no longer return us to ourselves (see section 4.5.1), the ability to attune to the other's conduct keeps us at a distance from the concerns of others. Remarkably, depression has the tendency to exacerbate the putative epistemic problem of "other minds" such that both the depressed person and those around her feel unable to fully understand one another. Anna Mehler-Paperny recounts a conversation that took place with her father about her time spent in hospital after an attempted suicide

> escorted outings [from the hospital] were not carefree ones for my parents [...] [My father said], "You once went into the bathroom at a Queen Street restaurant where we were out for our dinner and suddenly we were terrified that maybe you took a knife to the bathroom and were going to try and kill yourself again [...]" (I was oblivious to this. I just went to the bathroom)" (Mehler Paperny 2019, 16)

A respondent from Karp's study of depression draws attention to an almost inevitable contradiction that arises out of depression's interpersonal dimension, namely that the sufferer endures isolation and distance, from both others and the world:

> Depression steals away whoever you were, prevents you from seeing who you might be someday, and replaces your life with a black hole [...] Nothing human beings value matter any more – music, laughter, love, sex, children, toasted bagels and the *Sunday New York Times* – because nothing and *no one can reach the person* trapped in the void (Karp 1996, 24, emphasis added).

A final example from Gask summarizes the circular problem that is elicited by depression:

> Like many of my patients, I was afraid of feeling isolated and cut off from the rest of the world [...] The problem is that when we become depressed, we often begin to actively isolate ourselves from others, because it's difficult to talk, enjoy company or trust anyone. This leads to a vicious circle whereby we become more isolated and, thus, even lower in mood. The solution isn't always as straight forward as simply being with people again [...] When we are depressed, we may feel particularly ambivalent about being out there in the world with other people (Gask 2015, 120-121).

Our otherwise normal ability to navigate (or gravitate toward) interpersonal life without explicit awareness belongs to the species of "practical action," and is thus equally prone to disturbance in depression. The three descriptions above draw attention to the way depression cleaves the self from the world. Even in difficult or uncomfortable interpersonal situations, we nevertheless remain affectively attuned to our interlocutors, perhaps even more so in different situations. Depression, on the other hand, inhibits the self from fully living in the intentions of others. Similarly, those who attempt to engage someone with depression are met with a reciprocal, affective prohibition, which likewise blunts their attempts to connect with the sufferer. This dynamic is indicative of a classic depression trope whereby the sufferer is accused of lacking empathy, which in turn renders the other person less likely to feel empathy for the sufferer.

Depressed experience is saturated with contradictions and ambiguities. As Ratcliffe astutely notes, the desire to fulfill certain practical actions may remain present but the conative drive or motivation is absent; I may *want* to meet my friend for lunch, or I may want to go out to exercise, but the world no longer draws me in in the way it once did. No matter the intentional aim of the self – be it interpersonal, work related, or imagining one's future goals – depressed experience is formally marked by spatial relations. That is, the ability to effortlessly enact one's self style is predicated on the extent to which one is able to take up disparate situations non-thetically. With this in mind, Bortolan (2017) has noted that descriptions of depression sometimes point to an erasure of boundaries. Arguably, the loss of boundaries illustrates one's inability to gear into a variety of everyday situations; the labile nature of space and time becomes rigid, and the self-style, which actualizes itself according to the specific demands of situational demands, is inhibited or neutralized in the absence of discreet situational boundaries. In the next chapter, part of our task will be to delineate two distinct ways situatedness and lived-space are clinically relevant to clinical diagnosis in the context of self-as-a-style. Taking the categories of major depressive disorder and persistent depressive disorder as our point of reference, I will illustrate two ways the phenomenological analysis of selfhood and depression may thicken the clinical use of the DSM-5. Broadly speaking, I will show that major depressive disorder is consistent with interrupted self-style, while persistent depressive disorder is indicative of a depressive self-style.

5.8 Conclusion

Having completed the phenomenological analysis of depression, a pertinent question remains on the horizon: to what extent is depressive self-style and interrupted self-style clinically salient? Why some people develop a depressive style while others experience an interruption of self-style, is a highly contingent question. As I have argued, what counts as significant for us in a given situation is always concomitant with the way in which our preferred habitual (and therefore, pre-reflective) ways of situational coping develop. It may be tempting to suggest that the trajectory of this development is linear and therefore – in principle – makes it possible to attribute habit with causal factors. Doing so would not only efface the contingency of self-development, it would likewise ignore the innumerable contingent factors involved in the way we take up our lives. In addition to our habitual comportment, because each individual is thrown into the world, the way one comports oneself is delimited by immutable, and therefore insurmountable constraints. Many of our physical capabilities to navigate the world are predicated on the bodies we are born with; we are tall, short, long-limbed, near-sighted, sensitive to some smells and sounds over others, and so on.

The central point to be drawn here is that our capacity to be beings that sense and are sensible is an admixture of determined and indeterminate features, which ultimately makes it futile to attribute, beyond doubt, causal pathways to habitual expressive behavior. This does not mean that it is an impossible endeavor or that we cannot derive reasonable inferences concerning the "cause" of certain habitual styles. I will say more on this topic in the final chapter in the context of therapeutic interventions for depression.

This chapter considered some of the influential phenomenological accounts of depression, all of which share the basic premise that depressed experience expresses an affective change between body and world. However, it was my contention that a proper understanding of this change between self and world demands that we uncover how this affective change is manifested through embodied perception. Through phenomenological analysis, I illustrated that depressed experience is, first and foremost, spatial in nature, which subsequently led me to argue that an overlooked component of depressed experience is the way in which depression is intrinsically related to the existential dimension of depth. By investigating the phenomenological function of depth, it became clear that the loss of possibilities, change in bodily resonance, or altered bodily attunement, may all be aspects of depression, but that these changes are also fundamentally dependent on how sense or significance of the world is structured by the self.

Over the course of this investigation we have become broadly acquainted with selfhood and depression from multiple perspectives, including historical, clinical, theoretical, and phenomenological viewpoints. But what we have yet to consider is what, if any, are the implications of these intersecting perspectives? The task in the final chapter will be to situate the phenomenological findings in the broader context of clinical psychiatry. Drawing on the analysis of selfhood from Chapter 4, where I proposed that selfhood is characterized by habitual self-style, in Chapter 6 I will propose two possible ways that self-style may be relevant to the clinical diagnosis of depression. Using the experiential distinctions of depressive-self-style and the interruption of self-style in depression, I will demonstrate how these two forms of experience may be interpreted as overlapping with the DSM-5 diagnostic category of depression. Moreover, I will provide an overview of how our phenomenological investigation may support and re-imagine the goals of talk-therapy as a project of self-transcendence.

CHAPTER 6

The ends of therapy: Phenomenological implications for diagnosis, treatment, and well-being

6. Introduction

Throughout this investigation I have approached the phenomena of depression and selfhood from historical, clinical, and phenomenological perspectives. This has permitted me to articulate what I consider to be the essential structures of depressed experience. In the preceding chapter, I argued that depression is experientially marked by a contraction or restriction of lived-space. It also became evident that the contraction or restriction of lived-space expresses altered self-experience through perceptual depth. We also acquired novel insights into depression and selfhood by looking at clinical *praxis* (Chapter 2), insights that we subsequently used as a springboard for phenomenological analysis in chapters four and five. The final task for this investigation will be to address several practical implications that may be derived from the phenomenological findings in the previous two chapters.

In this final chapter, I consider three different ways that our investigation of depression and selfhood may positively contribute to clinical practices in psychiatry. The first practical consideration concerns the phenomenological relevance of self-style in the context of depression diagnosis. I contend that altered self-style in depressed experience is diagnostically identifiable in two basic ways: first, I argue that depressive *style* is diagnostically indicative of persistent depressive disorder (PDD); second, I argue that the *interruption* of self-style is diagnostically indicative of major depressive disorder (MDD). Recall, if you will, from the interviews in Chapter 2, where clinicians overwhelmingly reported tension between the clinical imperative to provide a diagnosis and the "impersonal" diagnostic criteria that are used to identify depression. By employing a diagnostic distinction between depressive style and interrupted style, clinicians who had expressed ambivalence concerning the diagnostic process will find that a phenomenologically-inspired approach to depression diagnosis may help assuage concerns that DSM-5 depression criteria result in an "impersonal" sketch of the person being diagnosed.

The second practical implication of our phenomenological study of depression addresses the way in which selfhood is implicated in determining therapeutic goals.[64] Specifically, based on the account of self-as-style I developed in Chapter 4, it would be inaccurate to assume that the overarching therapeutic aim for people with depression is to return to a "previous" state of self, or to recover a non-depressed version of oneself. From a phenomenological perspective, the temporal dimension of selfhood precludes the possibility of characterizing selfhood as an entity that remains self-same over time. In Chapter 3, I argued that metaphysical conceptions of selfhood, according to which the self is understood as an enduring entity, only make sense if abstracted from lived-experience. Accordingly, depression cannot be reduced to a mere "moment" or isolated experience in one's life; like all experience, depressed experience is an extension of past experiences that shape and orient our future experiences, and as a consequence prevents us from characterizing selfhood as a static phenomenon.

The third (and final) implication of this investigation concerns the way in which our phenomenological description of selfhood and depression maybe used to establish basic (meta) goals that I believe to be fundamental to any psychotherapeutic method, irrespective of particular professional norms and professional competencies that guide a particular psychotherapeutic orientation (e.g. cognitive behavioral therapy, psychodynamic therapy, dialectical behavioral therapy, art therapy, and so on). Hence, even though a clinician's psychotherapeutic competence will depend, to a large extent, on his or her professional training, we can nevertheless develop essential therapeutic goals that will subtend any modality of therapy, irrespective of a clinician's theoretical or practical training.

But rather than developing a novel set of meta-goals to guide therapeutic approaches to depression, I want to instead elaborate on existing goals that are formulated in Russon's account of psychotherapy as a *therapeutic project* (Russon, 2003). In addition to the fact that Russon's notion of a therapeutic project is deeply indebted to the philosophy of Merleau-Ponty, Russon's proposal is particularly appealing since the nature of a psychotherapeutic project is remarkably consistent with the nature of an *existential*-project. Importantly, it is also an intersubjective project that is com-

—

[64] I use the term therapy broadly to denote psychotherapeutic (or similar) approaches.

prised of individual responsibilities that must be upheld by both patient and clinician respectively. This said, even if both patient and clinician were to successfully fulfill his or her respective *individual* therapeutic responsibilities, it must be kept in mind that a therapeutic project is also rooted in the inviolable intersubjective demand to be recognized and confirmed by an other self (the therapist). Put plainly, it is an ongoing project, the success of which depends upon intersubjective engagement. This means that a satisfactory vision of therapy should not be one that prioritizes self-directed introspection. Instead, therapeutic goals subtend the therapeutic relationship and must be navigated by both parties. However, the psychiatric professional is not just another person with whom a patient seeks out for help. The psychiatric clinician acts as a surrogate on behalf of reality, and of others, in general, the overarching aim of which is to make it possible for persons with depression to be oneself.

6.1 A Fork in the depression road: Two directions for selfhood

Over the course of this investigation I have stressed that depression is rooted in a dynamic relationship between self and world. In normal everyday experience, the self-world relation is a reciprocally structured dyad: between a self who senses, and a self who is sensitive to the sensible world. Contemporary phenomenological accounts of depression (see sections 5.1.1 and 5.1.2) have rightly noted that in depression this reciprocal dynamic is affectively modified. Whether this experiential modification is characterized as a loss of possibilities (Ratcliffe, 2015), a change in bodily resonance (Fuchs, 2001), or a change in affective attunement (Svenaeus, 2014), all three characterizations express variations of a shared theme: *affective changes in depression are attributed to pre-operative, intentional self-experience.* Still, though I concur with this characterization, I have also argued that depressed experience elicits a reorganization of structured perceptual habits *vis-à-vis* self-style, which in turn underscores how a loss of possibilities, a loss of resonance, or altered attunement, are all operative with an implicit, perceptually grounded, notion of selfhood. Furthermore, because my argument stipulates a mutual dependence between selfhood and depression, we can make a fine-grained phenomenological distinction about the way in which selfhood is diagnostically implicated in both major depression (MDD) and persistent depression (PDD), something that extant phenomenological accounts of depression are unable to achieve.

At the outset of Chapter 1, I provided a schematic of the American Psychiatric Association's DSM-5 diagnostic criteria that enable clinicians to identify two categories of depression: persistent depressive disorder (PDD) and major depressive disorder (MDD). A diagnosis of persistent depression is obtained when depression symptoms have persisted for at least *two years* or longer. In major depression, by contrast, a person need only to experience symptoms for a minimum of two weeks, which means the crucial diagnostic difference between PDD and MDD is that of duration. My phenomenological analysis of depression in the previous chapter, which specified two ways that selfhood is implicated in depression (depressive-style and interrupted style), supports the distinction between PDD and MDD based on duration. For instance, since self-style develops early in infancy, I argued that depression may sometimes be the outcome of a person's repeated inability to deal with situations that he or she was unable to satisfactorily resolve. The inability to cope with the demands of one's situation, over a protracted period of time, engenders a situated and embodied habitual style that I want to characterize as a depressive style; a manner of habitual comportment that becomes privileged over time.

For clinicians, then, the notion of depressive-style diagnostically coincides with the DSM-5 category of persistent depression (which must be experienced minimally for at least two or more years) by virtue of temporal duration. Conversely, with respect to major depression, the symptoms of which need only be present for two weeks, rather than a depressive-style, we witness an *interruption* to self-style. So, while the phenomenological perspective permits us to discern differences between MDD and PDD by drawing on lived-experience, these two divergent forms of depression share an underlying phenomenological insight, namely that depression inhibits the ability to be oneself.

It is important that we do not overstate the transformative power of our phenomenological insights with respect to depression diagnosis. Even if clinicians are (or become) clinically adept at identifying depressive-style and interrupted style, it would be naïve to presume that this phenomenological distinction remedies diagnostic problems of reliability and validity that were discussed at length in Chapter 1. The phenomenological distinction between depressive-style and interrupted style is intended to provide clinicians with a diagnostic aid that supplements existing diagnostic protocols and (if necessary) permits clinicians to make fine-grained distinctions based on lived-experience, should such a need arise. Hence, though this phenomenological distinction between depressive-style and interrupted style will not radically transform psychiatric practice, it nonetheless serves as a gentle reminder to clinicians that encounters with depression are likewise encounters with selfhood.

The emphasis placed on lived-experience also helps make clinicians mindful of the fact that the appropriate therapeutic goals for depression treatment should also attend to the way in which patients have habituated their relations with the world. Clinicians who find the phenomenological findings from Chapter 5 compelling, may choose to supplement the diagnostic process by drawing on the phenomenological descriptions of depression that were provided in the previous chapter. In addition to the DSM-5 diagnostic criteria for depression, clinicians may elect to further probe patients with questions aimed at lived-experience: how do you experience things in the world? Do you feel connected or detached to things and to people? How do certain situations solicit embodied habits that are often taken for granted? These examples are merely intended to illustrate that it is possible for clinicians to adopt phenomenological sensibilities should he or she identify a need for more fine-grained descriptions. All the while, the distinction between self-style and MDD/PPD gently reminds clinicians that depression is ultimately a disorder of the self, the source of which is rooted in the patient's pre-reflective contact with the world.

6.1.1 Persistent depressive disorder: Fitting a round peg in a square hole

In Chapter 5 I characterized depressive-style as an intelligent behavior that expresses a specific habitual way of skillfully coping with certain situations. When this situation is repeatedly encountered over time, our intelligent behavior or self-style is embodied as a preferred way of dealing with the situation in question. In the case of the "depressed person," whose parents failed to exhibit genuine interest in her life, we should not understand her depressive style as pathological, in the bio-medical sense. Instead, her depressive style in adult life is an elaboration of embodied habits that, as a young child, enabled her to cope with the intersubjective tensions that were a predominant source of disquiet. However, in adult life, this coping style, which had proven successful as a child, can prove problematic when encountering situations that resemble those from her childhood. For this reason, to suffer from persistent depressive disorder is comparable to repeatedly attempting to fit a round peg in a square hole; no matter how many times the woman attempts to transcend the problematic situation, the sedimented habits from her youth – which were previously fruitful – enact a style that repeatedly proves itself to be inadequate to satisfy the demands of her situation as an adult.

Staying for a moment with the case of the "depressed person" from Chapter 5, whose parents, recall, were so caught up in their own interpersonal struggle that, as a young child, the depressed person learned to comport herself toward the world as inconspicuously as possible. And because this situation could not be satisfactorily overcome, her embodied stance toward the world established itself as one of guilt and in turn reinforced her sense of being burdensome to and for others. To repeatedly experience oneself as the source of discord between others motivates a particular way of situational coping that, over time, engenders sedimented habits that stultify interpersonal situations.

A potential objection from a cognitive-scientific perspective might claim that the child's feelings of guilt are associated with a cognitive-schema that disposes her to evaluate reality negatively. But as I have stressed throughout this investigation, we must recognize that the existence of a cognitive-schema is only possible by first abstracting lived-experience; that is, a cognitive-schema is predicated on the presence of a non-cognitive body-schema that is perceptually sensitive to the world prior to conceptual thought, which as a result, enables us to habituate intelligent behavior without the use of mediating concepts or propositions.

The young child's inability to deal with the interpersonal situation compromises her future ability to *spontaneously* establish new levels of significance in similarly structured situations. I want to cite once more Merleau-Ponty's existential characterization of depth, which we addressed early in Chapter five. It reiterates that self-style is expressed by "lived distance [that] links me to things that count for me and exist for me, and links them to each other. At each moment, this distance measures the 'scope' of my life" (Merleau-Ponty 2012, 299). Therefore, the scope of one's life in long-term depression is only as expansive as one's habits will permit: "a habit precisely anticipates the world to which we are habituated" (Morris 2004, 47). The extent to which some things stand out as more significant than others is, among other things, indicative of how the self has organized and stylized lived-space through sedimented habits. As a result, one's preferred – but ineffective – ways of dealing with a situation may institute a depressive style; that is, a habit anticipates a certain outcome because the style establishes a set of practices which are simultaneously prolonged or carried into one's present concerns. This process of prolongation is depicted in Merleau-Ponty's reference to Goethe, to whom he attributes the saying, "genius is posthumous productivity" (2010c, 9). Put in the context of our discussion here, the self establishes a relation with the world that continues to "work" long after it was initially instituted, which is why a depressive style should be considered to be a particular embodied relation to the world that has developed successively over time.

At the most basic level, I am claiming that self-development – and hence self-style – is expressed through our preferred ways of encountering the world. Reciprocally, these preferred ways are motivated by a situation. It would be remiss to characterize depressive-style as a secondary expression that derived, first and foremost, from a primary tension between "nurture versus nature," since neither "nature" nor "nurture" capture the way in which situations are always *contingent upon the way in which we take up those situations*. Hence, a phenomenological analysis encourages us to recognize that self-style in long-term depression expresses a habituated style at odds with certain situational demands that are repeatedly encountered over the course of one's life.[65]

6.1.2 Interrupted self: Constricted space in major depression

In contrast to PDD, where self-style manifests as a depressive style, self-style in MDD is instead *interrupted*. This does not mean that a person diagnosed with major depression lacks a self-style. On the contrary, major depression disrupts or inhibits the "effortless" ability with which self-style is enacted. A peculiar feature of major depression, then, is that one becomes acutely aware of the inability to be oneself.

The phenomenological analysis in Chapter 5 helped illuminate how depressed *experience* is often "silent" or "hidden." Hence, although a competent clinician may be adept at identifying the salient depression symptoms upon encountering a patient, he or she may nevertheless fail to fully tease out the extent to which the cluster of objective symptoms is discontinuous with the phenomenological state of affairs:

> I looked at the trees turning [color] and I didn't care. I couldn't believe it. I'd be looking at this big flaming maple and I'd look at it and I'd think, "There it

---

[65] Anna Bortolan proposes a similar idea about the relationship between depression and narrativity. She posits that changes to affective world orientation in depression alter a person's narrative, and subsequently structure new narratives that are predicated on the configuration of affective background feelings (existential-feelings). This position, however, begins from the assumption that depression is characteristically a disturbance to the *narrative* self, whereas I am arguing that depression implicates the self *per se*.

> is, it's a maple tree. Its bright orange and red." And nothing in me was touched" (Karp 1996, 61).

Unfortunately, clinicians tend not to be recipients of rich descriptions such as this one. Nevertheless, this respondent's description of depressed experience underscores how objective signs and symptoms – which are intended to index the "realness" of depression – may very often fail to converge with lived-experience. Even in the brief passage above we can glean basic phenomenological insights into the experience of depression. The respondent's description of depression compels us to recognize that depression is not just, as the adage goes, like wearing dark tinted sunglasses. Depression is not a misevaluation of reality but rather an implicit change to the entire structure of intentional experience.

In otherwise normal circumstances, objects of perception – such as the maple tree – tear us away from ourselves. Perceptual awareness of the tree structures my perceptual foreground, simultaneously necessitating that my bodily awareness is shifted to the perceptual background. Interestingly, however, in the example of the maple tree, the respondent's description of depressed experience illustrates that precisely the opposite occurs: the respondent's bodily awareness assumes the perceptual foreground while the maple (as object of perception) recedes to the experiential background. She is no longer "touched" by the tree, presumably meaning she is not stirred by the tree's beauty or its vibrant colors. Put in phenomenological terms, major depression is marked by an altered capacity to affect, and be affected by, the world.

One of the central phenomenological distinctions between MDD and PDD concerns the reversibility of sensible experience. That is, the embodied ability to shift the focal awareness of the body as perceptual foreground or the body as perceptual background in intentional experience. Leder's work on embodiment deals extensively with the way in which bodily awareness is experientially modified in illness. For instance, he writes that when we are ill, "we are no longer dispersed out *there* in the world, but suddenly congeal right *here*" (1990, 75 emphasis original). In the context of major depression, the ubiquitous bodily feelings – which we said may be also be experienced as not have feeling – inhibits our capacity to be experientially drawn away from oneself.

Although Leder is mainly interested in the phenomenological significance of the body in somatic illness, his phenomenological account of bodily experience is nevertheless broad enough to encompass embodied illness experiences of depression. His characterization of embodied illness is especially pertinent to depression for the reason that it aptly captures the way in which depth is experientially modified in lived-space, such that the power of our hold on the world has changed. Aspects of the world fail to solicit us in the way they once did, the result of which subsequently reveals a disparity between our normal habitual style of meeting the world, and the inability to maintain this style.

It is understandable, then, that major depression often renders people feeling "unlike themselves," something J.S Park became acutely aware during his own experience of depression: "depression is a fog in which I collapse inward and lose all sense of myself. I know when it begins, like I've stepped into a sweeping cold, and I know when it ends, as if I've stepped into new air, like the cold was never there" (2009, 13). Here, I want to stress that in major depression, the dimensions of depth, affect, and world salience do not simply disappear, for they are necessary features of conscious experience. It is also important to emphasize that unlike self-alienation or self-dissolution, which often accompanies schizophrenia (Stephensen and Henriksen 2017), self-style in depression does not implode or disintegrate despite the apparent sense that one's world is disintegrating. And though Park's own experience of depression is somewhat at odds with this claim, I want to further argue that his description in fact *supports* the idea that selfhood remains "intact." When Park provides us with the image of stepping into fresh air, he tacitly describes depression – not as an alien invader or hostile intruder – but precisely as a way of establishing relations with the world, the ubiquitous feeling that depression is everywhere and nowhere: "I've stepped into new air, like the cold was never there."

Perceptual experience remains grounded in the concrete, shared world, of others. The overarching feature of major depression is an inability to "dilate" one's situation. As Artaud so eloquently puts it: "we can accept life only on the condition of greatness, only if we feel ourselves at the origin of the phenomena, at least a certain number of them. Without the power of expansion, without a certain domain over things, life is indefensible" (1927, 17n 1). Artaud articulates the way in which intentional consciousness directs us toward the world as beings endowed with a capacity to dilate our lived-world. For Merleau-Ponty,

> [it is the] power of marking out borders and directions in the given world, of establishing lines of force, of arranging perspectives, of organizing the given world according to the moment, and of constructing upon the geographical

> surroundings a milieu of behavior and a system of significations that express, on the outside, the internal activity of the subject (2012, 15).

Both Artaud and Merleau-Ponty recognize that being-in-the-world is experientially prior to the common-sense view that we are *contained by* the world; from a phenomenological perspective, world significance or lines of force express the extent to which we are perceptually geared into the world without explicit awareness. By way of illustration, I have emphasized how lived-experience is marked by a double movement of sedimentation and spontaneity, that is, a capacity to both enact and transcend bodily-habits by virtue of being primordially open to perceptual sense; accordingly, world significance is expressed through the body as a self-style, and once we recognize that this "activity of the subject" may be read through the expressive body, we can no longer presume that the thoughts, desires, and inner-life of the other is forever inaccessible to us.

Having said this, and according to the perspective of objective thought, if we want to penetrate the world of the other, we need to pare back behaviors and linguistic expressions to discover his or her true intentions, desires, or feelings. Objectively observed physical symptoms commonly associated with major depression – including sluggishness, stupor, an inability to concentrate, or general malaise – qualitatively indicate a decrease in vitality. I believe that vitality is not an altogether uninstructive term, but only insofar as it signifies an openness or ability to take up countless possible scenarios that we encounter during our lives. Here, vitality is not a blind, life-preserving force, that lurks beneath conscious experience. This capacity to place ourselves in different situations, which we discussed earlier in Chapter 4, is nothing other than what Husserl (and later, Merleau-Ponty) call the "I can" of consciousness; that is, an embodied plasticity or preparedness to do things in the world without cognitive mediation. If we observe these "vital symptoms" such as languor and sluggishness, they do not simply indicate depression in the way that smoke is taken to indicate fire. Instead, these physical expressions are depression, as such. For this reason, one's reduced ability to engage with otherwise normal situations in MDD is underscored by a *contraction* or *narrowing* of lived-space. Restricted spontaneous action and capacity to affect and be affected by the world not only modifies self-style, it more generally interrupts one's ability to effortlessly enact it.

My phenomenological analysis of depression in Chapter 5 addressed the spatial nature of depressed experience. I supported this claim by suggesting that the word de-pression evokes a sense of *pulling away* from the world. I situated this meaning of depression in the context of operative-intentionality so as to illustrate that the common-sense notion that depression elicits feelings of being "pressed down" is more accurately a feeling of being distanced from the world. Using this sense of the word depression, I contended that in normal experience, the existential-dimension of depth expresses our voluminous or expansive hold on the world. But when we considered the descriptions of persons who have experienced depression, it became apparent that many of the respondents reported a sense of world detachment, as well as an explicit awareness of depression itself.

One way to characterize the experience of "detachment" and "explicit awareness of depression" is that it inhibits the ability to be oneself. The experience of depth in depression is one of contraction or narrowing, such that self-awareness becomes a prominent foreground feature of experience. This description of depressed experience dovetails with the notion of bodily corporealization (Fuchs) and altered affective resonance (Svenaeus) we considered in Chapter 5. In everyday life our embodied experience is oriented toward the world from the perspective of the *sensing* body; we are turned away from ourselves toward things in the world. But as Fuchs rightly points out, in major depression, our focal awareness is consumed by the *sensible* body. In other words, due to overwhelming feelings (or change in feelings) the body becomes object-like insofar as major depression renders the person acutely self-aware of being "object-like." As a result, a person's normal everyday affective engagement with the world, which is the basic experiential mode that permits self-stylization (i.e. effortlessly and pre-reflectively), is inhibited by bodily self-awareness.

6.2 Re-framing the clinical coping strategy

Now that we have considered how a phenomenological understanding of selfhood may be practically relevant to the diagnostic component of clinical practice, I want now to specify the way in which our phenomenological approach to selfhood is relevant to the therapeutic context. As we have seen, self-as-a-style is a developmental phenomenon that emerges from perceptual and practical experiences structured by meaning. This style is enacted through habitual or preferred ways of establishing contact with the world. For some people, there may have been a time – perhaps over an extended period of one's life – when the development of certain behaviors and habits were necessary for dealing with the demands of his or her milieu. As we mature, these established habits are retained as embodied sedimented structures for action, and although these habits may have been crucial to cope with one's situation at a pervious point in one's life, these habits may not be suitable for resolving situations of a similar kind later in life.

In the example of the "depressed person," whose childhood was marked by parental indifference, her habituated way of dealing with this type of situation was productive, even necessary. However, her inability in adult life to transcend what was a previously fruitful style of comportment is (eventually) expressed as a depressive self-style. Crucially, depressive-style does not represent stunted development, and it would be misguided to evaluate a depressive-style as "abnormal" or "negative," for at one point in her life this style *was* both a normal and positive way to make sense of her situated life.

Incorporating phenomenological language in the psychotherapeutic context can both compliment and support extant therapeutic goals that guide therapeutic practices. I want to stress that clinicians may become increasingly at ease with phenomenological insights, such as those we have discussed over the course of this investigation, without having to adopt entirely novel approaches to talk-therapy. For instance, I think it is essential that clinicians retain their empathic intuition to protect or shield patients from over-identifying with their diagnosis (see section 2.5.1).

An overarching goal that ought to guide the therapeutic process refers back to the clinician's coping strategy, which was discussed at length during Chapter 2 (section 2.3.1). Here, however, rather than distancing patients from the problem (i.e. you are not the problem, depression is the problem), the notion of self-as-a-style enables clinicians to invert their strategy. The impetus to protect patients can remain intact without severing depression from the person. Not only is it possible for clinicians to recognize that depression is inseparable from the sufferer, they can do so without fear of ascribing blame or guilt to the depressed patient:

> He or she is not simply thinking, feeling, desiring, etc., in ways that differ from what is normal in human beings, but in ways that significantly affect his or her chances of achieving a *satisfactory* human life. At the same time, he or she is not properly described as depraved, or corrupt, or blameworthy, since it seems clear that the condition is not correctable by a simple unaided choice on the part of the sufferer (Matthews 1999, 309, emphasis original).

Viewed this way, it is essential that clinicians retain their compassionate stance toward patients, but in doing so, there is no need to artificially separate the patient from the diagnosis. For clinicians, then, their strategy can be re-framed by characterizing a patient's depressive style as a reasonable practical response to what was – at one point in time – an otherwise stultifying situation. As Russon sees it, "our habitual behaviors *are intelligent*: they exist for discernable reasons rooted in the history of our development" (2003, 134, emphasis original). The phenomenological analysis of selfhood as a style can temper clinical worries that patients may be prone to over-identify with their depression diagnosis (section 2.5.1). Likewise, by acknowledging the tight-knit relationship between depression and selfhood, we can assuage clinical worries that depression diagnosis *negatively* affects the patient. Together, clinician and patient address *intelligent* (motivated) behaviors rather than behaviors that are flawed or engendered by negative evaluations of reality.

Framing a patient's behavior as intelligent rather than a moral or personal failure is an approach that can assuage a clinician's unease about the relationship between patient identity and depression. As a general overarching goal, this approach encourages clinicians to view a *patient's* self-style as an expressive coping strategy, an essential strategy that unfortunately proves to be anachronistic in similar situations during one's mature life. But the ultimate benefit of identifying selfhood as a behavioral style is that it invites clinicians to reconsider the goals of talk-therapy in general; it encourages clinicians to prefigure the project of therapy as self-education or self-transcendence. Because coping strategies are rooted in habitual engagement with the world, part of the therapeutic goal, then, aims at modifying self-style as a project of self-understanding, all of which takes place in the context of how one engages with the world at large.

6.2.1 The "normal" self is not a previous self

Throughout this study I have repeatedly invoked the claim that in depression not only is something different, *something is different with me*. What sets depressive disorders apart from physical injury and other forms of illness is that depression envelops the sufferer in such a way that he or she cannot attribute it to a specific location in (or on) the body. In the previous section, I suggested that depression is recognizable – not just as signs and symptoms but – through an embodied depressive-style. Then again, because this style is structured unreflectively, we should not presume that the depressed person experiences herself as being depressed, particularly given the all-encompassing nature of depressed experience.

How, then, should we understand the medical imperative to treat depression when clinicians encounter persons whose "loss [of a once-flourishing life] is not just profound, but senseless – loss without reason, without explanation, without meaning" (Hoffmaster 2014, 37)? A patient cannot locate the pain or problem; it feels everywhere and subsequently nowhere. But the analysis of both selfhood and depression in chapters four and five showed us that depression is indeed somewhere, insofar as self-experience is always situated. Thus, when depression is experienced as a pervasive feeling, the *is-ness* does not reside in phylogenetic dysfunction; rather, depression coalesces around the self: the expressive source through whom depression hangs together. By adopting the phenomenological perspective, we have been able to disclose the extent to which depressed *experience* is remarkably divergent from those symptoms used to classify that experience.

Without a phenomenological perspective our description of depression would be restricted to one *aspect* of embodied experience; we would only have access to embodied experience as a *sensible* body. As a consequence, our analysis of depression would exclude the obverse experience of being a *sensing* body; we would be unable to flesh out the way in which experiential awareness of the world changes. Consider, for example, the qualitative experiential difference between objective depression symptoms – such as decreased appetite, psycho-motor agitation – and the phenomenological description of depression where "one feels lost in this empty space in which it is not possible to grasp or to reach anything. Between the self and things, between the self and the other opens a gap in which one lives in a state of suspension" (Micali 2014, 216). The distance between self and world, as we have illustrated with the dimension of depth, is not an objective or quantifiable observation. This distance cannot be captured by objective thought given that it is affectively disclosed through the operative-intentional establishment of one's relation to the world. And it is precisely this relation to the world that remains inaccessible to non-phenomenologically grounded approaches to depression.

I want to elaborate further on Micali's excellent description of depressed experience and lived-space. Even if one rationally knows *that* the world is not measurably further away, the world nonetheless feels out of reach, which is itself a painfully unsettling feeling. This experience is nicely illustrated in Sylvia Plath's auto-biographical novel when she describes how depression has re-configured the significance of even banal features of everyday life:

> I knew perfectly well the cars were making a noise, and the people in them and behind the lit windows of the buildings were making a noise, and the

> river was making a noise, but I couldn't hear a thing. The city hung in my window, flat as a poster, glittering and blinking, but it might just as well not have been there at all, for all the good it did me (2005, 17).

Plath's description conveys how depression engenders an experiential dissonance between how things are and how they once were. Moreover, Plath's acute awareness of the "distance" between her milieu and herself is consistent with the way in which self-style is interrupted in major depression, which for Plath is punctuated by a heightened sense of being affectively impotent in the world.

Most people who experience depression are motivated to seek out psychiatric help by a basic desire to "feel like oneself" again. Put plainly, one wants to feel normal. Sometimes in somatic medicine, normality may be recognized as the absence of pathology, or in the case of pathology, one returns to a state of normality by eradicating the presence of a foreign entity. While this characterization of medical normality is over-simplified, it proves useful for assessing the therapeutic distinction between being depressed and being well. Accordingly, in the context of our phenomenological analysis of depression and selfhood, if an aim of the therapeutic process is to restore a patient's ability to "feel like oneself" again, it should not be understood as a *return* to a previous self or state of self: "Health after healing is not the same health as before. The lucid consciousness of the fact that *healing is not a return* helps the patient in his search for the state of least possible renunciation by liberating him from his fixation upon his previous case" (Canguilhem 2012b, 66, emphasis added). Canguilhelm views "normal" or healthy experience as a capacity or power to intervene in situations that are significant for us. A resumption of the previous self would belie the indeterminate nature of existence, which we previously characterized using Merleau-Ponty, as a double movement of "sedimentation and spontaneity" (Merleau-Ponty 2012). All experience modifies already acquired capacities and habits – even if only slightly – which are subsequently incorporated into one's pre-existing bodily disposition toward the world.

6.2.2 The project of therapy

The goals of therapy that I am endorsing for depression are not intended to represent indicators of success. Precisely, the goals of therapy I have in mind do not determine or measure what a successful therapeutic outcome ought to entail. It is important, of course, to recognize that therapy *can* establish and work toward outcome-based goals, such as improvement of personal functioning (e.g. daily activities, basic tasks, work, etc.).

However, since I have portrayed self-style to be deeply rooted in sedimented habits, which may later develop into depressed-style or interrupted style, the goals of a therapeutic project must support the *possibility* of self-change. Based on this broad therapeutic goal of self-change, the psychotherapeutic treatment of depression is, from the outset, a process of re-education. According to Matthews, psychotherapeutic oriented interventions are "not unlike a form of *education*, involving, like all genuine education, the active involvement of the 'student,' rather than anything like conventional medical treatment for bodily illness, in which the 'patient,' as that name itself suggests, is largely passive" (1999, 309, emphasis original). Within the phenomenological framework that has guided our investigation, therapy as "moral" education should be understood as (re)orienting one's life in accordance with a vision of what will constitute a satisfactory life. Interestingly, therapy understood in this way overlaps with Merleau-Ponty's claim that life is inherently an existential project: "I am the one who gives a sense and a future to my life, but this does not mean that I conceive of this sense and this future; rather, they spring forth from my present and form my past, and particularly from my present and past mode of coexistence" (2012, 472). Merleau-Ponty's sentiment is particularly poignant since it reiterates for us why there is no return to a pure self or previous self. Furthermore, it reminds us also that self-as-style is not causally fettered to the past. It is true that there are "facts" about our past, but the sense or meaning of these facts are not immutable. In fact, as Merleau-Ponty argues, that we understand ourselves through the past, follows from our orientation toward the world in the present.

I want to briefly draw attention to Merleau-Ponty's importance for existential-psychoanalysis and how it dovetails nicely with my characterization of therapy as a project of re-stylization. I discussed the historical legacy of Freud at length in Chapter 1, but said little of the psychoanalytic process itself. One significant reason for this omission is that psychiatry's desire to retain its status as a medical profession prompted the American Psychiatric Association to expunge analytic theory from its ranks. Unsurprisingly, as a result of psychiatric reform in the 1980s, psychoanalytic theory became anathema to the empirical scientific image that psychiatry desperately sought to emulate. It was a considerable fall from grace, since psychoanalysis, being the one-time dominant theoretical framework of psychiatric medicine, effectively became a fringe approach to problems such as depression. All the same, even though psychiatric medicine moved toward the medical model of treatment and care, the influence of analysis was not altogether vanquished. As psychiatrists began to focus on psychopharmacological interventions for depression, talk-therapy emerged as a therapeutic treatment that co-existed with psychiatry yet ultimately emerged as a practice independent of psychiatry with its own professional standards and internal norms. Today, though psychoanalytic treatment retains popularity in a small segment of the population, its legacy lives on through psychodynamic oriented approaches to therapy.

With respect to Merleau-Ponty's relationship to psychoanalysis, the former places confidence in the latter, not because psychoanalysis is theoretically sound or that it discloses Truth about oneself, but on account of the general process of analysis as such. Merleau-Ponty critically engaged with the work of Freud extensively over the course of his career and rejected, like most phenomenologists, the meta-psychological structure of the unconscious. For example, in a working note written just prior to his death, Merleau-Ponty writes: "The Id, the unconscious – and the Ego (correlative) to be understood on the basis of flesh" (1968, 270). The Freudian meta-psychological structure, Merleau-Ponty claims, maps onto the ontological structure of intentional consciousness. That is, while the notion of unconscious processes is phenomenologically dubious, we find nonetheless that the Ego-Id dynamic maps onto the ambiguous nature of consciousness: the reversibility (or aspect shift) of operative-intentional experience and thetic experience of consciousness. The main difference, however, is that neither aspect of intentional consciousness is ever *un*conscious. As Merleau-Ponty's working notes intimate, if psychoanalysis is to prove fruitful, it is only on the basis that our interpretations are ontological rather than psychical. So, while phenomenology and psychoanalysis are not entirely continuous with one another, they share the same overarching goal: disclosing the same "latent" content, which phenomenologically speaking, is existence; that is, the source of our unreflective and embodied existence.

The affinity between the structure of the psychoanalytic approach, on the one hand, and therapy as an existential project, on the other, lies in the process itself, whereby a therapeutic project is broadly defined as an open-ended process that aims to align (or re-align) one's sedimented habits with one's vision of a flourishing life. In one sense, both these approaches are quasi-genealogical, insofar as the source of the patient's suffering is bound up in his or her life history; likewise, psychoanalysis and therapy-as-a-project are both interested in identifying past "traumas" as a means to release the patient from her suffering. However, a crucial distinction between these two methods is the way in which traumas are resolved. In analysis, the analysand attempts to resolve his or her "traumas" (or micro-traumas) by bringing unconscious conflicts into consciousness, the trauma –in principle – will no longer elicit undesirable behaviors that developed out of the person's inability to overcome his or her situation.

A therapeutic project, by contrast, though concerned with the person's life history, cannot resolve a trauma by virtue of bringing it to conscious awareness. As I already claimed, becoming aware of one's self-style or behavior is insufficient to engender permanent change. The genealogical character of therapy indeed requires that we interrogate our past, but this interrogation is not one of causal explanation. Broadly construed, the goal of therapy is to make sense of one's intelligent behaviors in light of their relationship to a traumatic situation. Simply put, self-transcendence is the task of making sense of oneself in relation to temporal horizons (the past and the future) by re-organizing how one comports oneself to difficult situations in the present.

A therapeutic project, which is oriented around the development of new or modified habits that express self-style, does not consist in "a liberation from his childhood's *psychotraumata,* but of a liberation from the *significance* of the *psychotraumata* [...] the patient *learns to see* his past differently" (van den Berg 1972, 98, emphasis added). This "liberation," as van den Berg understands it, does not consist in approaching one's personal history as a series of causal events that, should we attempt to re-trace them, will deliver us to the causal origin of one's depression; liberation from one's past permits a patient to recognize that she may not have been "right about" herself; the "facts" of her past do not reify her future.

Hence, a therapeutic project shares features with psychoanalysis, but the two are far from interchangeable. The goal of self-transcendence is rooted, not in the "truth" of the past, but rather in the way in which we establish relations to the world according to the organization of sense; I cannot erase the "traumas" of my past, but I can gather together a new sense of these events. For example, in the case of the "depressed person" that we have considered already, her comportment toward the world and others is constrained by her sense of being a burden or imposition; her struggle with interpersonal relations is expressed by her comportment toward the situation; the sense of being invisible to her parents is witnessed in her literal attempts to be invisible, and when she cannot be invisible, the depressed person would "always implore any friend she was on the telephone with to tell her the very *second* she (i.e., the friend) was getting bored or frustrated or repelled or she felt that she had more interesting things to do" (Foster Wallace 2007, 44). In her adult life, the depressed person's way of establishing relations with both others and the world is habitually distanced and apologetic; her power to dilate the world is limited by her embodied habit of closing in around herself; her ability to deal with interpersonal situations as an adult is delimited by her habitual contact with otherness, which in turn is structured by her sense of being burdensome.

The therapeutic project is a concrete project, which is another way to say it is a process that is actively sustained and prolonged. It assumes that the possibility of self-transcendence is a two-fold achievement: first, patient and therapist work to re-organize sense or meaning that guides our habitual action, which is to say, interrogating one's sedimented past so as to uncover new structures of meaning that underscore undesirable behavior; second, this new sense or significance must eventually be re-habituated through action.

Crucially, however, therapy as "education" or existential project departs from cognitive-based approaches that typically focus on developing pragmatic solutions to resolve so-called negative evaluations of reality. Therapy is a project of re-education; the person engaged in therapy cannot simply think oneself out of depression; even if deep introspection or self-interrogation were to elicit novel self-insights, anyone who has engaged in talk-therapy will appreciate how difficult it can be to close the gap between awareness of one's behavior and changing that behavior. For instance, the "depressed" person may *know* that she is not a burden to others and yet she continues to experience herself as being burdensome. How, then, do we anchor a patient's vision of a satisfactory life *qua* existential project in the therapeutic process?

Because a therapeutic project is a joint project, both the patient and clinician are mutually implicated in achieving desirable therapeutic outcomes. For persons who are depressed, the subtending therapeutic goal is straightforward: to diminish suffering associated with depression, which is to say, to be oneself. In this process, both patient and clinician are bound by a shared therapeutic goal, despite the fact that both parties are tasked with fulfilling their respective individual responsibilities to evince the desired therapeutic outcome. Accordingly, I want to spend time delineating individual therapeutic responsibilities on behalf of both the patient and clinician respectively.[66]

6.2.3 Therapeutic responsibilities: The patient

Amelioration of suffering in depression via "talk therapy" is contingent upon several factors. First, unlike the psychopharmacological "magic bullet" treatment model, which was discussed in Chapter 1, a therapeutic project in the context of depression is a personal project, a project that does not attempt to uncover specific pathological processes, but instead seeks to uncover the way in which we establish relations with the world vis-à-vis sedimented and embodied habits. Second, the therapeutic project is a joint project; neither patient nor clinician alone can sustain therapy. A therapeutic project (minimally) presupposes that patient and clinician are mutually committed to the patient's endeavor of self-transcendence, which in phenomenological terms, is equivalent to re-habituating one' self-style. But mutual commitment alone cannot guarantee therapeutic success given that self-transcendence is, after all, a *project*. Having said this, what we *do* know in advance is that the relative "success" of a particular therapeutic project is interwoven with a person's ability (or inability) to enact his or her vision of a satisfactory life, which at the same time, coincides with being oneself.

The vision of what constitutes a satisfactory life for the depressed person is not reducible to what she *thinks* it ought to be. We can, of course, hold explicit ideas about what this vision might look like. Still, according to our phenomenological analysis in the preceding chapters, what constitutes a satisfactory life is not – first and foremost – a matter of what we *think*. In

[66] Because therapy aims to re-structure embodied habits, it is apparent that therapy as a project is more amenable to working through persistent depressive disorder rather than major depressive disorder on account of the fact that the former explicitly refers to a habitual *depressive* style. In principle, the therapeutic task is to establish a self-style that will enable oneself to successfully cope with otherwise difficult situations. In the case of major depression, on the other hand, because self-style is interrupted, it may well be the case that therapy will be the optimal solution in acute cases of depression. Often, major depression spontaneously remits on its own, though it is also the case that persons diagnosed with major depression are likely to experience relapses in the future. Hence, therapy as a project may not always be the most appropriate intervention for persons *newly* diagnosed with major depression. The chronic nature of persistent depression makes it more amenable to therapy as a project for the simple reason that the depressed person is compelled to seek help in an attempt to understand oneself. For this reason, I focus on the affinity between therapy as a project and persistent depressive disorder on account of the structural similarity. This does not mean that therapy is ineffective or impotent in the context of major depression, but it may not always be the most salient intervention for acute experiences of depression.

fact, what we explicitly believe to be constitutive of a satisfactory life may be at odds with the implicit way we establish our embodied and perceptual relationship with the world. How, then, should we characterize the therapeutic project from the perspective of the patient? To answer this question, I want to cite Russon at length to illustrate how we ought to characterize the depressed person's relationship to his or her therapeutic project:

> Therapy will thus to a large extent involve learning to describe the way in which one experiences objects, the way in which one *finds situations calling upon one*, how one's compulsions are experienced. This description is the first step toward the explication of these situated experiences in terms of the interpretative commitments they enact and embody, and subsequent re-education (sic) of one's most familiar interpretive reflexes. Therapy thus amounts, *not an escape, nor a return to some original purity, nor to advance to some preestablished goal of perfection*, but to a phenomenological process of self-interpretation and self-transcendence (2003, 137, emphasis added).

The above passage requires considerable unpacking. First, Russon reiterates my earlier claim that the goal of therapy should not be characterized as a return to a previous state of self. The therapeutic aim is, first and foremost, to reconfigure one's established habitual practices. This entails re-organizing the sense or meaning that motivated previously established habits. Following from this, the second implication of Russon's description is that the therapeutic project is likewise a pedagogical project. Moreover, not only is the project pedagogical, it is likewise a *phenomenological* endeavor. But what does this mean?

The therapeutic project is not unlike Merleau-Ponty's vision of his phenomenological project: "We witness, at each moment, this marvel that is the connection of experiences, and *no one knows how it is accomplished better than we do, since we are this very knot of relations* […] True philosophy entails *learning to see* the world anew" (2012, lxxxv, emphasis added). Hence, when viewed this way, philosophy and therapy share an affinity. As Ludwig Binswanger once opined, "philosophy is not here in any way being introduced into psychiatry or psychotherapy, but rather that the philosophical bases (sic) of these sciences are being laid bare" (1955, 312). As was the case in our qualitative study in the second chapter, we are not trying here to fit philosophy into existing theoretical therapeutic frameworks, but instead are interrogating the basic philosophical underpinnings of therapy as such, so as to clarify the aims and goals of therapy in the context of selfhood and depression.

Hence, if therapy entails learning to describe the way in which situations and objects solicit our "interpretive reflexes" (i.e. habitual actions), and phenomenology entails learning to see the world in a new way, then the therapeutic project *is* likewise a phenomenological project. In other words, if our goal is to acquire novel insights about one's self-style, we must attend to the embodied and perceptual structures that permeate one's lived-experience prior to reflective thought.

From the patient's perspective, a therapeutic project aspires to self-understanding by attending to descriptions of *how* the self-world dyad is experienced in depression. As a result, therapy will "involve a 'turn' (a 'conversation,' as it were) of one's attitude away from the world interpreted as 'objective' (i.e., the world interpreted in terms of the positivistic prejudices…) and towards oneself as the sense-giving power operative throughout one's situation" (Russon 2003, 136). This characterization of therapy dovetails with my claim from Chapter 4 that selfhood is a developmental phenomenon reflecting our inherent situatedness; self-style coincides with our pre-reflective relation to the world, a manner of self-comportment that denotes our pre-conceptual capacity to navigate situations.

I also argued in Chapter 4 that self-style develops as a movement from the pre-personal realm toward the personal realm. It involves the "taking up" of our given pre-personal corporeal capacities (such as perception and motility) in order to skillfully navigate our situation(s) by establishing increasingly complex corporeal habits. Over time, habits coalesce and sediment as behaviors that are expressed through self-style. Russon is right that therapy is a process of "re-education," but in the context of our investigation regarding depression and selfhood, therapy is in fact a process of re-stylization, an attempt to re-organize sense or meaning structuring our pre-conceptual and habitual way of relating to the world. Therapy is indeed pedagogical insofar as the aim is to alert oneself to taken for granted habitual commitments expressing one's relation to otherness. But based on our notion of selfhood as an expressive style, the acquisition of novel self-insight alone is insufficient to elicit concrete change. To reiterate an earlier sentiment from Russon, for the patient, the therapeutic process is not an intellectual exercise such that one "simply thinks one's way out of the problem along the model of the stoic who by an act of stern self-denial says, 'I will no longer do that'" (2003, 132). If self-transcendence is a real possibility, it must be recognized that *I am* the creative source of possible change; the possibility of re-stylizing oneself begins with self-insight, yet such insight is always flavored with ambiguity: I am the source of my habitual commitments even though I rarely explicitly experience myself as having been the author.

The process of re-stylization I am advocating is not an introspective accomplishment. Reflection alone cannot disclose inalienable truths about oneself or about the origins of depression. And even if it were possible to systematically work back through one's life to identify the cause of depression, such a discovery can only provide limited insight into our implicit existential commitments that are expressed vis-à-vis our situatedness. Interestingly, this notion of re-stylization is not entirely foreign to existing clinical practice. For instance, one of the significant findings from the qualitative study in Chapter 2 is that child psychiatry – in contrast to adult psychiatry – makes sense of the patient's life-world within a larger constellation of inter-personal relations. These relations not only reveal interpersonal dynamics, they likewise offer insight about self-stylization. According to Merleau-Ponty:

> The things of the world are not simply neutral objects which stand before us for our contemplation. Each one of them symbolises or recalls a particular way of behaving, provoking in us reactions which are either favourable or unfavourable. This is why people's tastes, character, and the attitude they adopt to the world and to particular things can be deciphered (2004, 63).

The self-world dyad unfolds through one's concrete situation, which is, first and foremost, a stylized dialogue with the world and others. One of the respondents in Chapter 2 offered an instructive case that exemplifies why embodied habits are nothing other than what Russon calls "intelligent behaviors." I noted earlier (section 6.3) that while many behaviors may have proved useful to cope with a situation during time A, they also risk becoming a source of stultification later in life, at time B.

The case in question involved a seven-year-old child exhibiting aggressive behavior toward the mother. The psychiatrist noted how in this type of case, when addressing a question to the child, it was not uncommon that

> immediately [the child's] eyes go to mamma and mamma starts answering the question because they've programmed each other to know that that's how this one communicates. And that's also part of a problem, and I don't think it's a problem for a 4-year-old to do that, but I think it's weird for a 14-year-old to do it...

He then went on to add that

> and that also seems to indicate problems in learning how to live a life, learning who to become a part of all of the groups one is a part of, how do you live there, how do you relate there, how do you talk there, how do you communicate there…

And he concluded by noting that:

> It's a very special situation that [the child] will be out of, they [eventually] won't even live with that person any longer, suddenly there's nobody to answer [the child's] questions.

This informant's case offers a hint as to why therapy may be understood as a project of "education." Rather than framing the situation as a tension between nature versus nurture – external social causes versus internal physiological causes – this psychiatrist implies that it is through family constellations that we are thrown into the existential-project of *learning how to live*. This sentiment is shared by Russon, who contends that

> our emotional life in general could thus be construed as the defenses we have constructed in order to cope with the challenges we have faced in our efforts to assert the centrality of the claim 'I matter.' The world confronts us with a variety of obstacles, challenges, and assaults, and *our emotional life is our developed style for carrying on* in the face of such opposition (2003, 77, emphasis added).

As I argued already in Chapter 4, situated coping skills emerge out of our encounter with otherness. Family relations are the most proximal source of frustration influencing our attempt to assert ourselves as free agents in a world of pre-given determinacies. Thus, when the child is asked a question by the psychiatrist, we can identify the way in which the child's situation is imbued with significance or meaning. The child looks to his mother to answer the question because he has learned that the best strategy to cope with the situation is to remain silent. It is plausible that he has learned from experience that speaking out against his parents may elicit negative consequences (e.g., yelling, hitting, shaming, and so on). Subsequently, he views himself to be untrustworthy, someone whose choices must be verified through others. Speculating further in this case, it is plausible to imagine that as a young boy, his learned habit of deferring to his mother may have been highly apposite behavior in light of potentially undesirable repercussions. However, the learned habit, which prompts him to deign to the opinions or imperatives of others, may engender a self-style in adult life that imbues him with a sense of being someone who is not self-reliant; a person for whom self-determination intersects with interpersonal conflict. Should this habit formation develop into a depressive style, the therapeutic project – as I have presented it thus far – should address the "problems [that] are rooted in the conflict inherent to the most deeply seated habits of making sense that found one's personality" (Russon 2003, 133). It is clear, then, that therapy will engage in self-explication, and yet this alone will not engender habitual change. Re-stylization of habits cannot be accomplished at the level of conceptual knowledge alone. The most significant challenge is the modification of non-conceptual habits that govern our immediate and unreflective action in and toward the world.

6.2.4 Therapeutic responsibility: The clinician

To be sure, re-stylizing one's habits is a formidable task. The project of therapy presupposes that the person seeking therapy not only *wants* to change, but that he or she is motivated to sustain change. Assuming that education is an end in-itself, so too is the project of therapy, meaning that we cannot know the outcome of this project in advance.[67] Likewise, therapy as an education addresses the "central question, 'Who am I?' For that reason, in picking a therapist, an individual is picking another individual to act as a representative of what it is to be human" (Russon 2003, 139). A person who initiates therapy implicitly acknowledges personal responsibility for his or her desire to change. However, as I argued earlier in the chapter, therapy is itself a project of mutual dependence. We have so far in this chapter focused on some of the responsibilities associated with the patient-side of the therapeutic project. Up to this point, I have argued that therapy aims to elicit the patient's vision of a satisfactory life by making sense of sedimented habits that inhibit his or her ability to enact a satisfactory life. As a process of re-education or re-stylization, therapy supports and facilitates patient self-transcendence. But if self-transcendence is fundamen-

—

[67] A case can be made that neither education nor therapy are ends in themselves, but rather means to an end. This would mean, for instance, that even if self-transcendence is the final aim, many people rely on education and therapy to satisfy acute problems or to develop practical ways to cope with depression. I concur that for some persons, therapy as a project is an overly-daunting prospect. However, I have tried to emphasize that even if education and therapy offer pragmatic solutions to acute problems, these solutions are only viable if one takes for granted that our situatedness in the world is always an existential predicament.

tally a pedagogical project, how should we characterize the responsibilities of clinician *qua* teacher-therapist?

We have seen that the project of therapy, as an end in itself, is a pedagogical and phenomenological project. Accordingly, therapy is first and foremost a dialogical enquiry that begins with a relationship of two or more interlocutors that "consists in the recognition of the potentiality of the object and the liberation of its presentative forces" (Natanson 1969 , 86). Therapy is tasked with disclosing the way in which depression manifests as a certain style or manner of comportment reflected in our non-conceptual relationship to objects and others. Put alternatively, therapy will involve *seeing* our relationship to the world anew, establishing a *new sense* of one's habitual behaviors.

A formidable obstacle to self-change is, of course, that habits *qua* self-style are non-conceptually structured. Consequently, when we attempt to grasp a particular behavior or action, we direct our attention to that behavior or action only to find that it slips away. This, as seen in Chapter 4, is the nature of intentional consciousness, namely that in order for something to move into my experiential foreground, whatever it is on which I am focusing my attention must shift to the background; to focus explicitly on a particular action or behavior presupposes that I am no longer *living* that behavior or action.

This structure of intentional consciousness complicates the possibility of self-change, but crucially, it does not prohibit self-change. The depressed person who enters a therapeutic relationship implicitly acknowledges that self-change is an intersubjective endeavor. When therapy is initiated, the clinician/therapist "is entrusted [with] the individual's own most intimate needs and powers, for the therapist is made the agent who works on behalf of the individual's own identity" (Russon 2003, 140). Before we explore this claim further, I want to draw a connection between this specific point and our discussion of speech acts in Chapter 2.

Recall that one of the conclusions drawn from the qualitative study was that many clinicians are attentive to the potential affective force that diagnosis exerts on patient identity. The clinicians' sensitivity to this affective capacity was expressed through clinician's desire to "distance" or shield patients from over-identifying with their depression diagnosis. Interestingly, this coping strategy, which we already discussed at length in Chapter 2, turns out to be a two-fold strategy. On the one hand, this strategy elicits patient recognition as someone worth protecting. On the other hand, by recognizing the patient as one worth protecting, the clinicians' strategy simultaneously recognizes the burden of their therapeutic responsibility, namely as someone "who works on behalf of the [patient's] own identity."

But what exactly does it mean to be responsible for the identity of another? This responsibility must be understood in the context of self-development itself. In Chapter 4 I argued that self-awareness is the result of an accomplishment rather than something pre-given. The argument further stipulated that an infant's distinction between self and other is a process of recognition, a process of self-awareness beginning once the infant has grasped that she is different from others by virtue of being *someone* (a self) who is recognized by others. Moreover, it is in response *to* others that self-style is nascently expressed: a style that develops in direct proportion to lived-experience, and is expressed as sedimented mature habits. With this in mind, the therapist's responsibility for the patient's identity is motivated by the therapeutic relationship itself

> one individual [patient] must be approaching the other-as-therapist with a desire to be educated in the context of the fundamental question, 'Can you tell me that I am right about me?' or something similar, while the other individual must correspondingly recognize that this is the scope of the undertaking and embrace the responsibility for caring for the unique demands of the perspective of the other as patient (Russon 2003 139).

A therapeutic relationship minimally requires two participants. And even if this relationship between patient and therapist (or clinician, guide, educator, etc.) remains one-to-one, the therapist nevertheless acts as a representative or a surrogate for the series of intersubjective relations that constitute the patient's world.

In the therapeutic project the therapist stands in as a representative of reality, by which I mean a person who endorses or confirms a patient's attempt at self-knowledge on behalf of others as such. If the patient-therapist relationship is to be fruitful, then it is essential that I (eventually) encounter my therapist *as someone who may be right about me*, while simultaneously accepting that I may be wrong about myself. Thus, the therapist is *this* person with whom I enact my self-style in order to disclose self-knowledge, as well as fundamentally being *this* person who is simultaneously a surrogate for *that* person (e.g. mother, father, sibling, friend, partner, etc.). Through this dyadic structure, the patient attempts to make sense of her habitual behaviors (or depressive style) as having developed out of her contact with others.

6.3 A final word on the ends of therapy

What I have outlined so far regarding the goals of therapy is not intended to be prescriptive for any specific modality of therapy. Our concern here is not whether a therapist is steeped in psychodynamic theory, cognitive behavioral theory, or other versions thereof, since these specific therapeutic frameworks entail their own set of practices and assumptions. The initiation of a therapeutic project will always presume that the depressed person seeks therapy because she cannot reconcile her current life with the life she wants to live. To a certain degree, the person suffering from depression wants to know what is "true" about herself. And because our everyday life is typically considered from the perspective of objective thought, it may well be the case that any initiation of therapy is, for some, a search for explanations: Why am I like this? What causes me to do that? Am I responsible for my own depression? Even if such questions elicit answers that possess some value, explanations – and self-insights – alone are insufficient for facilitating self-change. Why? Because self-style and embodied comportment are rooted in sedimented habits, and thus self-change necessitates more than self-awareness. Re-habituating self-style, as the word suggests, requires that I not only understand a behavior but that I modify that behavior.

Yet, if our developed habits and self-style are formed tacitly over the course of our lives, and if insight into these behaviors alone is insufficient to engender change, on what basis will change be possible? I want to answer this question by suggesting that the possibility of change is made viable, not by disclosing the "Truth" about oneself, but instead by disclosing new truths about oneself. Summarily put, our developed habits reflect the way in which we have *learned* to navigate the world, which I argued in Chapter four, are imbued with an embodied sense or meaning that proves elusive to reflection.

Habits cannot be established unless I am the source of those habits; they are not blind reflexes or senseless actions that restrict our capacity to act. But habits do nevertheless prefigure our future horizons, which is what Merleau-Ponty has in mind when he writes "events in an experience endow the experience with durable dimensions, in relation to which a whole series of other experiences will make sense, will form a thinkable sequel or history [...] events which deposit a sense in me, not just as something surviving or as a residue, but as the call to follow, the demand of a future" (Merleau-Ponty 2010c, 77). We have already shown that the meaningfulness of our milieu or environment is ambiguous; meaning is not given in advance and yet perceptual existence is irascibly meaningful. Through embodied-perceptual action our situations are meaningfully structured; or we can likewise say that our situated activity is the manifestation of that with which we find ourselves concerned. As a result, embodied action carries forward our past into the present, but also sketches out a general outline (or flavor) of the future.

The therapeutic possibility of disclosing new self-truths requires exploration of one's personal history. Despite the shared affinity with the genealogical process promoted by psychoanalysis, the success of a therapeutic project does not hinge on raising unconscious conflicts to the level of conscious awareness. As I have noted, self-awareness of one's behavior is insufficient.

The process of change is tantamount to establishing a new manner of establishing contact with the world vis-à-vis the patient's encounter with a therapist who acts as a surrogate of intersubjective reality. Accordingly, then, the project of therapy "is not just a conceptual challenge to the ideas that governed one's family life, but is the establishment of a new 'home'" (Russon 2003, 142), insofar as home imbues us with the power of expansion and domain over our lives (Artaud, 1927).

6.4 Conclusion

The vision of therapy I have proposed in this chapter is by no means a guaranteed remedy for depression. In fact, according to the way I have characterized it in this investigation, it may be rightly argued that many people with depression will lack the proper motivation to commit to such a demanding project. Having said this, I have noted that a therapeutic project is not unlike the existential project of life itself, since *who we are* is expressed by *living* a life. The significant distinction between a therapeutic project and our existential project is that the latter is implicitly taken up as the condition of existence itself while the former attempts to articulate an explicit vision of a satisfactory existential project. For this reason, it is unwarranted to view therapeutic efficacy objectively in terms of success or failure, since each individual who takes up therapy articulates his or her own sense of the "good life." By this I mean that the success or failure therapy, for the depressed person, is realized in action. And even if I cannot re-habituate my self-style in a satisfactory manner, the therapeutic process itself elicits change, though it may not conform to the ideal that I have outlined here in this chapter; initiation of therapy itself signifies change, a recognition that I am not who I want to be, or a recognition that I am no longer sure if I am right about myself.

There are, however, numerous factors that affect a therapeutic outcome, the most critical of which is the patient-therapist relationship. This relationship is not solely defined by a therapist's commitment to a specific psychotherapeutic model (e.g. psychodynamic, cognitive behavioral, dialectical behavioral therapy, etc.). Even though the practice of psychotherapy is guided by different professional and theoretical norms, the patient-therapist/clinician relationship transcends the therapeutic artifice. As I argued in this chapter, the clinician *qua* therapist is – as a representative of others and reality – the one through whom I seek to be recognized or confirmed. Here, I think, it is prudent to acknowledge that this type of relationship – if established – unfolds over time.

Consequently, the project of therapy as I have presented it is a therapeutic ideal. Not all depressed persons will find therapy to be the appropriate therapeutic medium. But I have attempted to underscore that therapy as a project is a meta-structure that ought to guide any form of psychotherapy. Whether therapy helps reduce the suffering of depression is determined less by the form of therapy than the patient-therapist relationship itself. Having said this, a stark fact about depression is that the efficacy of current depression treatments (pharmacological, psychotherapy, electroconvulsive therapy, trans-cranial magnetic stimulation) is ultimately unpredictable. Accordingly, the therapeutic project I endorse will not suit every person with depression.

One way to assess a person's suitability for therapy as self re-stylization is to draw on our earlier phenomenological distinction between major depression and persistent depression. I argued at the start of the chapter that major depression is characterized by interrupted self-style while persistent depression is consistent with a depressive self-style. While neither type of depression is inherently more amenable to the project of therapy, we have good reason to assume that a prerequisite for "success" is a person's willingness to initiate therapy.

In this chapter I have elected to focus on the potential merits of therapy as one of several possible treatments for depression. The notion of therapy as a project is structured by mutual recognition, the same form of recognition that occurs when the young child realizes that other people have a situated perspective on her. In other words, therapy and selfhood are both processes that tend toward individual recognition that one is indeed a someone to whom others relate themselves. I have not advocated for any one type of therapy nor have I proposed a novel therapeutic approach. Rather, I have opted to employ Russon's account of therapy (as a project of self-transcendence) as a guiding framework amenable to any therapeutic approach. I stressed that both patient and therapist have respective responsibilities to be fulfilled in a therapeutic project: the patient must be prepared to interrogate the way in which she has habitually established her contact with the world – a descriptive task that attempts to disclose the incompatibility of previously long-held habituated behaviors and the demands of one's current situation. A conflict between sedimented intelligent behaviors and the demands of one's present situation impels a patient to initiate therapy, which is to say, this conflict prevents a patient from fulfilling her vision of a satisfactory life. Consequently, patients – with their therapist – are responsible for re-establishing their vision of the "good life."

By contrast, the therapist or clinician is tasked with the responsibility of acting as a surrogate on behalf of others in general. Accordingly, the patient-therapist encounter is structured by intersubjective recognition. The therapist acts on behalf of others as one to whom patients turn to address the question "who am I?" and "can you confirm me?" The patient's attempt to re-habituate self-style necessitates a therapeutic partnership insofar as patients re-enact and recollect (and eventually re-habituate) their intersubjective world through their therapist.

The therapeutic project is akin to the phenomenological-existential project that characterizes being-in-the-world. The former, to the extent that it is possible, is tasked with bringing the latter to self-awareness. I argued that depression cannot be cured, if a cure implies a return to some baseline or previous state of self. In the words of Canguilhem, "to learn to heal is to learn the contradiction between today's hope and the defeat that comes in the end – without saying no to today's hope" (2012a, 66). Hence, therapy always entails the spectre of failure, yet it cannot proceed without an attitude of hope.

The clinical presentation of depressive style or interrupted self-style indicates the variable nature of depression. Irrespective of a specific cause, depression always implicates a "problem" of the self. Behaviors, preferences, or actions are not so much usurped by depression, they are rather the very expression of depression. This investigation began with a similar premise, namely that a robust understanding of depression necessitates that we understand the nature of selfhood. More specifically, I argued that if depression is a disorder of selfhood, then it is entirely warranted that we inquire into the way psychiatric clinicians understand selfhood. By drawing from existential-phenomenology my discourse on selfhood and depression not only encourages clinicians to adopt a new philosophically-inspired *way of seeing* depression, it likewise encourages clinicians to approach therapy as a stewardship, that is, as one who is willing to recognize the formidable existential task of *being oneself.*

Summary

The premise of this dissertation is that depression is a phenomenon that affectively alters the core of who we are. I argue that depression is (i) a disorder of the self and that (ii) it may be broadly characterized by the inability to be oneself. Phenomenological investigations of schizophrenia, personality disorders, and dementia, convincingly demonstrate that selfhood is prone to disintegration. In these disorders, self-disintegration may often involve changes related to *ipseity* (i.e. the experience of oneself), memory, and rationality. In this dissertation I argue that, while depression undoubtedly shares overlapping features with other psychiatric "self-disturbances", the structure of depression is existentially unique. The sense of "existential" here is unrelated to transcendental meaning or the meaning of life, though it is often remarked upon that persons with depression do indeed endure crises concerning loss of meaning in life. To say that depression is existentially-structured means that depressed experience is neither a problem of the mind nor of the biological body; rather, it is an entire reorganization of the way one finds herself in the world. That depression modifies one's way of being-in-the-world has already been well-established in the phenomenological literature. Yet, absent from this phenomenological literature is a detailed study of the relationship between selfhood and depression. This dissertation claims that, if we want to understand the essential structures of depressed experience, then we must simultaneously understand the nature of selfhood.

Based on this assumption, I argue that depression is effectively a disorder of the self. So-called disorders of self are typically associated with schizophrenia or personality disorders, both of which are believed to entail a person's experiential "break" with reality. This narrow view of self-disorders, however, is not capacious enough to entail altered self-experiences where one's connection to reality remains "intact." Having said this, psychiatric medicine is surprisingly silent on the concept of, or function of, the phenomenon of selfhood. Hence, not only does this investigation demonstrate why the notion of selfhood is essential to psychiatric practice, it likewise offers an account of selfhood that is derived from lived-experience rather than scientific enquiry.

The intrinsic appeal of a phenomenological approach is the impetus to re-discover lived-experience, something that is taken for granted in scientific-thought. This means that the psychiatric mandate to scientifically explain depression (objectively) fails to recognize that objective knowledge about depression is only possible by abstracting lived-experience. Thus, phenomenological philosophy reminds us that scientific explanations of phenomenon are *necessarily* preceded by experience of the world as it is lived. Crucially, though, theory alone is insufficient to fully appreciate the complexity of depression.

Psychiatry theory must also translate into psychiatric practice, which suggests it would be remiss to investigate depression without attending to the way in which depression is *done* in psychiatry. Likewise, if depression is a disorder of the self, and if persons with depression seek out psychiatric professionals for help, then it is imperative that we also investigate how clinicians conceptualize the notion of selfhood. In order to make sense of the way psychiatric theory intersects with psychiatric practice, the study is in part based on interviews conducted with psychiatric professionals at two clinics in Stockholm Sweden, as well as the psychiatric out-patient program at Karlstad hospital, two hours west of Stockholm.

The findings from the qualitative study reveal considerable insight into some of the vexing problems that psychiatric clinicians routinely encounter in clinical *praxis*. An overarching tension that continually appeared in the interview material is the clinicians' ambivalent relationship with psychiatric diagnosis. On the one hand, clinicians overwhelmingly reported dissatisfaction with the operationalized approach to psychiatric diagnosis on account of the "impersonal" and vague symptoms used to diagnose depression. On the other hand, the clinicians also recognize that, in spite of the imperfect diagnostic criteria, a clinical diagnosis of depression opens the gateway for patients to receive the appropriate care. But the especially salient finding from the qualitative study is that the way in which clinicians understand depression entails implicit assumptions about the nature of selfhood.

Although the qualitative findings related to psychiatric practice are interesting in and of themselves, the attitudes expressed by the interviewees need to be considered within the broader historical landscape of psychiatric medicine itself. That is, the informants' views regarding depression and selfhood are not *sui causa*; when we examine the historical contingencies of depression, as well as the influential figures in early psychiatry, such as Emil

Kraepelin and Sigmund Freud, it becomes clear that contemporary clinical attitudes regarding depression continue to be informed by the way in which depression and selfhood have been conceptualized historically in psychiatric medicine. At the same time, because the clinicians express dissatisfaction with the nature of psychiatric diagnostics, it is evident that their frustration is partly attributable to the fact that they lack a language that permits them to describe depression in a way that transcends the "scientific" discourse of psychiatric medicine.

To provide clinicians with a phenomenological vocabulary, I draw upon the philosophy of Maurice Merleau-Ponty and Erwin Straus in order to characterize selfhood phenomenologically as a *self-style*. The upshot of this conception of self is that it simultaneously entails aspects of contemporary accounts of selfhood, addressed in Chapter 3, without ever being reducible to any particular one of them. The phenomenological description of selfhood as being a self-style captures the way in which selfhood is an existentially grounded phenomenon that is remarkably uncanny; on account of the reversible nature of conscious experience, self-as-a-style is experientially that with we are intimately acquainted yet simultaneously remains foreign to us. More specifically, self-style is a perceptual and embodied phenomenon expressed through our habitual and practical actions. This means that self-style is a developmental phenomenon that is actively engaged in the world by virtue of being affectively sensitive to the way in which the world solicits meaningful activity. As a result, the relationship between depression and self-style may be traced through the situated of nature of lived-space and motivation.

Hence, I draw a connection between self-style and depression in the context of lived-space, a relationship that may initially appear somewhat curious outside the bounds of phenomenology. My analysis reveals the extent to which self-style is predicated on spatial experience; specifically, how embodied experience is motivated by experience of spatial depth (lived-space). In depressed experience, our embodied and perceptual hold on the world is modified such that our experience of both objects and people no longer solicit us to respond as one would in otherwise normal experience. Not only are the world and others experienced as being out of reach or far away, depression likewise reveals that spatial depth indexes the scope or extent of our hold on the world.

Consequently, depressed experience is marked by an inability to "be oneself." This means that in depression our expressive and habitual behaviors are not merely signs that, when taken as a whole, represent the presence of depression; this is particularly important to bear in mind as there are (at least) two distinct ways to characterize the way in which depression affects the inability to be oneself: I argue that in Persistent Depressive Disorder (PDP), the modification of selfhood is witnessed in a depressive-self-style. Conversely, in cases of Major Depressive Disorder (MDD), the otherwise effortless ability to enact one's self-style is *interrupted*.

I employ a phenomenological distinction between depressive style and interrupted style to illustrate the unique way in which selfhood is altered in PDP and MDD respectively, which is not only pertinent to clinical diagnostics, but it also informs the fundamental structure of the therapeutic encounter. With respect to "talk therapies" or psychotherapy, I show that therapeutic "success" first depends on the goals of therapy as such. The phenomenological description of selfhood and depression permits us to establish basic (meta) goals that are fundamental to any psychotherapeutic method, irrespective of particular professional norms and professional competencies that guide a particular psychotherapeutic orientation (e.g. cognitive behavioral therapy, psychodynamic therapy, dialectical behavioral therapy, art therapy, and so on).

Drawing on the work of Canadian philosopher John Russon, I make it clear that therapy is, first and foremost, a therapeutic *project*, the overarching goal of which aims at self-transcendence or re-stylization of self-style. For persons suffering from depression, actualization of this goal is contingent upon the extent to which they are able to successfully re-habituate sedimented behaviors that stultify their ability to cope with practical situations. Having said this, the possibility of self re-stylization is a formidable task. Pinpointing our behaviors, which are sedimented as embodied habits over time, is limited by the fact that these behaviors are both developmental and unreflective. In other words, because lived-experience is practical and therefore non-conceptual, and because our preferred ways of practically coping with the world emerge even at the earliest stages of life, our embodied way of contacting the world is overwhelmingly tacit.

Put plainly, therapy is an ongoing project, the success of which depends upon intersubjective engagement. This means that a satisfactory vision of therapy should not be one that prioritizes self-directed introspection. Instead, therapeutic goals subtend the therapeutic relationship and must be navigated by both parties, where the psychiatric acts as a surrogate on behalf of reality, and of others, in general, the overarching aim of which is to make it possible for persons with depression to be oneself.

Bibliography

Aho, Kevin. 2013. “Depression and embodiment: phenomenological reflections on motility, affectivity, and transcendence.” *Journal of Medicine, Health Care, and Philosophy* 16 (4):751-759.

Albahari, Miri. 2016. *Analytical Buddhism: The Two-tiered Illusion of Self*. Basingstoke: Palgrave Macmillan.

Antich, Peter. 2018. “Narrative and the Phenomenology of Personal Identity in Merleau-Ponty.” *Life Writing* 15 (3):431-445.

APA. 2013. *Diagnostic and statistical manual of mental disorders: DSM-5*. Washington, D.C: American Psychiatric Publishing.

Artaud, Antonin 1927. “Lettre a la Voyante. ” *La Révolution surréaliste* 1 (8):16-18.

Beck, Aaron T., John A. Rush, Brian F. Shaw, and Gary Emery. 1979. *Cognitive Therapy of Depression*. New York: Guilford Publications.

Bell, Emily, Ghislaine Mathieu, and Eacine Racine. 2009. “Preparing the ethical future of deep brain stimulation.” *Surgical Neurology* 72 (6).

Benjamin, Walter. 1968. “The Storyteller.” In *Illuminations*, edited by Hannah Arendt. New York: Houghton Mifflin Harcourt.

Berrios, German E. 1988. “Melancholia and depression during the 19th century: A conceptual history.” *The British Journal of Psychiatry* 153 (3):298-304.

Berrios, German E. 2012. “The 19th-century nosology of alienism: history and epistemology.” In *hilosophical Issues in Psychiatry II: Nosology*, edited by Kenneth S Kendler and Josef Parnas. Oxford: Oxford UP.

Berrios, German E, and Ivana S Marková. 2003. “The Self in Psychiatry: A conceptual history “ In *The Sellf in Neurosciecne and Psychiatry* edited by Tito Kircher and Anthony David. Cambridge: Cambridge University Press.

Berrios, German E, and Ivana S Marková. 2015. “Toward a New epistemology of Psychiatry.” In *Re-Visioning Psychiatry*, edited by Laurence J Kirmayer, Robert Lemelson and Constance A. Cummings, 41-68. Cambridge: Cambridge University Press.

Berrios, German E, and Roy Porter, eds. 1995. *A History of Clinical Psychiatry: The Origin and History of Psychiatric Disorders*. New Brunswick, NJ: Athlone Press.

Binswanger, Ludwig. 1955. “Existential Analysis and Psychotherapy.” Acta Psychotherapeutica, Psychosomatica et Orthopaedagogica, Zurich.

Bolton, Derek, and Johnathan Hill. 2004. *Mind, Meaning, and Mental Disorder*. Oxford: Oxford UP.

Bortolan, Anna. 2016. “A phenomenological discussion of Antonio Damasio’s theory of emotions.” *Phenomenology and Mind* 0 (1):142-150.

Bortolan, Anna. 2017. “Affectivity and narrativity in depression: a phenomenological study.” *Medicine, Health Care and Philosophy* 20 (1):77-88.

Bortolan, Anna. 2019. "Phenomenological Psychopathology and Autobiography." In *The Oxford Handbook of Phenomenological Psychopathology*, edited by Giovanni Stanghellini, Matthew Broome, Andrea Raballo, Anthony Vincent Fernandez, Paolo Fusar-Poli, René Rosfort and Anna Bortolan, 1052-1064. Oxford: Oxford UP.

Brampton, Sally. 2018. *Shoot the Damn Dog: A Memoir of Depression*. London: Bloomsbury Publishing.

Briggs Meyers, Isabel. 1962. *The Meyers-Briggs Ype Indicator*. Palo Alto: Consulting Psychologists Press.

Brinkmann, Svend. 2014. "Languages of Suffering." *Theory and Psychology* 24 (5):630-648.

Butler, Judith. 2001. "Giving an account of oneself." *Diacritics* 31 (4):22-40.

Callahan, Christopher M, and German E Berrios. 2004. *Reinventing Depression: A History of the Treatment of Depression in Primary Care, 194--2004*. New York: Oxford University Press.

Canguilhem, Georges. 2009. *Knowledge of Life*. Translated by Stefanos Geroulanos and Daniela Ginsburg. New York: Fordham University Press.

Canguilhem, Georges. 2012a. "Is a Pedagogy of Healing Possible?" In *Writings on Medicine*, 53-66. New York: Fordham University Press.

Canguilhem, Georges. 2012b. *Writings on Medicine* Translated by Stefanos Geroulanos and Todd Meyers, *Writings on Medicine*. New York: Fordham University Press.

Cooper, John E, and Norman Sartorius. 2013. *A Companion to the Classification of Mental Disorders*. Oxford: Oxford University Press.

Cooper, Rachel. 2004. "What is Wrong with the DSM?" *History of Psychiatry* 15 (1):5-25. doi: ß.

Cooper, Rachel. 2006. *Classifying Madness: A Philosophical Examination of the Diagnostic and Statistical Manual of Mental Disorders*. Dordrecht: Springer.

Cooper, Rachel. 2007. *Psychiatry and philosophy of science*. Stocksfield: Acumen.

Cosgrove, Lisa, and Sheldon Krimsky. 2012. "A Comparison of DSM-IV and DSM-5 Panel Members' Financial Associations with Industry: A Pernicious Problem Persists." *PLOS Medicine* 9 (3):e1001190.

Cuthbert, Bruce N., and Thomas R. Insel. 2010. "Toward New Approaches to Psychotic Disorders: The NIMH Research Domain Criteria Project." *Schizophrenia Bulletin* 36 (6):1061-1062.

Damasio, Antonio. 2010. *Self Comes to Mind: Constructing the Conscious Brain*. New York: Pantheon Books.

Davidson, Larry. 2003. *Living Outside Mental Illness: Qualitative Studies of Recovery in Schizophrenia*. New York: NYU Press.

Davies, Charlotte Aull. 2008. *Reflexive ethnography: a guide to researching selves and others*. Second ed. London: Routledge.

de Haan, Sanneke. 2017. "The existential dimension in psychiatry: an enactive framework." *Mental Health, Religion & Culture* 20 (6):528-535.

Decker, Hannah. 2013. *The Making of DSM-IIIR: A Diagnostic Manual's Conquest of American Psychiatry*. Oxford: Oxford University Press, USA.

Descartes, René. 1996. *Descartes: Meditations on First Philosophy: With Selections from the Objections and Replies*. Translated by John Cottingham. Cambridge: Cambridge University Press.

Disner, Seth G., Christopher G. Beevers, Emily A. P. Haigh, and Aaron T. Beck. 2011. "Neural mechanisms of the cognitive model of depression." *Nature Reviews Neuroscience* 12 (8):467-477.

Eghigian, Greg. 2011. "Deinstitutionalizing the history of contemporary psychiatry." *History of Psychiatry* 22 (86):201-14.

Elliott, Carl. 2011. *White Coat, Black Hat: Adventures on the Dark Side of Medicine*. Boston: Beacon Press.

Ellis, Albert. 1987. "A sadly neglected cognitive element in depression." *Cognitive Therapy and Research* 11 (1):121-146.

Feighner, John P., Eli Robins, Samuel B. Guze, Robert A. Woodruff Jr., George Winokur, and Rodrigo Munoz. 1972. "Diagnostic criteria for use in psychiatric research." *Archives of General Psychiatry* 26 (1):57-63.

Fernandez, Anthony. 2014. "Depression as existential feeling or de-situatedness? Distinguishing structure from mode in psychopathology." *Phenomenology and the Cognitive Sciences* 13 (4):595-612.

Fernandez, Anthony Vincent. 2019. "Phenomenology and Dimensional Approaches to Psychiatric Research and Classification." *Philosophy, Psychiatry, & Psychology* 26 (1):65-75.

Forrester, John. 1994. "'A whole climate of oppinion': Re-writing the history of psychoanalysis." In *Discovering the History of Psychiatry*, edited by Mark S. Micale and Roy Porter, 174-190. Oxford: Oxford University Press.

Foster Wallace, David. 2007. "The Depressed Person." In *Interviews with Hideous Men*, 37-71. New York: Back Bay Books.

Freud, Sigmund. 2004. *Civilization and its Discontents*. London: Penguin Books Limited. Original edition, 1941.

Fuchs, Thomas. 2001. "Melancholia as a Desynchronization: Towards a Psychopathology of Interpersonal Time." *Psychopathology* 34 (4):179-186. doi: 10.1159/000049304.

Fuchs, Thomas. 2005. "Corporealized and Disembodied Minds: A Phenomenological View of the Body in Melancholia and Schizophrenia." *Philosophy, psychiatry & psychology* 12 (2):95-107.

Gadamer, Hans-Georg. 1994. *Truth and Method*. Translated by Joel Weinsheimer and Donald G Marshall. Second ed. New York: Continuum.

Gallagher, Shaun. 2005. *How the body shapes the mind*. Oxford: Clarendon Press.

Gallagher, Shaun, and Kai Vogeley. 2011. "Self in the Brain." In *The Oxford Handbook of Self*, edited by Shaun Gallagher, 111-136. Oxford: OUP Oxford.

Gask, Linda. 2015. *The Other Side of Silence: A Psychiatrist's Memoir of Depression*: Summersdale Publishers Limited.

Gelder, Michael, and Hugh Freeman. 1999. "Adolf Myer (1866–1950)." In *A Century of Psychiatry*, edited by Hugh Freeman. London: Mosby.

Gibson, Eleanor J. 2006. "Ontogenesis of the Perceived Self." In *The Perceived Self: Ecological and Interpersonal Sources of Self Knowledge*, edited by Ulrich Neisser, 25-42. Cambridge: Cambridge University Press.

Gibson, James J. 2014 [1979]. *The Ecological Approach to Visual Perception: Classic Edition*: Taylor & Francis.

Gilbert, Jill Marie. 2014. "Toward a phenomenology of depression: Merleau-Ponty and the plunge into the present." PhD, Philosophy, University of Guelph.

Goldberg, David, and Ian Goodyer. 2005. *The Origins and Course of Common Mental Disorders*. London: Cambridge University Press.

Goldie, Peter. 2012. *The Mess Inside: Narrative, Emotion, and the Mind*. Oxford: OUP.

Griesinger, Wilhelm. 2000. "Hypochondriasis and melancholia." In *The nature of melncholy: From Aristolte to Kristeva*, edited by Jennifer Radden, 223-229. New York: Oxford University Press.

Grob, Gerald N. 1991. "Origins of DSM-I: A Study in Appearance and Reality." *The American Journal of Psychiatry* 148 (4):421-31.

Gruenberg, Alan M., Reed D. Goldstein, and Harold A. Pincus. 2005. "Classification of Depression: Research and Diagnostic Criteria: DSM-IV and ICD-10." In *Biology of Depression: From Novel insights to therapuetic stratigies*, edited by Julio Lincinio and Ma-Li Wong. Weinheim: Wiley-VCH.

Hadlaczky, G., A. Stefenson, and D. Wasserman. 2012. "The state of psychiatry in Sweden." *International Review of Psychiatry* 24 (4):356-62.

Halpin, Michael. 2016. "The DSM and Professional Practice." *Journal of Health and Social Behavior* 57 (2):153-167.

Healy, David. 1997. *The anti-depresant era*. New York: Harvard UP.

Healy, David. 2004a. *Let them eat prozac*. New York: New York UP.

Healy, David. 2004b. *Let Them Eat Prozac: The Unhealthy Relationship Between the Pharmaceutical Industry and Depression*. New York: NYU Press.

Heidegger, Martin. 2008. *Being and Time*. Translated by John Macquarrie and Edward Robinson. New York: HarperCollins.

Hempel, Carl G. 1965. *Aspects of scientific explanation: and other essays in the philosophy of science*. New York: Free Press.

Henckes, Nicolas. 2011. "Reforming psychiatric institutions in the mid-twentieth century: a framework for analysis." *History of psychiatry* 22 (2):164-181.

Hess, Volker, and Benoît Majerus. 2011. "Writing the history of psychiatry in the 20th century." *History of psychiatry* 22 (2):139-145.

Hindmarch, I. 2001. "Expanding the horizons of depression: beyond the monoamine hypothesis." *Human Psychopharmacology: Clinical and Experimental* 16 (3):203-218.

Hoffmaster, Barry. 2014. "Understanding Suffering." In *Suffering and Bioethics*, edited by Ronald Michael Green and Nathan.J. Palpant, 31-53. Oxford: Oxford University Press.

Holstein, James A, and Jaber F. Gubrium. 1995. *The Active Interview*. Thousand Oaks: SAGE Publications.

Horwitz, Allan V. and Jerome Wakefield. 2007. *The loss of sadness: how psychiatry transformed normal sorrow into depressive disorder*. Edited by Jerome C. Wakefield. Oxford: Oxford University Press.

Horwitz, Allan V., Jerome C. Wakefield, and Lorenzo Lorenzo-Luaces. 2016. "History of Depression." In *The Oxford Handbook of Mood Disorders*, edited by Robert J. DeRubeis and Daniel R. Strunk. Oxford: OUP.

Horwitz, Allan, and Jerome Wakefield. 2005. "The Age of Depression." *The Public Interest* (158):39-58.

Hume, D. 2007. *A Treatise of Human Nature*: BiblioBazaar.

Jablensky, Assen. 2012. "The Nosological Entity in Psychiatry: a historical illusion or a moving target?" In *Philosophical issues in psychiatry. II, Nosology*, edited by Kenneth S. Kendler and Josef Parnas, 77-994. Oxford: Oxford University Press.

Jackson, Stanley W. 1990. *Melancholia and Depression: From Hippocratic Times to Modern Times*. New haven: Yale University Press.

Jacobs, Kerrin. 2013. "The depressive situation." *Frontiers in psychology* 4:429-429.

Jacobson, Kirsten. 2015. "The Gift of Memory: Sheltering The I." In *Time, Memory, Institution: Merleau-Ponty's New Ontology of Self*, edited by David Morris and Kym Maclaren. Athens: Ohio University Press.

James, William. 1918. *The Principles of Psychology*. New York: Holt.

Jaspers, Karl. 1963. *General psychopathology*. Translated by J. Hoeing and Marian Hamilton. Seventh ed. Manchester: Manchester UP.

Karp, David Allen. 1996. *Speaking of sadness: depression, disconnection, and the meanings of illness*. New York: Oxford University Press.

Katschnig, Heinz. 2010. "Are psychiatrists an endangered species? Observations on internal and external challenges to the profession." *World Psychiatry* 9 (1):21-28.

Kelly, Michael R. 2015. "The Subject as Time." In *Time, Memory, Institution: Merleau-Ponty's New Ontology of Self*, edited by David Morris and Kym Maclaren. Athens: Ohio University Press.

Kendell, Robert E. 1976. "The Classification of Depressions: A review of contemporary confusions." *British Journal of Psychiatry* 129:15-28.

Kendler, Kenneth S. 2009. "An historic framework for psychiatric nosology." *Psychological medicine* 39:1935-1941.

Kendler, Kenneth S., Rodrigo A. Muñoz, and George Murphy. 2010. "The Development of the Feighner Criteria: A Historical Perspective." *American Journal of Psychiatry* 167 (2):134-142.

Kirk, Stuart A., and Herb Kutchins. 1992. *The selling of DSM: the rhetoric of science in psychiatry*. New York: A. de Gruyter.

Kramer, Peter D. 1994. *Listening to Prozac*. New York: Penguin Books.

Kramer, Peter D. 2016. *Ordinarily Well: The Case for Antidepressants*. New York: Farrar, Straus and Giroux.

Laing, R.D. 1971. *The Politics of the Family, and Other Essays*. London: Tavistock.

Lawlor, Clark. 2012. *From Melancholia to Prozac: A History of Depression*. Oxford: OUP.

Leder, Drew. 1990. *The absent body*. Chicago: University of Chicago Press.

Lilienfeld, Scott O, and Kristin Landfield. 2008. "Issues in Diagnosis: Categorical vs. Dimensional." In *Psychopathology : history, diagnosis, and empirical foundations*, edited by W. Edward Craighead, David Jay Miklowitz and Linda W. Craighead. Hoboken: John Wiley & Sons.

Lingis, Alphonso. 1996. *Sensation: intelligibility in sensibility*. New Jersey: Atlantic Highlands.

Locke, John. 1998. *An essay concerning human understanding*. London: Wordsworth.

Maclaren, Kym. 2008. "Embodied Perception of Others as a Condition of Selfhood?" *Journal of Consciousness Studies* 15 (8):63-93.

Maiese, Michelle. 2015. *Embodied Selves and Divided Minds.* Oxford: OUP Oxford

Maj, Mario. 2010. "Financial and non-financial conflicts of interests in psychiatry." *European Archives of Psychiatry and Clinical Neuroscience* 260 (2):147-151.

Mallin, Samuel B. 1979. *Merleau-Ponty's Philosophy.* New Haven: Yale UP.

Marchenko, Gillian. 2016. *Still Life: A Memoir of Living Fully with Depression.* Downers Grove: InterVarsity Press.

Marratto, Scott L. 2012. *The Intercorporeal Self: Merleau-Ponty on Subjectivity*: SUNY Press.

Martin, Brice, Nicolas Franck, Michel Cermolacce, Jennifer T. Coull, and Anne Giersch. 2018. "Minimal Self and Timing Disorders in Schizophrenia: A Case Report." *Frontiers in Human Neuroscience* 12:1-8.

Matthews, Eric. 1999. "Moral Vision and the Idea of Mental Illness." *Philosophy, Psychiatry, & Psychology* 6 (4):299-310.

Matthews, Eric. 2007. *Body-Subjects and Disordered Minds: Treating the 'whole' Person in Psychiatry.* OXford: OUP Oxford.

Mazis, Glen A. 2015. "The Depths of Time in the World's of Merleau-Ponty." In *Time, Memory, Institution: Merleau-Ponty's New Ontology of Self,* edited by David Morris and Kym Maclaren. Athens: Ohio University Press.

Mehler Paperny, Anna. 2019. *Hello I Want to Die Please Fix Me.* Toronto: Random House.

Merkin, Daphne. 2017. *This Close to Happy: A Reckoning with Depression.* New York: Farrar, Straus and Giroux.

Merleau-Ponty, Maurice. 1964a. "The Child's Relations with Others." In *The Primacy of Perception*, edited by James M Edie. Northwestern University Press.

Merleau-Ponty, Maurice. 1964b. *Signs.* Translated by Richard. C McCleary: Northwestern Univeristy Press.

Merleau-Ponty, Maurice. 1968. *The visible and the Invisible.* Translated by Alphonso Lingis. Edited by Claude Lefort. Evanston: Northwestern University Press.

Merleau-Ponty, Maurice. 1973. *Prose of the World.* Translated by John O'Neil. Edited by Claude Lefort. Evanston: Northwestrn UP.

Merleau-Ponty, Maurice. 2004. *The World of Perception.* Translated by Donald A. Landes. Abingdon: Routledge.

Merleau-Ponty, Maurice. 2010a. *Child Psychology and Pedagogy: The Sorbonne Lectures 1949–1952.* Translated by Talia Welsh. Evanston: Northwestern University Press.

Merleau-Ponty, Maurice. 2010b. "The Child's Relations with Others." In *Child Psychology and Pedagogy: The Sorbonne Lectures 1949–1952*, 241-315. Evanston: Northwestern University Press.

Merleau-Ponty, Maurice. 2010c. *Institution and Passivity: Course Notes from the Collège de France (1954–1955).* Translated by Leonard Lawlor and Heath Massey. Evanston: Northwestern University Press.

Merleau-Ponty, Maurice. 2012. *Phenomenology of Perception.* Translated by Donald A. Landes. Abingdon: Taylor & Francis.

Metzinger, Thomas. 2011. "The no-self alternative." In *The Oxford Handbook of Self,* edited by Shaun Gallagher. Oxford: OUP Oxford.

Micale, Mark S, and Roy Porter. 1994a. *Discovering the History of Psychiatry*. New York: Oxford UP.

Micale, Mark S., and Roy Porter. 1994b. "Reflection on psychiatry and its histories." In *Discovering the History of Psychiatry*, edited by Mark S. Micale and Roy Porter. Oxford: Oxford University Press.

Micali, Stefano. 2014. "The Alterationm of Embodiment in Melancholia." In *The Phenomenology of Embodied Subjectivity*, edited by Dillon Moran and Rasmus Thybo Jensen, 203-220. Heidelberg: Springer International.

Michels, Robert, and Allen Frances. 2013. "Should Psychiatry Be Expanding its Boundaries?" *The Canadian Journal of Psychiatry* 58 (10):566-569.

Moncrieff, Joanna, and David Cohen. 2006. "Do Antidepressants Cure or Create Abnormal Brain States?" *PLoS Medicine* 3 (7):e240.

Mora, George. 1994. "Early American Historians of Psychiatry: 1910–1960." In *Discovering the History of Psychiatry*, edited by Mark S Micale and Roy Porter. New York: Oxford UP.

Morris, David. 2004. *The Sense of Space*: State University of New York Press.

Morris, David, and Kym Maclaren, eds. 2015. *Time, Memory, Institution: Merleau-Ponty's New Ontology of Self*. Athens: Ohio University Press.

Moynihan, Ray, Iona Heath, and David Henry. 2002. "Selling sickness: the pharmaceutical industry and disease mongering." *British Medical Journal* 324 (7342):886-891.

Murphy, Dominic. 2006. *Psychiatry in the scientific image*. Cambridge: MIT Press.

Natanson, Maurice. 1969 "Psychiatry and philosophy." In *Philosophy and Psychiatry*, edited by Maurice Natanson. Verlag: Springer.

Neisser, Ulric. 2006. "The Perceived Self." In *The Perceived Self: Ecological and Interpersonal Sources of Self Knowledge*, edited by Ulrich Neisser, 3-21. Cambridge: Cambridge University Press.

Neisser, Ulric, and David A. Jopling. 1997. *The Conceptual Self in Context: Culture Experience Self Understanding*. Cambridge: Cambridge University Press.

Northhoff, Georg. 2013. "Brain and self – a neurophilosophical account." *Child and Adolescent Psychiatry and Mental Health* 7 (28):1-12.

Northhoff, Georg, and Alexander Heinzel. 2003. "The Self in philosophy, neuroscience, and psychiatry." In *The Sellf in Neurosciecne and Psychiatry* edited by Tito Kircher and Anthony David, 40-55. Cambridge: Cambridge University Press.

Parfit, Derek. 1971. "Personal Identity." *The Philosophical Review* 80 (1):3-27.

Parfit, Derek. 2011. "The Unimportance of Personal Identity." In *The Oxford Handbook of Self*, edited by Shaun Gallagher, 419-441. Oxford: OUP Oxford.

Park, J.S. 2017. *How hard it really is*: TWE Media.

Parnas, Josef, and Pierre Bovet. 2015. "Psychiatry made easy: operation(al)ism and some of its consequences." In *Philosophical Issues in Psychiatry III: The Nature and Sources of Historical Change*, edited by J Parnas and K Kendler, 191-212. Oxford: Oxford UP.

Parnas, Josef, Paul Moller, Tilo Kircher, Jorgen Thalbitzer, Lennart Jansson, Peter Handest, and Dan Zahavi. 2005. "EASE: Examination of Anomalous Self-Experience." *Psychopathology* 38 (5):236-58.

Pichot, Pierre J. 1997. "DSM-III and its reception: a European view." *The American journal of psychiatry* 154 (6 Suppl):47-54.

Pinker, Steven. 2011. *The Better Angels of Our Nature: Why Violence Has Declined.* New York: Penguin Publishing Group.

Plath, Sylvia. 2005. *The bell jar*. London: Faber and Faber.

Popper, Karl. 1963. *Conjectures and refutations.* London: Routledge and Keagan Paul.

Radden, Jennifer. 2002. *The Nature of Melancholy: From Aristotle to Kristeva.* New York: Oxford University Press.

Radden, Jennifer. 2003. "Is This Dame Melancholy?: Equating Today's Depression and Past Melancholia." *Philosophy, Psychiatry, & Psychology* 10 (1):37-52.

Radden, Jennifer. 2009. *Moody minds distempered: essays on melancholy and depression*. Oxford: Oxford University Press.

Radden, Jennifer, and Somogy Varga. 2013. "The Epistemological Value of Depression Memoirs: A meta-analysis." In *The Oxford Handbook of Philosophy and Psychiatry*, edited by K.W.M Fulford, Martin Davies, Richard Gipps, George Graham, Jonh Z. Sadler, Giovanni Stanghellini and Tim Thornton, 99-115. Oxford: OUP.

Ratcliffe, Matthew. 2008. *Feelings of Being: Phenomenology, Psychiatry and the Sense of Reality*. Oxford: OUP.

Ratcliffe, Matthew. 2015. *Experiences in Depression: A phenomenological study*. Oxford: Oxford Uiniversity Press.

Ratcliffe, Matthew. 2018. "Depression, Self-Regulation, and Intersubjectivity." *Discipline Filosofiche* XXVIII (2):21-42.

Ratcliffe, Matthew, and Matthew Broome. 2012. "Existential phenomenology, psychiatric illness and the death of possibilities." In *Cambridge companion to existentialism*, edited by Steven G Crowell. Cambridge: Cambridge University Press.

Ratcliffe, Matthew, and Achim Stephan, eds. 2014. *Depression, Emotion and the Self: Philosophical and Interdisciplinary Perspectives*. Exeter: Imprint Academic.

Reed, Geoffrey M. 2010. "Toward ICD-11: Improving the Clinical Utility of WHO's International Classification of Mental Disorders." *Professional Psychology: Research and Practice* 41 (6):457-464.

Regier, Darrel A., Irving. D. Goldberg, and Carl. A. Taube. 1978. "The de facto us mental health services system: A public health perspective." 35 (6):685-693.

Ricoeur, Paul. 1981. *Hermeneutics and the Human Sciences: Essays on Language, Action and Interpretation*. Translated by John B Thompson. Cambridge: Cambridge University Press.

Ricoeur, Paul. 1988. *Time and Narrative*. Translated by Kathleen Blamey and David Pellauer. Vol. III. Chicago: University of Chicago Press.

Ricoeur, Paul. 1992. *Oneself as Another*. Chicago: University of Chicago Press.

Rochat, Phillioppe. 2009. *Others in Mind: Social Origins of Self-Consciousness*. Cambridge: Cambridge University Press.

Rochat, Phillippe. 2001. *The Infant's World*. Cambridge: Harvard University Press.

Ross, Karen D. 2014. "A Review of "From Melancholia to Prozac: A History of Depression." *History: Reviews of New Books* 42 (2):67-68.

Russon, John. 2003. *Human Experience: Philosophy, neurosis, and the elements of everyday life*. Albany: SUNY Press.

Sandford, Stella. 2016. "Feminist Phenomenology, Pregnancy and Transcendental Subjectivity." In *Phenomenology of Pregnancy*, edited by Jonna Bornemark and Nicholas Smith. Stockholm: Södertörn University.

Sartorius, Norman. 2015. "Classification of Psychiatric Disorders: Challenges and Perspectives." *Emotion Review* 7 (3):204-208.

Sass, Louis, Elizabeth Pienkos, Barnaby Nelson, and Nick Medford. 2013. "Anomalous self-experience in depersonalization and schizophrenia: A comparative investigation." *Consciousness and cognition* 22 (2):430-441.

Sato, Yuji. 2015. "Depression in a biopsychosocioeconomic context." In *Philosophical issues in psychiatry III: The nature and source of historical change*, edited by Kenneth S. Kendler and Josef Parnas. Oxford: Oxford University Press.

Schechtman, Marya. 2011. "The Narrative Self." In *The Oxford Handbook of Self*, edited by Shaun Gallagher, 394-416. Oxford: OUP Oxford.

Schön, Donald. 1983. *The Reflective Practitioner: How Professionals Think In Action*: Basic Books.

Schön, Donald A. 1987. *Educating the Reflective Practitioner: Toward a New Design for Teaching and Learning in the Professions*. San Fransico: Wiley.

Scull, Andrew. 1999. "A quarter century of the history of psychiatry." *Journal of the History of the Behavioral Sciences* 35 (3):239-246.

Shorter, Edward. 1997. *A History of Psychiatry: From the Era of the Asylum to the Age of Prozac*. New York: Wiley.

Shorter, Edward. 2013. *How Everyone Became Depressed: The Rise and Fall of the Nervous Breakdown*. Oxford: Oxford University Press.

Siderits, Mark. 2011. "Buddihist Non-Self." In *The Oxford Handbook of Self*, edited by Shaun Gallagher, 297-315. Oxford: OUP Oxford.

Slaby, Jan, Asena Paskaleva, and Achim Stephan. 2014. "Enactive Emotion and Imparied Agency in Depression." In *Depression, Emotion and the Self: Philosophical and Interdisciplinary Perspectives*, edited by M. Ratcliffe and A. Stephan. Exeter: Imprint Academic.

Smith, Benedict. 2013. "Depression and motivation." *Phenomenology and the Cognitive Sciences* 12 (4):615-635.

Smith, Johnathan A. 2018. "'Yes It Is Phenomenological': A Reply to Max Van Manen's Critique of Interpretative Phenomenological Analysis." *Qualitative Health Research* 28 (12):1955-1958.

Solomon, Andrew. 2001. *The Noonday Demon: An Atlas Of Depression*. New York: Scribner.

Stegenga, Jacob. 2018. *Medical Nihilism*. Oxford: Oxford University Press.

Steinbock, Anthony J. 1987. "Merleau-ponty's concept of depth." *Philosophy Today* 31 (4):336-351.

Stephensen, Helene, and Mads Gram Henriksen. 2017. "Not being oneself: A critical perspective on 'inauthenticity' in schizophrenia." *Journal of Phenomenological Psychology* 48:63-82.

Strandberg, Gustav. 2018. "An A-subjective Coexistence." *Auc Interpretationes* 7 (1):86-101.

Straus, Erwin. 1963. *The Primary World of Senses*. Translated by Jacob Needleman. London: The Free Press of Glencoe.

Straus, Erwin. 1966a. “The Forms of Spatiality.” In *Phenomenological Psychology*. New York: Basic Books.

Straus, Erwin. 1966b. “Norm and Pathology of I-World Relations.” In *Phenomenological Psychology*, 255-276. New York: Basic Books.

Straus, Erwin. 1966c. *Phenomenological Psychology*. Translated by Erling Eng. New York: Basic Books.

Straus, Erwin. 1982. *Man, time, and world: two contributions to anthropological psychology*. Pittsburgh: Duquesne University Press.

Straus, Erwin W., Natanson Maurice, and Ey Henri. 1969. *Psychiatry and philosophy*. Verlag: Springer.

Styron, William. 2010. *Darkness Visible: A Memoir of Madness*: Open Road Media.

Summa, Michela, and Thomas Fuchs. 2015. “Self-experience in Dementia.” *Rivista Internazionale di Filosofia e Psicologia* 6 (2):387-405.

Svenaeus, Fredrik. 2001. *The Hermeneutics of Medicine and the Phenomenology of Health: Steps Towards a Philosophy of Medical Practice*. Dordrecht: Springer.

Svenaeus, Fredrik. 2014. “Depression and the Self: Bodily Resonance and Attuned Being-in-the-World.” In *Depression, Emotion and the Self*, edited by Matthew Ratcliffe and Achim Stephan. Exeter: Imprint Academic.

Svenaeus, Fredrik. 2018. “Why Heideggerian Death Anxiety is not Truly Uncanny: Existential Feelings and Psychiatric Disorders.” *Discipline Filosofiche* XXVIII (2):43-60.

Tekin, Şerife. 2011. “Self-concept through the diagnostic looking glass: Narratives and mental disorder.” *Philosophical Psychology* 24 (3):357-380.

Tellenbach, Hurbertus. 1980. *Melancholy: History of the Problem, Endogeneity, Typology, Pathogenesis, Clinical Considerations*. Pittsburgh: Duquesne University Press.

Theroux, Marcel. 2013. *Strange Bodies: A Novel*. London: Faber & Faber.

van den Berg, Jan. 1972. *A different existence: principles of phenomenological psychopathology*. Pittsburgh: Duquesne University Press.

van Manen, Max. 2014. *Phenomenology of Practice: Meaning-Giving Methods in Phenomenological Research and Writing*. Walnut Creek: Left Coast Press.

van Manen, Max. 2019. “Rebuttal: Doing Phenomenology on the Things.” *Qualitative Health Research* 29 (6):908-925.

Varga, Somogy. 2013. “From Melancholia to Depression: Ideas on a Possible Continuity.” *Philosophy, Psychiatry, & Psychology* 20 (2):141-155.

Wakefield, Jerome C., and Michael B. First. 2003. “Clarifying the Distinction Between Disorder and Nondisorder.” In *Advancing DSM: Dilemmas in Psychiatric Diagnosis*, edited by Katherine A. Phillips, Michael B. First and Harold A. Pincus. Washington D.C: American Psychiatric Publishing.

Welsh, Talia. 2013. *The Child as Natural Phenomenologist* Evanston: Northwestern University Press.

Whitaker, Robert. 2011. *Anatomy of an Epidemic: Magic Bullets, Psychiatric Drugs, and the Astonishing Rise of Mental Illness in America*. New York: Broadway Books.

WHO. 2017. Depression and other common mental disorders: Global heath estimates. Geneva: World Health Organization.

Wrathall, Mark A. 2004. "Motives, Reasons, and Causes." In *The Cambridge Companion to Merleau-Ponty*, edited by Mark B. N. Hansen and Taylor Carman, 111-128. Cambridge: Cambridge University Press.

Wyllie, Martin. 2005. "Lived Time and Psychopathology." *Philosophy, Psychiatry, and Psychology* 12 (3):173-185. doi: 10.1353/ppp.2006.0017.

Xenophon. 1929. *Memorabilia and Oeconomicus*. edited by Edgar Cardew Marchant and Otis Johnson Todd. Cambridge, Mass.: Harvard University Press.

Zahavi, Dan. 2008. *Subjectivity and Selfhood: Investigating the First-Person Perspective*. Cambridge: MIT Press.

Zahavi, Dan. 2009. "Is the Self a Social Construct?" *Inquiry* 52 (6):551-573.

Zahavi, Dan. 2014. *Self and Other: Exploring Subjectivity, Empathy, and Shame*. Oxford: OUP Oxford.

Zahavi, Dan. 2019. "Getting It Quite Wrong: Van Manen and Smith on Phenomenology." *Qualitative Health Research* 29 (6):900-907.

Zaner, Richard. 1981. *The Context of Self: A Phenomenological Inquiry Using Medicine As a Clue*: Ohio University Press.

Södertörn Doctoral Dissertations

1. Jolanta Aidukaite, *The Emergence of the Post-Socialist Welfare State: The case of the Baltic States: Estonia, Latvia and Lithuania*, 2004
2. Xavier Fraudet, *Politique étrangère française en mer Baltique (1871–1914): de l'exclusion à l'affirmation*, 2005
3. Piotr Wawrzeniuk, *Confessional Civilising in Ukraine: The Bishop Iosyf Shumliansky and the Introduction of Reforms in the Diocese of Lviv 1668–1708*, 2005
4. Andrej Kotljarchuk, *In the Shadows of Poland and Russia: The Grand Duchy of Lithuania and Sweden in the European Crisis of the mid-17th Century*, 2006
5. Håkan Blomqvist, *Nation, ras och civilisation i svensk arbetarrörelse före nazismen*, 2006
6. Karin S Lindelöf, *Om vi nu ska bli som Europa: Könsskapande och normalitet bland unga kvinnor i transitionens Polen*, 2006
7. Andrew Stickley. *On Interpersonal Violence in Russia in the Present and the Past: A Sociological Study*, 2006
8. Arne Ek, *Att konstruera en uppslutning kring den enda vägen: Om folkrörelsers modernisering i skuggan av det Östeuropeiska systemskiftet*, 2006
9. Agnes Ers, *I mänsklighetens namn: En etnologisk studie av ett svenskt biståndsprojekt i Rumänien*, 2006
10. Johnny Rodin, *Rethinking Russian Federalism: The Politics of Intergovernmental Relations and Federal Reforms at the Turn of the Millennium*, 2006
11. Kristian Petrov, *Tillbaka till framtiden: Modernitet, postmodernitet och generationsidentitet i Gorbačevs glasnost' och perestrojka*, 2006
12. Sophie Söderholm Werkö, *Patient patients? Achieving Patient Empowerment through Active Participation, Increased Knowledge and Organisation*, 2008
13. Peter Bötker, *Leviatan i arkipelagen: Staten, förvaltningen och samhället. Fallet Estland*, 2007
14. Matilda Dahl, *States under scrutiny: International organizations, transformation and the construction of progress*, 2007
15. Margrethe B. Søvik, *Support, resistance and pragmatism: An examination of motivation in language policy in Kharkiv*, Ukraine, 2007
16. Yulia Gradskova, *Soviet People with female Bodies: Performing beauty and maternity in Soviet Russia in the mid 1930–1960s*, 2007

17. Renata Ingbrant, *From Her Point of View: Woman's Anti-World in the Poetry of Anna Świrszczyńska*, 2007
18. Johan Eellend, *Cultivating the Rural Citizen: Modernity, Agrarianism and Citizenship in Late Tsarist Estonia*, 2007
19. Petra Garberding, *Musik och politik i skuggan av nazismen: Kurt Atterberg och de svensk-tyska musikrelationerna*, 2007
20. Aleksei Semenenko, *Hamlet the Sign: Russian Translations of Hamlet and Literary Canon Formation*, 2007
21. Vytautas Petronis, *Constructing Lithuania: Ethnic Mapping in the Tsarist Russia, ca. 1800–1914*, 2007
22. Akvile Motiejunaite, *Female employment, gender roles, and attitudes: the Baltic countries in a broader context*, 2008
23. Tove Lindén, *Explaining Civil Society Core Activism in Post-Soviet Latvia*, 2008
24. Pelle Åberg, *Translating Popular Education: Civil Society Cooperation between Sweden and Estonia*, 2008
25. Anders Nordström, *The Interactive Dynamics of Regulation: Exploring the Council of Europe's monitoring of Ukraine*, 2008
26. Fredrik Doeser, *In Search of Security After the Collapse of the Soviet Union: Foreign Policy Change in Denmark, Finland and Sweden, 1988–1993*, 2008
27. Zhanna Kravchenko. *Family (versus) Policy: Combining Work and Care in Russia and Sweden*, 2008
28. Rein Jüriado, *Learning within and between public-private partnerships*, 2008
29. Elin Boalt, *Ecology and evolution of tolerance in two cruciferous species*, 2008
30. Lars Forsberg, *Genetic Aspects of Sexual Selection and Mate Choice in Salmonids*, 2008
31. Eglė Rindzevičiūtė, *Constructing Soviet Cultural Policy: Cybernetics and Governance in Lithuania after World War II*, 2008
32. Joakim Philipson, *The Purpose of Evolution: 'struggle for existence' in the Russian-Jewish press 1860–1900*, 2008
33. Sofie Bedford, *Islamic activism in Azerbaijan: Repression and mobilization in a post-Soviet context*, 2009
34. Tommy Larsson Segerlind, *Team Entrepreneurship: A process analysis of the venture team and the venture team roles in relation to the innovation process*, 2009
35. Jenny Svensson, *The Regulation of Rule-Following: Imitation and Soft Regulation in the European Union*, 2009
36. Stefan Hallgren, *Brain Aromatase in the guppy, Poecilia reticulate: Distribution, control and role in behavior*, 2009
37. Karin Ellencrona, *Functional characterization of interactions between the flavivirus NS5 protein and PDZ proteins of the mammalian host*, 2009

38. Makiko Kanematsu, *Saga och verklighet: Barnboksproduktion i det postsovjetiska Lettland*, 2009
39. Daniel Lindvall, *The Limits of the European Vision in Bosnia and Herzegovina: An Analysis of the Police Reform Negotiations*, 2009
40. Charlotta Hillerdal, *People in Between – Ethnicity and Material Identity: A New Approach to Deconstructed Concepts*, 2009
41. Jonna Bornemark, *Kunskapens gräns – gränsens vetande*, 2009
42. Adolphine G. Kateka, *Co-Management Challenges in the Lake Victoria Fisheries: A Context Approach*, 2010
43. René León Rosales, *Vid framtidens hitersta gräns: Om pojkar och elevpositioner i en multietnisk skola*, 2010
44. Simon Larsson, *Intelligensaristokrater och arkivmartyrer: Normerna för vetenskaplig skicklighet i svensk historieforskning 1900–1945*, 2010
45. Håkan Lättman, *Studies on spatial and temporal distributions of epiphytic lichens*, 2010
46. Alia Jaensson, *Pheromonal mediated behaviour and endocrine response in salmonids: The impact of cypermethrin, copper, and glyphosate*, 2010
47. Michael Wigerius, *Roles of mammalian Scribble in polarity signaling, virus offense and cell-fate determination*, 2010
48. Anna Hedtjärn Wester, *Män i kostym: Prinsar, konstnärer och tegelbärare vid sekelskiftet 1900*, 2010
49. Magnus Linnarsson, *Postgång på växlande villkor: Det svenska postväsendets organisation under stormaktstiden*, 2010
50. Barbara Kunz, *Kind words, cruise missiles and everything in between: A neoclassical realist study of the use of power resources in U.S. policies towards Poland, Ukraine and Belarus 1989–2008*, 2010
51. Anders Bartonek, *Philosophie im Konjunktiv: Nichtidentität als Ort der Möglichkeit des Utopischen in der negativen Dialektik Theodor W. Adornos*, 2010
52. Carl Cederberg, *Resaying the Human: Levinas Beyond Humanism and Antihumanism*, 2010
53. Johanna Ringarp, *Professionens problematik: Lärarkårens kommunalisering och välfärdsstatens förvandling*, 2011
54. Sofi Gerber, *Öst är Väst men Väst är bäst: Östtysk identitetsformering i det förenade Tyskland*, 2011
55. Susanna Sjödin Lindenskoug, *Manlighetens bortre gräns: Tidelagsrättegångar i Livland åren 1685–1709*, 2011
56. Dominika Polanska, *The emergence of enclaves of wealth and poverty: A sociological study of residential differentiation in post-communist Poland*, 2011
57. Christina Douglas, *Kärlek per korrespondens: Två förlovade par under andra hälften av 1800-talet*, 2011

58. Fred Saunders, *The Politics of People – Not just Mangroves and Monkeys: A study of the theory and practice of community-based management of natural resources in Zanzibar*, 2011
59. Anna Rosengren, *Åldrandet och språket: En språkhistorisk analys av hög ålder och åldrande i Sverige cirka 1875–1975*, 2011
60. Emelie Lilliefeldt, *European Party Politics and Gender: Configuring Gender-Balanced Parliamentary Presence*, 2011
61. Ola Svenonius, *Sensitising Urban Transport Security: Surveillance and Policing in Berlin, Stockholm, and Warsaw*, 2011
62. Andreas Johansson, *Dissenting Democrats: Nation and Democracy in the Republic of Moldova*, 2011
63. Wessam Melik, *Molecular characterization of the Tick-borne encephalitis virus: Environments and replication*, 2012
64. Steffen Werther, *SS-Vision und Grenzland-Realität: Vom Umgang dänischer und „volksdeutscher" Nationalsozialisten in Sønderjylland mit der „großgermanischen" Ideologie der SS*, 2012
65. Peter Jakobsson, *Öppenhetsindustrin*, 2012
66. Kristin Ilves, *Seaward Landward: Investigations on the archaeological source value of the landing site category in the Baltic Sea region*, 2012
67. Anne Kaun, *Civic Experiences and Public Connection: Media and Young People in Estonia*, 2012
68. Anna Tessmann, *On the Good Faith: A Fourfold Discursive Construction of Zoroastripanism in Contemporary Russia*, 2012
69. Jonas Lindström, *Drömmen om den nya staden: stadsförnyelse i det postsovjetisk Riga*, 2012
70. Maria Wolrath Söderberg, *Topos som meningsskapare: retorikens topiska perspektiv på tänkande och lärande genom argumentation*, 2012
71. Linus Andersson, *Alternativ television: former av kritik i konstnärlig TV-produktion*, 2012
72. Håkan Lättman, *Studies on spatial and temporal distributions of epiphytic lichens*, 2012
73. Fredrik Stiernstedt, Mediearbete i mediehuset: produktion i förändring på MTG-radio, 2013
74. Jessica Moberg, *Piety, Intimacy and Mobility: A Case Study of Charismatic Christianity in Present-day Stockholm*, 2013
75. Elisabeth Hemby, *Historiemåleri och bilder av vardag: Tatjana Nazarenkos konstnärskap i 1970-talets Sovjet*, 2013
76. Tanya Jukkala, *Suicide in Russia: A macro-sociological study*, 2013
77. Maria Nyman, *Resandets gränser: svenska resenärers skildringar av Ryssland under 1700-talet*, 2013

78. Beate Feldmann Eellend, *Visionära planer och vardagliga praktiker: postmilitära landskap i Östersjöområdet,* 2013
79. Emma Lind, *Genetic response to pollution in sticklebacks: natural selection in the wild,* 2013
80. Anne Ross Solberg, *The Mahdi wears Armani: An analysis of the Harun Yahya enterprise,* 2013
81. Nikolay Zakharov, *Attaining Whiteness: A Sociological Study of Race and Racialization in Russia,* 2013
82. Anna Kharkina, *From Kinship to Global Brand: the Discourse on Culture in Nordic Co-operation after World War II,* 2013
83. Florence Fröhlig, *A painful legacy of World War II: Nazi forced enlistment: Alsatian/Mosellan Prisoners of war and the Soviet Prison Camp of Tambov,* 2013
84. Oskar Henriksson, *Genetic connectivity of fish in the Western Indian Ocean,* 2013
85. Hans Geir Aasmundsen, *Pentecostalism, Globalisation and Society in Contemporary Argentina,* 2013
86. Anna McWilliams, *An Archaeology of the Iron Curtain: Material and Metaphor,* 2013
87. Anna Danielsson, *On the power of informal economies and the informal economies of power: rethinking informality, resilience and violence in Kosovo,* 2014
88. Carina Guyard, *Kommunikationsarbete på distans,* 2014
89. Sofia Norling, *Mot "väst": om vetenskap, politik och transformation i Polen 1989–2011,* 2014
90. Markus Huss, *Motståndets akustik: språk och (o)ljud hos Peter Weiss 1946–1960,* 2014
91. Ann-Christin Randahl, *Strategiska skribenter: skrivprocesser i fysik och svenska,* 2014
92. Péter Balogh, *Perpetual borders: German-Polish cross-border contacts in the Szczecin area,* 2014
93. Erika Lundell, *Förkroppsligad fiktion och fiktionaliserade kroppar: levande rollspel i Östersjöregionen,* 2014
94. Henriette Cederlöf, *Alien Places in Late Soviet Science Fiction: The "Unexpected Encounters" of Arkady and Boris Strugatsky as Novels and Films,* 2014
95. Niklas Eriksson, *Urbanism Under Sail: An archaeology of fluit ships in early modern everyday life,* 2014
96. Signe Opermann, *Generational Use of News Media in Estonia: Media Access, Spatial Orientations and Discursive Characteristics of the News Media,* 2014
97. Liudmila Voronova, *Gendering in political journalism: A comparative study of Russia and Sweden,* 2014
98. Ekaterina Kalinina, *Mediated Post-Soviet Nostalgia,* 2014

99. Anders E. B. Blomqvist, *Economic Natonalizing in the Ethnic Borderlands of Hungary and Romania: Inclusion, Exclusion and Annihilation in Szatmár/Satu-Mare, 1867–1944*, 2014
100. Ann-Judith Rabenschlag, *Völkerfreundschaft nach Bedarf: Ausländische Arbeitskräfte in der Wahrnehmung von Staat und Bevölkerung der DDR*, 2014
101. Yuliya Yurchuck, *Ukrainian Nationalists and the Ukrainian Insurgent Army in Post-Soviet Ukraine*, 2014
102. Hanna Sofia Rehnberg, *Organisationer berättar: narrativitet som resurs i strategisk kommunikation*, 2014
103. Jaakko Turunen, *Semiotics of Politics: Dialogicality of Parliamentary Talk*, 2015
104. Iveta Jurkane-Hobein, *I Imagine You Here Now: Relationship Maintenance Strategies in Long-Distance Intimate Relationships*, 2015
105. Katharina Wesolowski, *Maybe baby? Reproductive behaviour, fertility intentions, and family policies in post-communist countries, with a special focus on Ukraine*, 2015
106. Ann af Burén, *Living Simultaneity: On religion among semi-secular Swedes*, 2015
107. Larissa Mickwitz, *En reformerad lärare: konstruktionen av en professionell och betygssättande lärare i skolpolitik och skolpraktik*, 2015
108. Daniel Wojahn, *Språkaktivism: diskussioner om feministiska språkförändringar i Sverige från 1960-talet till 2015*, 2015
109. Hélène Edberg, *Kreativt skrivande för kritiskt tänkande: en fallstudie av studenters arbete med kritisk metareflektion*, 2015
110. Kristina Volkova, *Fishy Behavior: Persistent effects of early-life exposure to 17α-ethinylestradiol*, 2015
111. Björn Sjöstrand, *Att tänka det tekniska: en studie i Derridas teknikfilosofi*, 2015
112. Håkan Forsberg, *Kampen om eleverna: gymnasiefältet och skolmarknadens framväxt i Stockholm, 1987–2011*, 2015
113. Johan Stake, *Essays on quality evaluation and bidding behavior in public procurement auctions*, 2015
114. Martin Gunnarson, *Please Be Patient: A Cultural Phenomenological Study of Haemodialysis and Kidney Transplantation Care*, 2016
115. Nasim Reyhanian Caspillo, *Studies of alterations in behavior and fertility in ethinyl estradiol-exposed zebrafish and search for related biomarkers*, 2016
116. Pernilla Andersson, *The Responsible Business Person: Studies of Business Education for Sustainability*, 2016
117. Kim Silow Kallenberg, *Gränsland: svensk ungdomsvård mellan vård och straff*, 2016
118. Sari Vuorenpää, *Literacitet genom interaction*, 2016
119. Francesco Zavatti, *Writing History in a Propaganda Institute: Political Power and Network Dynamics in Communist Romania*, 2016

120. Cecilia Annell, *Begärets politiska potential: Feministiska motståndsstrategier i Elin Wägners 'Pennskaftet', Gabriele Reuters 'Aus guter Familie', Hilma Angered-Strandbergs 'Lydia Vik' och Grete Meisel-Hess 'Die Intellektuellen'*, 2016

121. Marco Nase, *Academics and Politics: Northern European Area Studies at Greifswald University, 1917–1992*, 2016

122. Jenni Rinne, *Searching for Authentic Living Through Native Faith – The Maausk movement in Estonia*, 2016

123. Petra Werner, *Ett medialt museum: lärandets estetik i svensk television 1956–1969*, 2016

124. Ramona Rat, *Un-common Sociality: Thinking sociality with Levinas*, 2016

125. Petter Thureborn, *Microbial ecosystem functions along the steep oxygen gradient of the Landsort Deep, Baltic Sea*, 2016

126. Kajsa-Stina Benulic, *A Beef with Meat Media and audience framings of environmentally unsustainable production and consumption*, 2016

127. Naveed Asghar, *Ticks and Tick-borne Encephalitis Virus – From nature to infection*, 2016

128. Linn Rabe, *Participation and legitimacy: Actor involvement for nature conservation*, 2017

129. Maryam Adjam, *Minnesspår: hågkomstens rum och rörelse i skuggan av en flykt*, 2017

130. Kim West, *The Exhibitionary Complex: Exhibition, Apparatus and Media from Kulturhuset to the Centre Pompidou, 1963–1977*, 2017

131. Ekaterina Tarasova, *Anti-nuclear Movements in Discursive and Political Contexts: Between expert voices and local protests, 2017*

132. Sanja Obrenović Johansson, *Från kombifeminism till rörelse: Kvinnlig serbisk organisering i förändring, 2017*

133. Michał Salamonik, *In Their Majesties' Service: The Career of Francesco De Gratta (1613–1676) as a Royal Servant and Trader in Gdańsk*, 2017

134. Jenny Ingridsdotter, *The Promises of the Free World: Postsocialist Experience in Argentina and the Making of Migrants, Race, and Coloniality*, 2017

135. Julia Malitska, *Negotiating Imperial Rule: Colonists and Marriage in the Nineteenth century Black Sea Steppe*, 2017

136. Natalya Yakusheva, *Parks, Policies and People: Nature Conservation Governance in Post-Socialist EU Countries*, 2017

137. Martin Kellner, *Selective Serotonin Re-uptake Inhibitors in the Environment: Effects of Citalopram on Fish Behaviour*, 2017

138. Krystof Kasprzak, *Vara – Framträdande – Värld: Fenomenets negativitet hos Martin Heidegger, Jan Patočka och Eugen Fink*, 2017

139. Alberto Frigo, *Life-stowing from a Digital Media Perspective: Past, Present and Future*, 2017

140. Maarja Saar, *The Answers You Seek Will Never Be Found at Home: Reflexivity, biographical narratives and lifestyle migration among highly-skilled Estonians*, 2017

141. Anh Mai, *Organizing for Efficiency: Essay on merger policies, independence of authorities, and technology diffusion*, 2017
142. Gustav Strandberg, *Politikens omskakning: Negativitet, samexistens och frihet i Jan Patočkas tänkande*, 2017
143. Lovisa Andén, *Litteratur och erfarenhet i Merleau-Pontys läsning av Proust, Valéry och Stendhal*, 2017
144. Fredrik Bertilsson, *Frihetstida policyskapande: uppfostringskommissionen och de akademiska konstitutionerna 1738–1766*, 2017
145. Börjeson, Natasja, *Toxic Textiles – towards responsibility in complex supply chains*, 2017
146. Julia Velkova, *Media Technologies in the Making – User-Driven Software and Infrastructures for computer Graphics Production*, 2017
147. Karin Jonsson, *Fångna i begreppen? Revolution, tid och politik i svensk socialistisk press 1917–1924*, 2017
148. Josefine Larsson, *Genetic Aspects of Environmental Disturbances in Marine Ecosystems – Studies of the Blue Mussel in the Baltic Sea*, 2017
149. Roman Horbyk, *Mediated Europes – Discourse and Power in Ukraine, Russia and Poland during Euromaidan*, 2017
150. Nadezda Petrusenko, *Creating the Revolutionary Heroines: The Case of Female Terrorists of the PSR (Russia, Beginning of the 20th Century)*, 2017
151. Rahel Kuflu, *Bröder emellan: Identitetsformering i det koloniserade Eritrea*, 2018
152. Karin Edberg, *Energilandskap i förändring: Inramningar av kontroversiella lokaliseringar på norra Gotland*, 2018
153. Rebecka Thor, *Beyond the Witness: Holocaust Representation and the Testimony of Images – Three films by Yael Hersonski, Harun Farocki, and Eyal Sivan*, 2018
154. Maria Lönn, *Bruten vithet: Om den ryska femininitetens sinnliga och temporala villkor*, 2018
155. Tove Porseryd, *Endocrine Disruption in Fish: Effects of 17α-ethinylestradiol exposure on non-reproductive behavior, fertility and brain and testis transcriptome*, 2018
156. Marcel Mangold, *Securing the working democracy: Inventive arrangements to guarantee circulation and the emergence of democracy policy*, 2018
157. Matilda Tudor, *Desire Lines: Towards a Queer Digital Media Phenomenology*, 2018
158. Martin Andersson, *Migration i 1600-talets Sverige: Älvsborgs lösen 1613–1618*, 2018
159. Johanna Pettersson, *What's in a Line? Making Sovereignty through Border Policy*, 2018
160. Irina Seits, *Architectures of Life-Building in the Twentieth Century: Russia, Germany, Sweden*, 2018
161. Alexander Stagnell, *The Ambassador's Letter: On the Less Than Nothing of Diplomacy*, 2019
162. Mari Zetterqvist Blokhuis, *Interaction Between Rider, Horse and Equestrian Trainer – A Challenging Puzzle*, 2019
163. Robin Samuelsson, *Play, Culture and Learning: Studies of Second-Language and Conceptual Development in Swedish Preschools*, 2019

164. Ralph Tafon, *Analyzing the "Dark Side" of Marine Spatial Planning – A study of domination, empowerment and freedom (or power* in, of *and* on *planning) through theories of discourse and power*, 2019
165. Ingela Visuri, *Varieties of Supernatural Experience: The case of high-functioning autism*, 2019
166. Mathilde Rehnlund, *Getting the transport right – for what? What transport policy can tell us about the construction of sustainability*, 2019
167. Oscar Törnqvist, *Röster från ingenmansland: En identitetsarkeologi i ett maritimt mellanrum*, 2019
168. Elise Remling, *Adaptation, now? Exploring the Politics of Climate Adaptation through Post-structuralist Discourse Theory*, 2019
169. Eva Karlberg, *Organizing the Voice of Women: A study of the Polish and Swedish women's movements' adaptation to international structures*, 2019
170. Maria Pröckl, *Tyngd, sväng och empatisk timing: Förskollärares kroppsliga kunskaper*, 2020.
171. Adriá Alcoverro, *The university and the demand for knowledge-based growth: The hegemonic struggle for the future of Higher Education Institutions in Finland and Estonia*, 2020
172. Ingrid Forsler, *Enabling Media: Infrastructures, imaginaries and cultural techniques in Swedish and Estonian visual arts education*, 2020
173. Johan Sehlberg, *Of Affliction: The Experience of Thought in Gilles Deleuze by way of Marcel Proust*, 2020
174. Renat Bekkin, *People of Reliable Loyalty…: Muftiates and the State in Modern Russia*, 2020
175. Olena Podolian, *The Challenge of 'Stateness' in Estonia and Ukraine*, 2020
176. Patrick Semiuk, *Encountering Depression In-Depth: An existential-phenomenological approach to selfhood, depression, and psychiatric practice*, 2020

www.ingramcontent.com/pod-product-compliance
Ingram Content Group UK Ltd.
Pitfield, Milton Keynes, MK11 3LW, UK
UKHW041635190726
13854UKWH00006B/2503